THE CAREER GAME
CHAMPIONSHIPS
and How to Win

Larry J. Linden, Ph.D.
and Joseph Parker

Order this book online at www.trafford.com/07-2792
or email orders@trafford.com

Most Trafford titles are also available at major online book retailers.

Co-authored by Joseph Parker.

Cover design/artwork by Michael Duval.

Note for Librarians: A cataloguing record for this book is available from Library
and Archives Canada at www.collectionscanada.ca/amicus/index-e.html

Printed in Victoria, BC, Canada.

ISBN: 978-1-4251-6130-9

*We at Trafford believe that it is the responsibility of us all, as both individuals and corporations,
to make choices that are environmentally and socially sound. You, in turn, are supporting this
responsible conduct each time you purchase a Trafford book, or make use of our publishing services.
To find out how you are helping, please visit www.trafford.com/responsiblepublishing.html*

*Our mission is to efficiently provide the world's finest, most comprehensive book publishing
service, enabling every author to experience success. To find out how to publish your book, your
way, and have it available worldwide, visit us online at www.trafford.com/10510*

 www.trafford.com

North America & international
toll-free: 1 888 232 4444 (USA & Canada)
phone: 250 383 6864 ♦ fax: 250 383 6804 ♦ email: info@trafford.com

The United Kingdom & Europe
phone: +44 (0)1865 722 113 ♦ local rate: 0845 230 9601
facsimile: +44 (0)1865 722 868 ♦ email: info.uk@trafford.com

10 9 8 7 6 5 4 3 2

Larry's Dedication

This is dedicated to Margie who has stood by me through thick and thicker, thin and thinner, and helped me believe that I had what it took to get this work done.

Joe's Dedication

This is dedicated to Phyllis Parker for always believing and Professor John Trimbur, who got me started in non-fiction.

Acknowledgements

Over the years many people have worked with me and became so enamored with the material that forms this book, they strongly urged me to get it into print and make it available to the general public. My dream has always been to help people obtain jobs they like. The Career Game Championships and How To Win is my way of giving that dream to them.

I want to thank the many people who made this book possible, for their support and encouragement to continue on and take a work that performed at a high level of excellence in action and create a powerhouse in print.

Linda Ostrander, D.M.A., Ph.D. was the first person to suggest that I should continue my education and go for my doctorate, a vision that I'd previously never imagined in my wildest thinking. She later became crucial in advising me as a member of my doctoral committee, which is where the original research material for this book began. For her inspiration and belief in me, I owe her more than I can put into words.

One of the first friends who genuinely believed that I should step up and put my ideas and advisement into print was Doris Klietmann. She saw a significant difference in my methods and pushed me into taking my work to a higher level.

Mark Joswicki has also been a good friend and professional who provided numerous key perspectives. It was he who gave me the inspiration to focus my attention on the technical world, a field where jobs continue to vaporize all over the USA. Through his eyes I was able to take the field of career counseling—known to be very "touchy-feely"—and give it a logical and strategic approach that made more sense to the technical world.

Susan Tordella-Williams offered some great writing tips as the book took shape. Her own experience in changing careers and using my concepts helped to prove that it really did work. She helped me develop my writing into readership language.

Rev. Judith Wright was my balance through the tough times and helped me keep perspective when it seemed darkest. A Unitarian Universalist minister and devout Buddhist, she reminded me many times and in different ways that I would likely never know what lay ahead of me around the corners of life, but if I kept believing and trusting in a positive vision, it would manifest accordingly. It has.

I think any budding author needs an experienced writer willing to acknowledge and offer testimony. This has particular meaning when that person is also a colleague in the same industry. I have respected Wendy Enelow's professionalism for many years and when she agreed to critique my work I was truly honored.

Jack Prather, Ph.D. was very unique. He knew absolutely nothing of the career advisement industry nor the work I'd created. In that, he was as objective as anyone could possibly be. I was a bit nervous when he agreed to read and critique my work. As a fully retired Public Relations expert, I knew that he'd be tough and probably not easily impressed. Jack, I thank you for your candor and your gracious thoughts.

Lynn Kuefler for providing a last set of eyes when we got too close to the words to see.

Mike Duval for coming in at the eleventh hour and doing a spectacular job creating a book cover worthy of the text.

What can I say about Joseph Parker? No Joe Parker, no book. It's as simple as that. He went far beyond making sure the syntax was correct and the book flowed well. His technical creativity, probative questions, and depth perspective brought this work to an entirely different level. We worked extraordinarily well together to develop this into the successful text it is today. I am eternally grateful for your preponderance of initiative.

Thank you one and all.

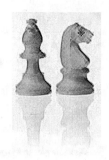

Table Of Contents

The Career Game Championships

The Self

Transition Theory, Concepts, and Principles

Tools

Process Quality Assurance

Integration

Appendices

Introduction

It used to be easier. If you needed to change jobs, you looked at the "want ads" and told your friends, relatives, and associates that you were looking. When you saw or heard about a job that fit, you mailed out a résumé that showed your work and education history. If the company representative liked your résumé, you got an interview; if you and the representative "clicked," you got the job.

Today, the process of job and career transition seems far more difficult: it is far from quick, far from easy, and for most people, a long way from fun. With the advent of the Internet as a job search medium, economic uncertainty, and global markets, the reward of a good job that pays well and is personally gratifying has become a much sought-after—but rarely achieved—prize. The average working professional searches doggedly for this reward, but in the end usually takes whatever job happens to come along.

That's the bad news. The good news is that it doesn't have to be this way. Here's even better news: I can show you how to land the prize.

...the reward of a good job that pays well and is personally gratifying has become a much sought-after—but rarely achieved—prize

As a Career Consultant for more than fifteen years, I have advised countless individuals. In that time, I have developed specific techniques that have been proven to work effectively. After honing these techniques in a one-on-one setting, I now want to take my ideas and concepts—which have helped my clients land excellent, appropriate, rewarding jobs with great salaries—to a broader audience. That's where *The Career Game Championships* comes in.

Let's use the analogy that a job search is like trying to win Olympic Gold. Often, the difference between the prestige of a medal and being a mere runner-up is tenths of a point or hundredths of a second. The job search process is no less competitive. The difference between getting the job offer and losing to the competition can be one poorly researched fact or a single ineffective answer to an interview question. And that's why I call this process "the Career Game Championships.™"

The key, whether it is athletic competition or job search, is upgraded training and excellence in applied technique. Without these, a gifted athlete is still unlikely to win the gold. I believe that with good training and improved technique your career and job search game will be at a significantly higher level.

With many of the techniques I will be sharing with you in the pages to come, the differences between what I'm teaching and what you're used to may seem subtle and in many instances you'd be correct. However, nearly two decades of development and results verification have convinced me that the fine-tuning I've done makes an incredible difference in how short and predictable an effective job search can be. These differences will come in the form of better presentation methods for both documents and direct interactions, carefully crafted differences in use of language, unique approaches, and a definitive frame of mind. When combined, these can make you a winner in the strategic game of your career management.

I can teach you to... take your job search to a different, higher level.

Experience has shown me that most people want to be in control of their searches and careers; they really want to win. All they need is a good coach to show them how. That is why many professionals eventually arrive at my door: I can teach you to overcome the challenges, make the most of your talents, and take your job search to a different, higher level. So, one of the things this book is designed to do is to teach you how to better manage your career and—more to the point—help you take control of your job search and not be a "victim of the system."

In today's business climate, you can be laid off, fired, downsized, right-sized—whatever the buzzword of the day might be—at a moment's notice. The reality is that companies will do whatever it takes to survive in a highly competitive marketplace. They owe that to the people who invested money into the company, and unfortunately in those instances, loyalty to employees takes a back seat. This fact of business life can put you in the situation of being an unwitting and unwilling victim of the system of enterprise. You cannot control that, but what you *can* control is how you react to such a turn of events. If you have the empowering knowledge to conduct an effective search in a way that keeps you from being a victim and remain in control of where you want to go with your career, great things will happen. Layoffs and the like are just speed bumps on your career path. They don't have to completely derail you, your family, or your financial security.

I hear you saying "Why should I change? I've always managed to get jobs in the past, and with the information available on the Internet today, it's so much easier." Sure, the information on how to get a good job that's right for you *is* out there. There are hundreds of books, videos, and CDs, as wells as endless hyperlinks on the Internet. Many provide good information, but the information on some will hurt you more than help you. How do you efficiently sift through the information? How do you separate the good information from the bad? And if you do have the time to take on such a huge task, will you have the expertise to be able to effectively apply the information to your particular situation?

Look no further than *The Career Game Championships*. Not only does it put the information you need on how to get the job that's right for you in one place, it also shows you how to apply the information.

> *While the skills and expertise you've gained are without question important to your search, you shouldn't be placed in a box because of them.*

Moreover, I find that typical search approaches tend to focus only on what the candidate has done in the past: they demonstrate *previous* experience, show the competencies he or she may have gained with regard to the *previous* jobs they have held, and in which industries they have *previously* performed. I believe this is a very narrow bandwidth for establishing an entire career path over a person's lifetime and it does little, if anything, to demonstrate marketing savvy critical to articulating how the candidate can specifically meet a target company's current needs. While the skills and expertise you've gained are without question important to your search, you shouldn't be placed in a box because of them.

There are a few things that distinguish the career change/ job search processes contained in this book from other approaches:

- My philosophy that to be successful in a career/job transition, you must *stand out*, and to do that you must do things in a different and better way than your competition; otherwise you are looking at a long, difficult exercise with little assurance of a positive outcome.
- My processes are specifically designed to be *pro-active* and articulate a searcher's motivational skills and expertise as they strategically relate to the business needs and profitability goals of target organizations.

- I encourage the use of a variety of measurable criteria and quality assurance parameters that allow you, the searcher, to make strategic corrections in your campaign, which contributes to *significantly shorter* transition time frames and *positive* outcomes.

- I utilize *subliminal imagery* and *neuro-linguistic programming techniques*—these are defined in the glossary—to bring about powerful self-empowerment, efficiency, and effectiveness. My deep research has led to finding simple yet unique and powerful ways of designing résumés and other search tools. These make use of exceptionally powerful language techniques that psychologically cause people to react favorably to the well-trained candidate, which usually results in strikingly short job searches. Transition times are often half the norm.

I will discuss these in detail throughout the book, except for the last bullet. I don't spend a lot of time discussing the imagery and language techniques beyond cursory descriptions, but rest assured that if you use the processes I talk about *just as they're described*, these powerful visual and linguistic techniques are implicit to them.

After using my processes, many people have mentioned that they were surprised that this knowledge had escaped their scrutiny and often-intensive research. Really, it's not so surprising. People typically spend some weeks or months around the time of a job search looking for applicable information. In contrast, I've spent a large part of my career researching and thinking about job search and career change issues and how to solve the problems associated with those activities. This knowledge is my expertise.

People who read this book and take the time to learn and implement its processes will be the beneficiaries of that experience and learning. I firmly believe that the information contained here can be particularly helpful to many professionals for the following reason: While they may be extremely skilled at their particular area of expertise, when it comes to the job transition process, most professionals are simply not very effective.

...when it comes to the job transition process, most professionals are not very effective.

It's not because they can't do it, but rather that they have never been shown how to conduct an intensive, focused job search. As a result, I have found that they seldom have the skills to evaluate their job or career *options*; they are seldom able to put together a good *strategic plan* to reach their goals; and they seldom have the *effective tools* to reach those goals. To compound the problem, most people do not know how to put together a *marketing plan* for themselves. This combination makes it tough to get into well-paying jobs that are rewarding for them.

This book contains processes that provide real and substantive answers to perplexing and difficult issues facing professionals, regardless of economic conditions or the state of the job market. It will help you objectively determine a number of career options and guide you in making good decisions about which direction makes the most sense for you. Then you will be given information on how to develop the appropriate tools to help you achieve your goals. You will find in tough economic times that the processes outlined here will make you stand out from the pack, and in better conditions, they will help you make your desired change even quicker and with higher returns than you may have imagined.

The Career Game Championships can help you learn many seemingly subtle, yet strikingly effective techniques that, when used together, provide higher marks across the many competitive events throughout the search process. Perhaps more important is the fact that this information will be useful for the rest of your working career and can help you to advance yourself to be as successful as you would like to be.

The techniques that I will show you include:

- **Cover Letters and Résumés**—How to create high impact, marketing-oriented materials that get measurable results in as little as 24 hours.
- **Interviewing**—How to prepare answers to interview questions that are personally tailored to your situation and are specifically designed with the hiring company's needs in mind—something every hiring manager is looking for.
- **Marketing Plan**—How to develop an effective job search management plan with ingredients—quality assurance and discipline—that few traditional plans offer, but are actually critical to an effective search.
- **Negotiating**—How to use a simple, yet effective way to approach negotiating more money, better benefits, and gain a greater sense of confidence about "asking" for what you deserve.
- **Process**—How to conduct a search using multiple and simultaneous methods. I believe this is the most important piece of all, because most people conduct their searches randomly and mostly on the Internet—a very weak process approach.

I want to specifically state here that comparing the components above to other search techniques is like comparing components of competing automobiles. All cars have an engine, tires, brakes, etc. Yet, there are significant differences between the models of various manufacturers.

In this case, my model is greatly different in how these search techniques are applied, and that separates my clients from the general population. I have used this information to instruct my clients in the subtleties of the process. I provide insight and instruction on the application of all these critical elements.

...my model is greatly different in how these search techniques are applied...

I believe that my approach is at least five to ten times more effective than traditional approaches. It substantially streamlines the search process and provides searchers with strategic and critical knowledge that the general public simply does not have, and is not typically provided by career counselors who want to continue to charge large fees for job search assistance. Further, the rewards will be mind-bending. For many of you this will be the very first time you've actually been in control of your own career destiny instead of being at the mercy of the market.

I can say to you without reservation that I think my way is a better way. So let's get to it.

The Career Game

Championships

The Career Game Championships

The Problem: The LIMP Method

Most people think they know how to perform an effective job search. Certain techniques have been passed down through the years and touted as "the way" to go about getting a job. To be sure, by and large, people do get jobs when they use them. So those methods keep getting reused, time and time again, whenever the time to change jobs or change careers comes around.

What I've found in my years as a career counselor is that the old methods aren't even close to efficient and instead tend to lock people into patterns that have them continually landing in jobs that they don't enjoy, without even the hope of breaking out into the *perfect job* that everyone hopes for.

Lately, technology—most obviously in the form of the Internet—has provided us with new ways to quickly get information about companies not only within miles of our homes, but around the globe. This new addition to the old bag of tricks has been heralded as a revolution in job or career change searches.

But even with all of the new information now available at our fingertips, people are still relying heavily on the same old methods, are not using the new technology in ways that leverage its full potential to benefit their searches, and absolutely are not using innovative and effective methods that separate them from the competition.

The approach that the vast majority of job seekers use can be summed up quite easily, and as you'll see, there isn't a lot of variation on the theme between searchers. Let's take a look at the "typical" approach that I see people using and its drawbacks. After that, we'll discuss how these typical methods ignore crucial elements that are critical to a successful search.

The LIMP Method

For as long as I have been working with professionals, I've noticed that nearly every single one goes about the career and job search process the same way. They use what I call the **LIMP** method:

- **L**ook at job listings in newspapers or on the Internet
- **I**nquire to see if anyone knows of any jobs or of any companies that are hiring
- **M**eet with a recruiter or temporary agency
- **P**aper the world with résumés in the hopes that one sticks and they get hired.

Does this sound familiar to you? While not all job searchers follow these exact steps, they happen more often than not. And even if the process doesn't match exactly, my experience tells me that a mere handful of people use a complete search methodology that covers all of the pieces of the puzzle from initial inquiries to signing on the dotted line.

...most of those I've talked to agree that when it comes down to it, they usually take... whatever job comes along.

Using the LIMP method will probably get you a job at some point, but there are a number of serious drawbacks to this method. First and foremost, it is quite simply *not* the most efficient way to perform a search, and it is not likely to net you the dream job that you have been hoping for. In fact, most of those I've talked to agree that when it comes down to it, they usually take what is referred in the business as "the low hanging fruit"—whatever job comes along. Sometimes it's a good, satisfying job in a decent company and sometimes it isn't. What it tells me is that most people are not in control of their career and are usually at the mercy of the business world. By taking the first thing that comes along, they are sacrificing the very things that are likely to make them happy in a job. I always find this to be a bit tragic because I know the result can be so much better. But instead of being a victor in their job search, they more often end up being a victim.

Direct Drawbacks of the LIMP Method

As I mentioned, there are a number of direct drawbacks to the LIMP method.

The first one, as you may have guessed, is that nearly everyone uses it. That means that almost every person trying to change jobs or careers is going through *exactly* the same steps that you are. This does nothing to distinguish you from all the other searchers.

Don't underestimate the power of being unique. If you want to have a successful and effective career or job transition, then everything that you use during your search—both your process and your materials—must be very different and of higher quality than what everyone else is using. Most people want to be unique in their job search, but they don't know how to achieve that goal, so they fall back on the LIMP method.

The second drawback to the LIMP method is that it places the power completely in the hands of the hiring organization. How can it be *your* dream job when *they* are setting the parameters? You have no control over the process; you are completely at the mercy of those on the hiring end of the equation. This not only has a negative effect on your self-worth, but in the vast majority of cases, you will end up with a "job in a box"—trying to shoehorn your skills into a job

> *If you want to have a successful and effective career or job transition, then everything that you use... must be very different and of higher quality than what everyone else is using.*

offered by the company instead of being able to generate a job that is tailored for your skills.

I know you're probably looking at the last statement and saying to yourself "that's impossible, I cannot get a company to *create* a new job tailored specifically to my skills." Let me assure you that it's not impossible, and in fact if you follow the processes laid out in this book, you will realize at the end of your search that you have done just that. I'll tell you how to make it happen.

But first, let's look at the specific drawbacks to each piece of the LIMP method.

Looking at Job Listings

The first element of the LIMP method is to "Look at job listings in newspapers or on the Internet."

This seems like the obvious place to start, doesn't it? While that may be true, for most people, that's also where the search ends.

The problem with relying solely on job listings is that they're available to everyone. By using only this source, you've placed yourself into the heaviest competition for those jobs. Any person on your block that has similar skills to yours can look in that newspaper's classified listings and have access to the very same opportunity that you do.

I'll let you in on a secret here: The Internet has only made it worse. People often think that Internet job sites have revolutionized the job search, opening up access to jobs in a way never before available. In fact, Internet sites *have* revolutionized the process: now, instead of a job listing being available only to people who can purchase your local newspaper, they're available to *any person across the globe*. Instead of competing with people in your local area, you're literally competing with millions of people anywhere in the world who can log on to that Internet site. The reality is, with those listings being so available, your odds of capturing the attention of the hiring company have actually *gone down*.

The second challenge with job listings is that

Revolt of a Different Kind

A former client of mine was able to land a position using the methods described in this book. When the time came to hire people for his own group, his boss told him to use a well-known Internet job posting site.

He dutifully filled out the listing. Though the job they were listing required using elements of the Internet, it was in no way a Web Design or Development job. In fact, he explicitly stated so in the listing.

Over the next two weeks he was bombarded with dozens of résumés, most of them from Web Designers or Software Developers. After trying in vain to keep up with them, he eventually got disgusted and stopped looking through them at all.

He eventually filled the position through his own business to business and personal network.

Still think Internet job sites are a revolution?

in most cases, once the listing has been prepared and placed, the parameters have been locked in. The hiring organization has settled on a very specific set of skills that they are looking for in a candidate, and by that time it's very difficult to change their mind. If your skills *are* an exact match, the match is still based on your past, not on where you want to go. If your skill set differs even slightly, you may not get consideration because it is very likely that so many people have responded to that ad that someone else's skill set *is* a perfect fit.

The third problem with relying on published listings is that it puts you at the mercy of the market. If the job market is down, fewer job listings are generated, so in turn there are fewer opportunities for you to follow. If the market is hot, there may be a plethora of listings at any one time, but they may still not be a good match for your skill set.

The Career Game Championships will show you how to use job listings to your benefit, but as one portion of a comprehensive job search process. It will show you how to find ways to open up the doors to opportunity using methods beyond prepared job listings that are also independent of the whims of the current job market. Finally it will open you up to the "Unpublished Job Market" that takes you beyond job listings entirely.

Inquiring about Jobs

The second element of the LIMP method is to "Inquire to see if anyone knows of any jobs or of any companies that are hiring."

First, when performing this inquiry step, the searcher's focus is often very narrow, limited only to people "in the industry" or to those that they think may have the proper connections. As we'll show later, this narrow vision is an impediment in itself, since the networking contact that will bear fruit may be someone you know in a completely unrelated field, or more often still, someone you *don't even know* at the start of your search.

Second, a serious drawback to this method is often the way it's presented and the limited scope of the people you come in contact with.

A Word About Networking

Many people think of the process of inquiring to their friends, colleagues, and perhaps past co-workers as "Networking." In a very simplistic way it is, but as we'll discover later, it's not the best way, nor is it true networking.

Many searchers also believe that networking will be the answer to all their problems, and that by calling only on their network, that this will somehow provide them with a short, easy job search.

My experience has shown me while networking is a critical element of a complete job search, the expectation by a searcher that networking will lead to a quick and easy job search is not valid.

By asking people specifically "Do you know of any companies that are hiring?" or "Do you know of any jobs?" you put them on the defensive. The honest answer in both cases may simply be "No." But you are also subconsciously putting the impetus of finding a job on them; the psychological message is that they actually need to do the legwork for you.

In addition, if they were to point you toward—or even more specifically, recommend you for—a job, they are now in the "hot seat." In that scenario their reputation is now at stake, since they were the one that recommended you or at the very least told someone that you were suited for the job. If for some reason you don't work out in the position, they become exposed and their personal relationship or reputation with that person or organization may be tarnished. This alone may prevent them from connecting you to the right people and pointing you toward an opportunity.

The Career Game Championships will show you innovative and attractive ways to network—we'll actually call it Resource Development—that go beyond people in the industry or people you know personally. It will also show you ways to approach people that not only prevents them from feeling defensive, but in fact makes them *want* to help you and provide better leads.

Meeting with Headhunters

The third element of the LIMP method is to "Meet with a recruiter or temporary agency."

> *Recruiters and Temporary Agency personnel are only interested in placing you in jobs most like the ones you've already been in.*

In and of itself, there is nothing wrong with this step but it is fraught with the same dangers that you find with relying solely on job listings.

First, despite appearances, recruiters—also known colloquially as "headhunters"—are not looking out for your best interest. They typically are paid by the hiring company and as such are interested in providing a perfect match between the résumés they have on file and the specifications laid out by the hiring organization. They generally only want to assist you if they happen to have a matching "job requisition" sitting on their desk at the time your résumé arrives. If your list of skills doesn't exactly match the criteria laid out in the listing, you aren't likely to get a call from the recruiter.

Second, Recruiters and Temporary Agency personnel are *only* interested in placing you in jobs most like the ones you've already been in. This may be helpful, but only if you want to stay in the same box. For the majority of the population who would like to get out of their old patterns and into new situations this method will most likely work against you. The result is no call. This can be particularly frustrating since these organizations actually do have open jobs waiting to be filled—just not for you.

Third, there are hundreds of recruiters out there and many hiring companies will use only one or two of them. In addition, recruiters typically want you to sign up exclusively with their organization. When you put these two things together, the result is a severely limited set of opportunities that will be presented to you.

The Career Game Championships will show you how to use recruiters to your benefit, as one portion of a comprehensive job search process. It will also show you how to open up opportunities outside of recruiters that will allow you to move beyond the situation you are currently in and leverage your skills in new ways.

Papering the World with Résumés

The last element of the LIMP method is to "Paper the world with résumés in the hopes that one sticks and you get hired."

...if you are sending out résumés to anyone who may have a job, you are not focusing your efforts...

There are a number of difficulties with this element.

First, if you are sending out résumés to anyone who may have a job, you are not focusing your efforts on companies and positions that suit you best, that will make best use of the skills you most like to employ, and that you are likely to enjoy working in. Again, your chances of getting your dream job are slim.

Second, in the interest of sending out as many résumés as possible in the shortest amount of time, typically the searcher sends exactly the same résumé and cover letter to every company on their list. Without any customization to these items based on the specific goals and needs of the organization to which you are applying, the result is a generic résumé, which, in turn, makes you seem generic.

Third, most searchers tend to use cover letters and résumés as "brain dumps" that merely present the standard chronological regurgitation of job tasks. Additionally, most searchers focus on "style over substance" when it comes to cover letters and résumés, believing that a slick presentation and the use of the latest trendy formats are the key to getting noticed.

The Career Game Championships will show you how to design your cover letters and résumés as *marketing instruments* designed to sell yourself to the organization while still gearing them towards the needs of the specific company. It will also show you how to supercharge the résumé that you submit so that it stands out from the rest and highlights your skills, experience, accomplishments and motivations rather than being a simple list of tasks performed in previous positions.

Indirect Drawbacks of the LIMP Method

There are a number of other drawbacks to relying solely on the LIMP method when performing a job or career search.

Ignoring Motivations

Using the LIMP method completely ignores your motivations. The key to a truly successful job or career change is that the resulting position allows you to employ the skills that you most enjoy using in your job. Keep in mind that the skills that most motivate you may not be the skills that you are currently using most often in your current job, and therefore may not be reflected in your list of accomplishments.

The Career Game Championships will help you identify your motivations and apply them to your job search.

Ignoring the Follow-Up

Quite possibly the biggest drawback of trying to perform a search using the LIMP method is that it is woefully incomplete. Look once again at the four major elements and you quickly realize that they may get you in the door, but no farther. They completely leave out interview, follow-up, and negotiation skills, which are by far the more important pieces of the puzzle.

The Career Game Championships will teach you important interviewing skills which will allow you to control the interview process, show you how to provide dynamic answers to tough interview questions, and show you how to recognize "hidden" questions lurking within seemingly innocent interview questions. It will show you how to follow up with the hiring organization after the interview is over. And it will also teach you important negotiating skills that can help you avoid leaving thousands on the table in salary, benefits, and perks—all in a calm, non-confrontational manner.

Ignoring Quality Assurance

This is an element that I find is missing from almost every job search. Usually when I ask if they've used any kind of quality assurance in their process all I get is a blank stare. People just don't consider it; some outright ignore it.

Since the typical methods revolve around getting you in the door, the only criterion that is typically used to measure success is the number of interviews that the searcher gets, and beyond that, the number of offers received. But if you look at the job search as an ongoing process, there is much more to it than that. The process *must* be managed.

> *Usually when I ask if they've used any kind of quality assurance in their process all I get is a blank stare.*

The Career Game Championships will show you numerous benchmarks and measurable keys that you should implement and examine throughout your search campaign. It will show you how to recognize problems and make critical adjustments along the way.

In summary, the methods typically used by those seeking to change jobs or careers fall far short of a complete process designed to result in the job you've always wanted. The process that I'm about to show you, starting with the next chapter, addresses all of these shortfalls and provides what I believe to be the most complete job search process available. It's a process designed to take all of your motivations and skills into account, while providing you with all the tools you need to finally find the job in the "right" organization, that you truly enjoy, pays well, and is personally gratifying.

The Breakthrough: The SOLID Method

Everyone hopes for a job that pays well and is personally gratifying. Most people are looking for a job that they enjoy and that makes good use of their skills—not just any skills, but those that they particularly like to employ. You may be a great accountant, but if it doesn't motivate you—if you don't enjoy it—you aren't going to find an accounting job particularly gratifying.

As we discovered, the LIMP method does nothing to address your motivations. In fact, it puts you totally at the mercy of the job market; you find yourself in a position where you must shoehorn your skills into a predetermined job description. I find it very frustrating when people rely on the same old things, not realizing the drawbacks of the tasks they are performing, and not recognizing the critical tasks that they are leaving out. Most people, possibly yourself included, have gone through this LIMP routine time and time again because no one has ever told them that there might be a better way.

I'm here to tell you that there *is* a better way.

The Career Game Championships aims to change the way that you prepare for, execute, and complete a job or career search. This is a process that empowers individuals to be in control of their search and to implement a career plan with direction and goals, taking into account the things that motivate them, and using tools that assist them in achieving those goals in both the short and long run.

The combination of enjoyment and favored skills is different for everyone, and that's a good thing because it ensures that there are people to fill all of the different types of jobs out there. People are complex, and that makes the Career Game Championships complex. It also means that everybody's idea of the ideal job is different, and a "job in a box" is not likely to fulfill the criteria of your ideal job.

So if the LIMP method only gets you a job in a box, obviously a new method is needed. I have such a method and it can be learned and implemented by anyone. A method that, if followed correctly, can place the searcher in a position of strength so that they find themselves winning regularly at the Career Game Championships.

The SOLID Method

The key to a successful job or career search is that you take the best of "the old way" and add a number of concepts that will result in a comprehensive process. Much of what I'm going to teach you is common sense, but I find that very few people use these methods in their search.

Some of what I'm going to teach you may also require some changes to your mindset. But what you'll find is that the method laid out here, in direct opposition to the method in the last chapter, is **SOLID**. This method emphasizes:

- **S**trategy—An approach combining marketing-oriented thinking, tools, and processes.
- **O**rganization—A complement of well thought out and planned search activities with planned results.
- **L**ogic—A logical, common-sense approach tells you that if your current actions aren't working, then you must adapt, adjust, and change.
- **I**nnovation—A commitment to learning new methods and techniques for marketing yourself that differentiates you from everyone else.
- **D**etermination—A demonstrated effort to combine and use all of the required search processes throughout your search—avoiding or leaving out any part at any time is a formula for failure.

In addition, once you've seen how my method works, I believe you will agree that is it both **U**ser-friendly and **R**ealistic. The final result? U R SOLID as opposed to LIMP.

Following this method will get you a much better job than you could have using other methods and one that is likely to be much more satisfying. It is also likely to get you a job in one-third to one-half the time it would take using more typical methods. It is also very likely that you won't feel pressure to simply settle for the low-hanging fruit, because you'll have more choices available to you. Many of my clients have found that they get a number of job offers almost simultaneously, giving them the ability to select the best option for themselves.

Direct Benefits of the SOLID Method

Just as there are drawbacks to the LIMP method, there are significant benefits to using the SOLID method.

The first is that it is unique, in two ways. The techniques described in this book help you discover the unique combination of talent and motivation that leads to the discovery of your ideal job. I will show you how to implement a process that is much different than the typical job search, and show you methods that stand head and shoulders above the usual "process," if you can even use that term to describe what most people do.

When you are finished, you will know how to present yourself as the unique candidate in the eyes of prospective employers, one that stands out from the pack. I'll let you in on another secret: If you follow my method correctly *there will be no pack*. This method is so proactive, you will be making opportunities for yourself without facing much competition, because you will be making your mark before a job listing is even prepared.

This method is so proactive, you will be making opportunities for yourself without facing much competition...

Which brings me to the second benefit: you are in control. Instead of relying on posted job listings that force you to shoehorn your skills into the "job in a box,"—a job that is already defined with specific tasks and certain required skills and criteria—this method allows you to control the process, and the end result is often a job that is tailored to your skills and motivations. As I alluded to in Chapter 1, you have the opportunity to generate your own position, possibly one that the company had not considered before. So much better than the jobs in a box that are typically very confining and seldom represent positions that will utilize all the skills you would most enjoy.

So let's look at the pieces of the SOLID method and investigate how they help you to be unique and bring a measure of control over the search process that you are likely to find is unprecedented in your career.

Strategy

The first element of the SOLID method is "Strategy." A truly effective job search is not a series of unplanned coincidences and unconnected encounters. Rather, it must be well thought out—a strategic process that combines marketing-oriented thinking, tools, and processes.

Marketing-oriented thinking refers to the fact that your job search process is really no different from a business project that markets a product. That business project totally focuses on the different ways to make the consumer aware of the product by using a combined marketing plan to raise awareness of the product using many different methods.

In this case, the product is you and the consumer is the hiring organization.

If your job search is a loose, mostly coincidental string of occurrences, you are not likely to get "the win"—a new, personally rewarding job. However, if as I suggest, you treat the job change process as a business marketing project and manage it accordingly, you are much more likely to be successful.

Management of the process requires time and

"Yeah, but I Hate Marketing…"

Many people say and think this because they believe a search becomes about "selling" themselves, an act that is counter to much of our society.

When I use the language of "marketing," my system is more about applying the tactical excellence—dotting the I's and crossing the T's—of an effective project management approach. When this is done, the marketing aspect will take care of itself quite well without having to compromise your work values or ethics.

effort, but I believe that the time and effort is all worthwhile, and when you've completed the process and moved into a position that you truly enjoy, I think you'll agree.

The Career Game Championships will show you how to put together a strategy for tackling the job search process. It will show you how to build a multi-faceted approach that will raise awareness of you and your skills. By using this strategic approach, prospective employers will take notice of you.

Organization

The second element of the SOLID method is "Organization." A truly effective job search is not simply thrown together, but instead is a well-organized set of planned search activities that lead you towards your desired results. During the process, you will plan each week's search activities, and know at that time what your expected outcome is.

By putting together an organized set of tasks that you can repeat on a scheduled basis, you not only have knowledge of the upcoming steps, but you can also better plan your tasks, responses, and alternatives.

The Career Game Championships will show you how to organize your job search so that it is the most thorough, complete process you've ever used. The organized process of the Career Game Championships shows you how to set up a methodology to track your progress, ways to continually grow your network, and how to use control measures to always improve your activities.

Logic

The third element of the SOLID method is "Logic." If the process you're using doesn't make sense to you, it's not going to be very successful. I believe that the process described in the following pages is extremely logical—it just makes sense. It has a flow. In fact, as we move through the process, you may find yourself saying to yourself, "That seems so obvious. Why didn't I think of that before?"

Logic should also tell you that if your current methods are not working, then something must change. This applies not only to methods you have used in the past, but also to the tasks that you happen to be performing at any given time as you implement the processes described by *The Career Game Championships*. There will be things along the way that may require adjustments, adaptations, and changes throughout the process. My program will accommodate such requirements as they arise.

If the process you're using doesn't make sense to you, it's not going to be very successful.

The Career Game Championships will lead you through this logical, common-sense approach. As you move through the process, you will see that logical thinking continually leads you along the path towards a successful outcome. It will help you learn how to discover real answers to hard questions, provide a methodical approach, and point you toward the logical conclusion.

Innovation

The fourth element of the SOLID method is "Innovation." This relates not only to my method itself, but also to your acceptance of it. I believe that this method is the most innovative way to conduct a job search that you will find. The richness of the method as well as its complete, thorough nature combine to form what for most people will be a completely new way of looking at the job search process.

In addition, you will be bringing innovation to your own search in the form of a commitment to learning new methods and techniques for marketing yourself. You will quickly see that these innovative methods and techniques are what are going to differentiate you from everyone else during your search.

I urge you to be innovative throughout the entire process. You will see that much of my method revolves around the concept of marketing yourself just as you would a business product. There are many ways to do this, and the more creative you are in finding ways to market yourself, the more flexible you are to find the methods that work best for you, the more successful your search will be.

The Career Game Championships will teach you an entirely new way to look at the job search process, teach you many new tasks and methods to use during the search, and teach you how to innovate during the process in the form of using new, inventive methods to market yourself.

Determination

The fifth element of the SOLID method is "Determination." I can't stress enough how important this element is to the process. No job search is easy, but I assure you that if you show your determination in following the techniques I'm describing to you, you *will* be successful. I also assure you that if you follow the methods I describe here closely, the length of your job search *will* be less than if you were relying on traditional methods. But in order to see the fruits of success, you must be determined to see it through.

> *...I assure you that if you show your determination in following the techniques I'm describing to you, you will be successful.*

The Career Game Championships has much to show you. You are going to have to put forth a demonstrated effort to combine and use all of the tools and methods described in this book throughout your search. The process is designed specifically to be used as a complete, all-encompassing set of tasks, methods, and activities; avoiding or leaving out any part at any time is a formula for failure.

I do believe, however, that if you remain determined throughout the process and follow the process closely, that your determination will be rewarded. The payoff will be better than you imagined.

3

The Solution: The Career Transition Model

While the SOLID method generally describes the desirable traits of a successful search, it doesn't say much about the actual nuts and bolts of performing one. It's kind of like having all the parts of a car but no manual on how to assemble it. You might put it together, but who knows how it will run?

There are many elements to a successful search and as I've mentioned, I believe it takes a cohesive combination of those elements to put together a truly successful job or career change search—one that's going to result in a well-paying, satisfying position that plays on your strengths, favored skills, and motivations.

So how do you put it all together and what *are* the crucial parts? The parts come out of all the pieces of the SOLID method. It is important to remember that to be successful, *all* the parts must be included. So to describe this, I have developed a theory around the process and created a model to visually illustrate how it works. To my knowledge, it is the first of its kind. I call it the Career Transition Model™ (CTM).

The CTM is the culmination of years of research, consideration, and observation throughout my counseling career. It visually describes that combination of elements that I believe are at the core of every successful search. Let me reiterate: to me, a "successful search" is not simply getting a job; it is landing a well-paying, personally gratifying job that challenges you, motivates you, and that you actually enjoy.

Let's take a look at the model, shown in Figure 1.

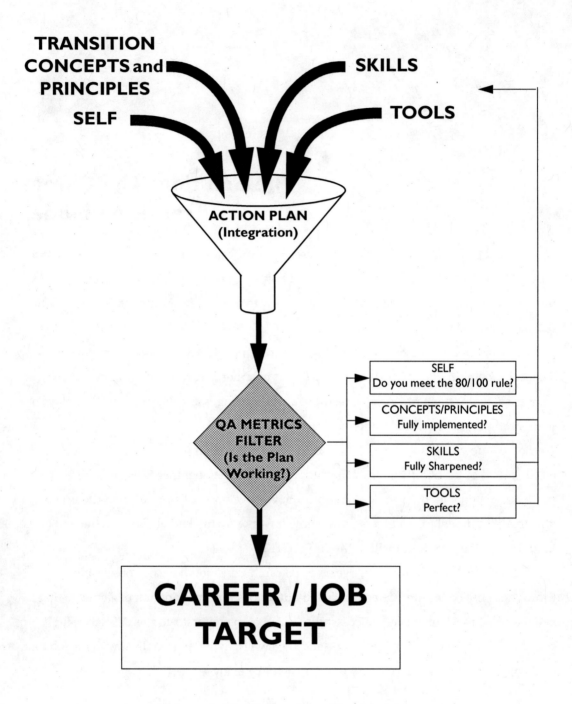

Figure 1: The Career Transition Model

As the model illustrates, the key to any successful career or job change within a planned, expedient time frame is the development of an action plan that integrates the four core elements—Knowledge of the Self, Skills, Tools, use of the Transition Concepts, and Marketing Principles. As I mentioned, the CTM is a visual representation of my Theory of Career Transition, which states:

> The optimal potential for expected outcomes for career or job change is contingent upon the application and integration of certain key elements which include, but are not limited to: intimate knowledge of Self; self-marketing principles and strategic thinking concepts; self-marketing tools; transition skills; and finally, quality assurance metrics that are woven into a circular-oriented, measurable process.

Of everything in this book that we're going to cover, the Transition Theory may be the hardest to grasp. It's very academic, much more abstract than the rest, and not as obvious at first glance. While it may not be quite what you're used to when thinking about a job change, when you break it down to everyday language, it's pretty simple and straightforward. The success of the search is based upon inclusion and implementation of all the elements illustrated in the model:

The success of the search is based upon inclusion and implementation of all the elements illustrated in the model.

- Self—Genuine knowledge of yourself as it relates to your job search.
- Transition Concepts and Principles—Structured ideas regarding the best way to approach a career or job change.
- Tools—The "tools of the trade" that are needed in every search, such as résumés, cover letters, and so on.
- Skills—Developed abilities to perform certain tasks involved in the search process; for example, interviewing abilities that are at a significantly higher standard than the norm.

These together form the four core elements of the Transition Theory. However, the other illustrated components are critical to the process:

- Action Plan—The integration of the four core elements.
- Process Quality Assurance Metrics—Determination if the search is working well enough to achieve the planned outcome in a reasonable, specified timeframe.
- Career/Job Change Target—Where you want to be. The right job, in the right organization, earning the right income.

Once an action plan is developed it is absolutely necessary to filter the process through Quality Assurance Metrics to determine positive, measurable results. If you aren't seeing the results that you expect, you must re-examine the four core components and determine if one or more are not performing to expectations. If you discover something lacking in the plan, you must re-evaluate, make changes where necessary, and once you put the updated action plan in place, continue running it through the QA filter until the desired results have been met. This is the key to successfully moving forward to the new position.

> *The vast majority of those who do not have knowledge of the model or those who have not used it become discouraged at their early attempts.*

The vast majority of those who do not have knowledge of the model or those who have not used it become discouraged at their early attempts. They tend to abandon the dream altogether or end up settling for yet another mundane job; they simply repeat old history. I'm not trying to frighten you, but rather to impress upon you the importance of using the complete, integrated process.

Consider this: Job search is a competition no matter what you do. Assume for a moment that you've entered into a statewide baking competition. Do you think you'd do well if you submitted a single layer box cake entry in a loaf pan? Yet, this is what most people do when it comes to their job searches. They use cookie-cutter processes, box-like resumes they found on the internet, and plain "loaf pan" methods. This isn't a criticism; it's a reality. And most people are simply unaware that there is another way.

The plain truth is that job search *is* a competition and more of a game of strategy, like chess. So let's use that kind of example since it's most like what is actually going on. Many people believe that they know how to play the game of chess fairly well. In fact, many do. They know the rules and the fundamentals of the game; they may have learned some good strategies and even achieved a reasonable level of skill. However, those that play it best have a complete command of everything going on in the game. They know the rules, they've studied the strategic concepts and principles, and they've developed their skills to recognize certain situations and respond accordingly.

Further, during the game itself, the truly skillful player is not just thinking about the current move, but also thinking ahead a number of moves to consider the implications of each possible action. They know how to use their tools—the pieces—to their best advantage. As you can imagine, if they are not thinking about the whole process, their game will be less successful and may even fall apart entirely.

The process of a job or career change, like chess, is a game of strategy. And likewise, most people believe they know how to conduct a job search. They've gotten jobs before, know the fundamentals of the job search, and possibly learned some good techniques along the way. But those who have a command of the entire process are those who excel at the search, those that get *the* job. The Career Transition Model is that process.

By following the Career Transition Model and exploiting its potential to the fullest, you can uncover and implement your championship-level job search skills. It can be used equally effectively by individuals who are changing positions as it can by someone who's changing careers completely.

There is one area where chess and the Career Game Championships diverge: In chess, a single misstep may cost a player the game. The beauty of the Career Game Championships is that you have many possibilities to recover from a mistake, and you can still clinch a significant win *provided that you return to the model when you discover a misstep*. In this game, individuals can easily refer back to this book or their notes and recalculate strategies for their next moves. This gives you a lot of flexibility and infinitely more opportunities.

> *The beauty of the Career Game Championships is that you have many possibilities to recover from a mistake...*

An Overview of the Model Components

Again, the key to a successful job or career change is having the knowledge and skill to integrate each of the core elements. While I listed them briefly, I'd like to expand upon them a bit here. In subsequent chapters I'll discuss and explain them all in depth, explain how to integrate them, and show how each plays its part in the game.

Self

In order to determine what it is that you really want in a job, you must genuinely and intimately know what you like and what you are all about. I call this the Self. This is the first core element that I discuss because it is imperative that you understand certain things about yourself before jumping into the process. Here, the self-evaluation process is a key factor in being able to establish the right career/job direction and avoid repeating bad history.

It always surprises me that most people take a new job or make a career step without taking the time to evaluate where they've been and where they are currently beyond "I'm not happy at my job." I suspect this may happen because they are unable to objectively evaluate the information and come up with viable job or career options on their own.

> *They may know that they dislike what they do or the company they work for, but they don't think about the root cause... or how they got there.*

They may know that they dislike what they do or the company they work for, but they don't think about the root cause or how they got there. As a result, they often continue the cycle of working for bad companies or in unsatisfying jobs. The Self section helps you objectively determine career options and guides you in making more informed decisions about which direction makes the most sense for you.

Another critical component of self-analysis is in the area of your current attitude and frame of mind. I have seen many job searches crumble because this part of the house was not in order. The Self section has been designed and carefully prepared to specifically provide you with knowledge and awareness that leads to a sense of hope, belief, and the confidence that you can truly achieve your career and job search goals.

Transition Concepts and Principles

The next core element to understand is the transition concepts and principles. A successful and well-managed job change or career transition adheres to certain strategic concepts and principles. Ignoring them results in a much less effective transition process.

Let's break these down a little bit.

- Business-minded Game Plan—An effective plan that includes business project best practices and marketing, as well as measurement and improvement of products and processes throughout the search project.
- Self-Marketing Principles—Effective use of time and energy that are consistent with efficiency and mirror marketing of products and services. Approaching the career or job change as a business project and managing it with that concept in mind.
- Strategic Thinking Concepts—Tactical processes and actions that are different than and superior to traditional views regarding job search. You must use strategic thinking throughout the search processes and activities.
- Innovative Thinking—You must be open-minded and willing to be flexible in adopting innovative concepts. This is critical when engaging in the quality assurance process.

- Commitment—You must be committed to the process, even if your materials and possibly your methods require modification, or during any "flat periods."

These are the same principles that come into play when you are managing a business project. This business project is about promoting a product—you. Like all products, this one must be marketed, and marketed effectively.

> *This business project is about promoting a product—you.*

Adopting the theory with its concepts and principles is as important to a successful, well-managed job/career search campaign as knowing the basic rules of chess if you expect to win a competition.

The Transition Concepts and Principles section discusses ways to identify these concepts and principles. It investigates various business concepts and good marketing techniques you can apply directly to your job search to make it as effective as possible.

Tools

This core element of the model revolves around the awareness and use of the appropriate tools—those that are actually designed to get the job done—and the realization that they all need to be in place. This is one area where most individuals typically have at least a little experience. Just about anyone who has ever looked for a job has a basic awareness about résumés, cover letters, and maybe some others. A savvy few may have also used some planning tools. There are some who have a level of expertise with these tools, but unfortunately, most people do not. Even with résumés and cover letters—areas where most people think they have a good command of how the tools should be used—I find most people are woefully misinformed and under-prepared.

The Tools section describes the proper use of résumés and cover letters. You'll learn to use them as proper marketing tools rather than a pretty introduction and list of past jobs. You'll also learn how to create an action plan, make the best use of your contacts, and the best ways to negotiate to get the best compensation—both financial and benefits—that you can.

Skills

The final core element is concerned with a number of important skills that must be learned in order to successfully complete a successful search. This is another area where individuals probably have a little experience. Interviewing is a part of almost any job search at any level, most people are familiar with the concept of negotiation, and many people have heard of networking, even if they have never used it. However, the vast majority of job searchers are not masters of these skills and they may even be hindering their progress by using them incorrectly. Very few have a sound understanding of the best way to practice and implement these skills and how they can be used in combination to "close the deal" in a way that benefits you most. Overall, the skills of the job search are usually not among any individual's premier strengths.

In the Skills section, you'll learn how to effectively create a network of resources that you can use to get information about and gain entry into the companies that you target, all without making your friends and colleagues feel uncomfortable and without forcing them into a recommendation. You'll learn how to identify the "real" question behind the questions asked by interviewers and ways to skillfully answer even the most difficult of them. You'll also learn how to negotiate a compensation package—one that goes beyond what you may have ever expected—for your desired position in a way that is non-confrontational, non-stressful, and easy.

Integration

This is the key to the model. By integrating all the core elements and not attempting to isolate or avoid certain parts, such as only engaging in activities that are "fun" or "easy," you gain significant advantage over the competition. Engaging in all of the elements as a single coordinated process dramatically increases the potential for a successful and desirable outcome.

Who is The Competition?
Simple: Everyone.
Technology has made it easy to search for positions down the street or across the globe at the click of a button. Therefore, anything that gives you a competitive advantage is a bonus.

This is not as easy as it might seem. Most clients tell me, "I had no idea that this was so involved." My response is usually, "It always was, you just didn't know it." And knowing the information does not necessarily mean that everyone can implement the program as they are instructed. Old habits are hard to break. My experience has shown that most people think they are engaging in all the activities they need to in order to achieve their job search goals. In reality, my clients—almost without exception—have, when challenged, been able to identify something that they were either leaving out or not fully leveraging in the complex process we call a job search.

Most people have one or more areas of expertise in their life. Job and career search is not usually one of them. The simple truth is that you need to be good at it if you really want to be in control of your career. And so, the final sections of the book deal with effectively integrating everything we discuss and ways to ensure that you aren't leaving anything out. I'll also demonstrate ways to streamline the process and make it simpler.

Process Quality Assurance

As I mentioned in Chapter 1, this is quite possibly the most overlooked of the core elements of the model. In all the years I've been consulting and coaching I've yet to hear a client say that they had used quality assurance in their search campaigns.

I can't stress this enough: *Quality Assurance is absolutely necessary.* If you can't measure your process, you cannot manage it. If you're not managing it, you have little to no control over it.

The Process Quality Assurance section provides numerous benchmarks and measurable keys to be implemented and examined all along the way of your search campaign. When you apply quality assurance to the program you can recognize problems and make critical adjustments along the way. Those adjustments can easily make all the difference in whether or not you have a successful outcome.

Getting Started

While the approach described in the Career Transition Model does require work, if you follow the program as I describe it and don't leave anything out you'll find it is not difficult.

It's a thorough, effective, and easily manageable process. Perhaps more importantly, it is quite unique. The techniques described in this book help you discover the one-of-a-kind combination of talent and motivation that reveals your ideal job, show you how to approach the job search using methods

> *It's a thorough, effective, and easily manageable process. And... it is quite unique.*

overlooked by the average job seeker, and possibly most important of all, present you as the distinctive candidate in the eyes of prospective employers.

The following pages contain clever moves, strategies, and control devices to check measurability, which in turn inspire a keen sense of confidence that comes from knowing how to win the Career Game Championships.

There is nothing here that is rocket science. The challenge is that most people think in a very linear fashion. They want to move from point A to point B to point C and so on. Therefore, people like to have this information presented in a linear manner. While I've tried very hard to do just that, the difficulty is that career change and job search is not linear in any way. It is much more of a quantum perspective, that is, it has many interdependent threads running through and around it, circling back on each other constantly, and ultimately creating a fabric of concentrated effort.

As a result, you will see references to other topics and concepts throughout the book, even some that we haven't covered yet as they're mentioned. Don't worry, if you are serious about implementing the process and read through and digest the contents of this book, it will all make sense in the end.

In fact, when you finish reading you'll probably realize that what I have shared is common sense and very obvious, but amazingly enough, the average person looking to change jobs or careers almost never uses these techniques. Just as in the game of chess, there are only so many pieces and so many ways the pieces can be moved. Yet, truly proficient participants can accomplish startling results when they know key approaches and techniques that are most likely to get them to "the win."

I want to share one more thing before we begin the journey. When you have completed the reading and implemented your search project I believe you'll have discovered something else unique about this process.

Are you ready for this?

Here goes: I've led any number of people through this process and those who have followed this program with a positive mindset have—on many occasions—expressed to me a feeling rarely experienced in conjunction with a job search: It's fun!

Believe it.

It is my personal quest to dispel the myth that there is never any pleasure in looking for a job and replace it with the reality that when you are in control, job searches can be an enjoyable experience. You may not believe it now, but when you win at the Career Game Championships, you'll understand.

With that said, let's get into the meat of the Career Transition Model and tackle each of the core elements in detail. I've broken each core element out into its own section. Within each section, the chapters cover components of the element in detail. Once we've covered each core element, we'll discuss how to integrate them, and then summarize the process.

The Self

The Self

Mindset

Before we get too deep into analyzing the Self, I want to make sure that your house is in order, so to speak. For this process to work, we need to put you into the right mindset, as there are many differences with my method when compared to the typical job search. So, I'd like to spend some time going through the potential shifts in thinking that you'll encounter throughout this process.

Evaluating Your Situation

Some readers may find it necessary to make a few mental adjustments by way of getting into the correct mindset. The process I'm going to describe to you is very effective for those who are mentally and emotionally ready to undertake it. However, if:

- you are hoping my method will be a "quick fix" that will magically get you a job without actually conducting a search
- you've got to get a job very quickly
- you feel that rejection is too difficult to deal with *at this time*
- your skills aren't up to industry standard
- you are in a "toxic" situation at your current job

then we need to take a step back. If any of these items describe you or your situation, then you may want to try something else in the short term. Any of these situations put a certain type of pressure on the process and will seriously hinder your efforts towards an effective search—the operative word here being *effective*.

The purpose of my method is to get a job that pays well and is personally gratifying—a job that you are going to love. That job isn't going to magically fall into your lap; if that were possible, it probably would have happened already. So there will be an active search component to my method. A job search of any value whatsoever is labor intensive.

In addition, done correctly, the process is going to take some time. This material is *not* designed to be a bandage for a hemorrhage situation. If the lack of financial resources is forcing an urgent need to take a job, I often suggest that you get some cash flow by taking a temporary or contract position. Such measures not only bring in some much-needed revenue, they also give you some breathing room to perform a thorough job search. These short-term positions also help to fill unwanted résumé gaps. I can tell you, though, that if you follow the program diligently, you will find that the overall search campaign is significantly shorter in length than searches employing other methods. I usually shoot for 90 days.

As with any job search, there is likely to be some rejection involved. It is exceedingly rare for a person to walk into their first meeting or interview, make an instant connection, be a perfect fit for the company, and get the job. Having said that, I would remind you that nearly every job search involves some rejection, no matter what method you use. I can assure you, though, that if you follow through with this program, you will see a dramatic reduction in rejection compared to past searches.

A Success Story

Recently, a client came in and as a result of using this material had three interviews in a single week and received two offers from the effort. He had been "launched" for only two weeks, and was searching in a job environment where most other searchers have been hard pressed to even get any interviews.

While not typical, that's my idea of a shorter search and near elimination of rejection!

However, based on what is taking place in your life or your emotional makeup, you may be in a position where it is difficult to handle that rejection. For example, you may be dealing with events in your life that make it hard to handle rejection in the short term. If this is the case, I suggest taking some time to deal with what is taking place in your life and then tackling the job search using this method when you are better able to handle the process.

You may be of the makeup where you have a difficult time with rejection overall. If this is the case, you may be thinking that this method might not be for you. Before you throw up your hands, consider this: True, there is likely to be some rejection involved, but if you recall, I also stated that there should be a dramatic reduction in rejection compared to other search methods. Having been fully engaged with clients who had some real issues with rejection, I found that the material I presented to them helped them tremendously in getting past those issues.

If you are in emotional turmoil, any job search is probably not going to be as quick as it would if you were feeling 100%. However, my method has been shown to cut job search time by up to half, even when the searcher is dealing with other stressful life events. In other words, no matter what method you use, when you are experiencing difficult circumstances your search would have taken longer than might be normally expected. But by using my method you will still cut your overall search time, especially as compared with other "traditional" methods.

An important strategic concept that I want to pass on to you is that a good career plan is one that is "market resilient"; that is, no matter what direction the market wind blows, the professional can easily adapt. Today's professional knows what they can do, what skills companies are willing to pay for, the value of those skills, and makes strategic moves before their career

> ### The Family Impact of Unemployment
> In the event that unemployment is a result of job loss, there may be some other issues to deal with: family issues.
> Nearly every unemployed person I've worked with has talked about the impact that being jobless has had on their family, both immediate and extended. Relations and spouses, male or female, have come right out and asked the searcher, "what is wrong with you? Why can't you find a job?" And, the longer the search took, the worse the comments and criticisms became.
> Alienation, depression, seclusion, substance abuse, divorce, and on rare occasions, domestic violence have been some of the results associated with being unemployed. Make no mistake—research shows that job loss ranks among the top ten emotional traumas in life.
> It is situations like those I mentioned above that were one of the driving factors for me to develop a better, more effective way to get through this difficult event. It was no surprise to me that a benefit to my method is the opportunity for not just a job, but for a better-fitting job with better pay within a company that is a good match for you.
> That said, if you are in a situation similar to the one I described above, you may want to go to "Plan B," jump to the Tools section of the book, and use them to get a short-term position to fulfill your immediate need. Then come back here to implement the full program when the situation is more stable.

reaches obsolescence. To avoid making common strategic errors today you must thoroughly know yourself, know the market, and have the expertise to maneuver within such fluid markets. It is important to stay on top of current industry trends and requirements, because it is very difficult to make a move if your skills are not up to par. Before you can make a move using this method, you need to spend some time making sure that your skill level matches—and if possible, exceeds—current standards. In other words, make yourself more market resilient.

It is also critical that your job search begin before the work environment becomes toxic, that is, the situation is so bad that you can no longer stand it and must get out immediately. When work environment toxicity occurs, it is already too late; the searcher has placed themselves in a victim role and must "react" as quickly as possible. The result is the need to get a new job immediately, which we've discussed is not an ideal match for this method.

Your Search is About... Them?

A major strategic concept that I want to discuss is the pervasive belief that the process of finding a new position is about you. I've seen it in almost every client I've ever had and it shows up everywhere—cover letters, résumés, and most often in interviews. The truth is, in successful searches, the focus, first, last, and always should be on the hiring company. What you want is of little relevance to the company.

> *...if the company can't use your skills and talents, they aren't going to hire you just because you're a whiz.*

I want to make this point as clearly as I can because it will be one of the most crucial concepts you learn.

A job search is 100% about the hiring company. After all, if the company can't use your skills and talents, they aren't going to hire you just because you're a whiz. The more times you integrate that thinking into your cover letters, your résumés, and the responses you offer at interviews, the greater your chances of getting the opportunity you seek.

This may seem counter to my earlier statements about controlling the process to get *your* dream job. Let me be clear. I am not saying that what you want isn't important. That will come later in the discussions with people in organizations, but just as the opening moves of a chess game are strategically critical to the desired outcome of the game, it is just as critical to demonstrate strategic awareness by showing the hiring organization what they need to see and hear. *The more you can connect the dots between what you do well and the specific needs of the company the greater your chances of landing the correct position in a target organization.* If you understand this statement and implement it, you are far ahead of your competition right from the start.

The Job Search Methodology

This may be the most important of the mindset shifts that I'm going to ask you to make. It is at the heart of the Career Game Championships.

Most of you who are reading this are thinking about the process in these terms: "getting a job." There is nothing wrong with that concept; we all have to live, and most of us need to work to do that. But I want you to think a little outside of the box so we can take that concept to a grander scale.

Think about it. Do you really want "just another job?" Or would you like to find *the* job? To land the "right" job, with the "right" company, in the "right" environment, and making the "right" money. Sound like a dream? I assure you, it's out there and it's attainable. All you have to do is reach out, take it, and not settle for less.

So far, so good. But this is where you start to think I'm crazy: The way to get all of these "right" things is to **not** look for a job.

That's not a typo... I'll say it again.

The way to get all of these "right" things is to **not** look for a job.

From this moment on, I don't want you to look for a job. Instead I want you to engage in a job search research project. By treating the process as a business project it's going to put you in a different frame of mind. As part of the project, you're going to:

> *By treating the process as a business project it's going to put you in a different frame of mind.*

- gain large amounts of information about companies
- obtain great insights about specific organizations and their cultures
- find out if those organizations actually have opportunities available

The most critical thing to understand here is that this process is *not* about looking for the job but rather looking for the company that is the best fit for you. The most productive way to do that is to research companies and find out something about them *before* you think about the position within that organization. This concept is quite different than the way that nearly all searchers—probably including yourself until now—think about gaining a position. Be different, target the company.

Once you have discovered which companies offer the best potential for you, the rest of the process is generally easy. In many instances when using this method the candidate has not had to ask for a job at all; the company has, instead, asked the candidate if they would consider a particular position in their organization.

The Unpublished Job Market

The last major mindset shift is in understanding and accessing the Unpublished Job Market. Unpublished markets are those that organizations have *not* paid for. These could take the form of internal postings, press releases, and so on. We will cover the Unpublished Job Market in depth and discuss the ways to leverage it.

As you can see, this process will have you thinking differently about your job search in a number of ways. You need to wear a very different mental hat to be effective in this effort. However, the results of this mindset shift are remarkable. With all this in mind, let's begin to take a good look at yourself—what you're about and what makes you tick.

5

Analyzing the Self

Now that we've gotten you into the right mindset, it's time to go deeper into the Self and focus on self-evaluation. I can't stress enough how important it is to the job or career search process to know and prepare the Self.

What is the Self, you ask? For the purposes of this book, it is all of the pieces of the process that are housed inside of you. Here, establishing an appropriate frame of mind, having a positive attitude, and going through a comprehensive self-evaluation process are key to being able to develop a foundation for career/job direction. This foundation is critical to avoid repeating the undesirable history of working in companies that are not suited to you or being in unsatisfying jobs.

I consider the job search process to be an important, life-changing event. Yet, my experience has shown that few people have ever gone through any type of self-preparation exercise prior to engaging in the search process. I thoroughly believe that when fundamental exercises are performed *before* the job search begins, the chances for a favorable outcome increase greatly.

Self Assessment

Whether you are looking for career options or simply changing jobs within the same industry, I always recommend that you take a little time and evaluate your work history and current situation. Some of you may have taken some time to examine your accomplishments, capture your work duties, look at what expertise you have gained, as well as to think about your latest professional development and what new skills you've learned. These are some of the typical things that appear on the professional résumé, and this process is very good.

While being able to document and articulate professional accomplishments and responsibilities are certainly important, I believe there is a significant list of other considerations—such as transferable skills and key motivations—that are critical for establishing career direction and discovering valuable options. I call these the *Seven Facets*.

The Seven Facets

Let's take the time to capture some data about you, a multi-dimensional, complex, highly diverse, and talented creature. Every individual has many facets that make them unique. I have determined that seven of them come into play for a comprehensive career assessment of the self. I've also determined that it is rare to come across anyone who has taken the time to think about all of them.

The seven facets to an effective career self-assessment are:

1. Work History
2. Personality Traits
3. Work Activity Preferences and Aversions
4. Skill Competencies
5. Functional Activities that Highly Motivate You
6. Work Values and Ethics
7. Environmental and Cultural Preferences

Each facet plays a critical role in determining appropriate career paths and, most importantly, provides the tactical ammunition you need to be successful in your efforts. We will use a variety of assessment tools designed to identify and elaborate on specific information in each area. A note of warning: some of the exercises will take some time to accomplish. I often recommend that a person do these self-assessment exercises in several stages over a period of a few days. While some people have only a short history to document, others' experience might be extensive and the general time frame for completing the seven facets below is expected to be several hours.

Before you begin I recommend you create a computer folder/file for working on the material or get hold of a fresh pad of paper and a pen so that you can keep the material together.

Work History

A primary component for establishing career direction begins with a thorough understanding of your work history. However a simple extraction from a résumé is not sufficient for the purposes of this exercise. We need to capture as much detail about each job you've had as you can remember. These include the following:

- Title of position
- Years of employment (months not required)
- Where you worked, including city and state
- Beginning and ending salary
- Number of direct and indirect reports
- Position Responsibilities (duties) and Accomplishments

For this last item, you should capture what you accomplished within each of your positions in as much detail as possible. It is essential to provide quantifiable information, that is, dollars, percentages or numbers for as many projects and activities as you can remember. For example: "I increased revenues by x dollars," or "I cut costs by approximately y percent or z dollars in a year." Another valuable figure is represented by the number of employees you have managed.

This information is an excellent baseline. Due to the level of detail, this exercise can take several hours to complete depending upon your experience, but it is invaluable in solidifying your understanding of what you have to offer prospective employers. In addition, for your own history knowledge you should be able to articulate the *full* extent of your responsibilities, along with a comprehensive listing of your accomplishments or results for each position you've held. This information comes in handy when you need to communicate your value to a potential employer.

Personality Traits

Once the work history portion of your personal assessment is completed, other assessments will be very important to you. One is the assessment of your personality type. Your personality type not only has an effect on the type of jobs you are likely to enjoy, but also on the type of work environment you prefer. Many employers are interested in hiring people who "fit in" and for this reason it can be very helpful to be aware of which types of positions are best-suited to a given personality type or profile. While this is not "cast in stone," it can be valuable to know what situations are likely to work best for you.

One of the most widely known personality assessment instruments is the Myers-Briggs Type Indicator® or MBTI®. Early in the 20th century, noted psychologist Carl Jung developed an instrument that has stood the test of time and has subsequently been used by many career consultants to help individuals learn about themselves from the perspective of personality "type." Isabelle Myers further developed the instrument and it has been named after her.

> *It's a well-known fact that people who select work environments most to their liking are more inclined to remain and succeed there.*

It's a well-known fact that people who select work environments most to their liking are more inclined to remain and succeed there. It would stand to reason, then, that determining your preferred environment should be very important to you. The instrument can be accessed and taken online at www.mbti.com. The website will take you to CPP which is the publisher of the Myers-Briggs® instrument.

The assessment provides a variety of useful information. There is also a section of the Myers-Briggs assessment that specifically provides career options. You should print this material and hold on to it. We will discuss application of this information later when we have accumulated all the data we need to develop a short- and long-term career plan.

Work Activity Preferences and Aversions

The next task is to identify the types of activities you prefer in your work life. It is just as important to determine which, of all the things you do day-to-day, activities you genuinely dislike. You may not always get your wish in this regard, but you will have a much clearer handle on those activities you want to avoid as much as possible.

Another self-assessment tool has been designed specifically for this type of exercise. John Holland's Self-Directed Search® is a great instrument to help you determine what functions have a potential of becoming a new direction. You can go to www.self-directed-search.com and the site will guide you through a comprehensive assessment of your likes and dislikes and will provide a listing of numerous job titles you could consider based upon the results of the assessment. I highly recommend this activity along with the MBTI. In fact, when I consult one-on-one, I cross-reference the material to gain added value to these instruments.

In addition to the general likes and dislikes regarding careers and jobs according to the Self-Directed Search, you should also consider the activities you have engaged in at your various jobs.

- Work Activity Preferences—List as specifically as you can what you liked about each job. For person A, the list may include working with colleagues, competition, problem solving, training, team building, traveling, and so on.

Just as important is the consideration of some of the various activities that you have done in your job that may have driven you to the point of distraction.

- Job Activities to Avoid—List as specifically as you can what you did *not* like about your job. For person B, that may include tons of paperwork, traveling, long hours, commute time, a seemingly endless stream of employee reviews, team building, negative reinforcement management models, training, etc.

Note that for some of you what I've just mentioned does not fit into the category of bad scenarios. Also note that for some activities, the same item appeared on both lists. This is to point out that these lists will be different for each individual and what may appear on one person's list as a preference may appear as another's aversion. However, these distinctions are what makes the process so important to perform.

> *Just as important is the consideration of some of the various activities that you have done in your job that may have driven you to the point of distraction.*

Skill Competencies

I find it rare that a person who has been thinking about making a career or job change takes into consideration the skills where they are especially competent. This is interesting because those skills are typically the very thing that companies want to know about you and more importantly are most willing to pay substantial dollars for. I am not necessarily talking about the fact that you may have computer skills or can solve problems. Most professionals today have those skills.

What I am suggesting is that you document the skills that you are exceptionally good at. In other words, if colleagues or superiors come to you because of a particular skill, that is the kind of skill you want to capture. One component of John Holland's Self-Directed Search considers this set of attributes and I *strongly* urge professionals to include this in their self-assessment process. You will find that the top six to ten items will be very helpful to you as we move forward.

Functional Activities that Highly Motivate You

Once the primary assessments have been completed I always require my clients to assess what kinds of things motivate them *in the workplace*. This is extremely important, because they are the kinds of activities from which a great deal of personal reward can be derived. An example might be that you are truly motivated to solve complex problems because of the challenge the process represents to you and for the personal high from figuring out a very complex issue.

These activities may be very different from ones you've discovered up to this point because you may be very good/competent at something but not be particularly motivated to do it. Further, you may enjoy doing it, but not want to make a career out of it. An example might be that you truly enjoy singing or painting, but have no desire to make a living out of it.

The instrument I often use to assess and evaluate a person making a career or job change is called "The Career Path Indicator". This instrument can be found in Appendix A. It is an instrument that very specifically identifies your core work motivations. I have long believed that it is these things that lay at the very foundation of a person who truly enjoys their work. Perhaps more importantly, identifying these areas and including them as an integral component of your search generally ensures a higher productivity level that is in turn visible to employers and often results in promotions and salary increases.

The Importance of Assessing

I recall a client who was looking to make a dramatic transition from the legal world into the private business sector. We discovered that she had a gift for analyzing businesses and from that information she could generate strategic plans that were easily implemented and led to favorable and dynamic bottom line results. Once we identified this talent, it took very little time for her to locate a number of positions in private organizations where she could make the most of those talents. It was one of many top motivations she identified.

These motivational items are generally *so* integral to what you do that they should be pervasive in any job that you seek. As you conduct your job search, consider that they may not occur every single day, but should occur at least several times a week. You may find these motivations expressed in job descriptions and you may know that they are typical in certain positions. If you are not sure if your top motivations are included in your day-to-day job activity it then becomes a function of questioning at the interview which I'll discuss later. The key here is to avoid sacrificing these motivations in the name of money, very short commutes, and so on. Even though these may be very important to you, chances are the "honeymoon" part of the new job may be over in as little time as a few weeks and you'll find yourself realizing that you are unhappy and right back in a bad situation... again.

Work Values and Ethics

I cannot count the number of people I've come across who took positions and later found out that they did not see eye-to-eye with the company or a superior. Usually this occurs for two reasons—the candidate has not assessed what their core values and work ethics are and what they are willing to sacrifice.

"The Career Path Indicator" included in Appendix A will help you determine your core values and ethics. For instance, knowing that family time is very important to you should mean that as you look for a new position you should concentrate on organizations that share that same philosophy.

No matter which assessment you select, you should have come away with a short list of motivations that will be very helpful to you in the next major step, Establishing Direction. It is time to become more focused on which industries and which functions within those industries would be right for you.

Environmental and Cultural Preferences

Last but not least in the self-assessment process is capturing some important data about the type of environment and culture that is the best fit for you. Knowing in advance whether you prefer purely hierarchical, matrix, or perhaps even "quantum"-oriented (everyone is considered equally integral) organizations is usually a very good thing to know before starting a search. It helps to be able to ask good questions at interviews regarding the organization's mission, philosophy, and management style as they relate to you. A section of "The Career Path Indicator" in Appendix A is dedicated to capturing this information.

Summary

Now that you've completed your assessment, you are in an excellent position to start your search knowing exactly what you want and what it's going to take mentally to get there. With this information at your disposal, it's time to start talking about the theory behind my method and exactly what is so different about it.

Transition Theory, Concepts, and Principles

Transition Theory, Concepts, and Principles

6

Transition Theory Concepts and Principles

Now that you've gone through the exercise of learning a little more about yourself and identifying your core motivations, it is much easier to perform the activities critical to an effective career change and job search.

A successful and well-managed job change or career transition adheres to certain strategic concepts and principles. If you ignore them, the transition process won't be nearly as effective and may, in fact, break down completely.

A major differentiator of my process, which we touched on briefly in Chapter 3, "The Solution: The Career Transition Model" is that I've created a theoretical model that actually defines what changing careers or jobs is all about. Up to now, most searchers only knew bits and pieces of what was needed to successfully make a change. My theory brings everything together and makes sure that you're using the components in a manner that greatly enhances the chances for success in your search.

To reiterate, the Career Transition theory states:

> The optimal potential for expected outcomes for career or job change is contingent upon application and integration of certain key elements that include, but are not limited to: intimate knowledge of self, self-marketing principles, concepts inclusive of strategic thinking, self-marketing tools and skills, and quality metrics that are woven into a circular-oriented process.

Read it again. None of it is rocket science. What it is saying is that if you want to do the transition right then you need to do all these things, all the time, with no exceptions.

The success of the search is based upon inclusion and implementation of all the elements of the model, which takes into account the whole person and your desire to find a career that satisfies both financial security and personal fulfillment. If any one of the elements is missing from the activity, the likelihood for achievement of the goal—in this case a successful job or career change in a timely manner—is greatly diminished and may even lead to disastrous results.

As I mentioned earlier, the concepts and principles you need to apply can be broken down into five main areas:

- Business-minded Game Plan
- Self-Marketing Principles
- Strategic Thinking Concepts
- Innovative Thinking
- Commitment

... if you want to do the transition right then you need to do all these things, all the time, with no exceptions.

These are all business project management techniques. And make no mistake, your job search is a business project promoting yourself. Like all products, it must be marketed and to market it most effectively you must be flexible, open to new ideas, committed, and perhaps most important, be as emotionally detached from the process as possible. Applying business project best practices and marketing techniques will make your job search the most effective it can be.

Adopting these five principles is critical to your successful campaign. So, we're going to look at each of these areas and discuss how to apply them to your transition. Then throughout the book, I'll demonstrate examples to help you.

The Business-Minded Game Plan

Again, I have found that the most successful way to approach the job search is as a business project. Most professionals know how to approach a new project, but flounder a bit when faced with a job search. By preparing for your search as you would a business project, you apply a familiar framework that helps you set priorities, identify needs, and set schedules. As I mentioned, this project is about promoting a product—you—which must be marketed and the results measured.

Flexibility, openness to new concepts and commitment are important, but possibly the most important element is to be as emotionally detached from the process as possible.

I realize this is a difficult thing to do. Job and career search can be one of the most emotional, stressful and draining tasks you ever face. It can certainly be a life-changing event. However, if you get into a mindset of emotional detachment like you would a business project, you can avoid potential stress and remain much more objective. When it comes down to it, job search is about business, both for the company and you. The less you can take the process personally—especially in times of rejection—the better off you will be.

Self-Marketing Principles

You must effectively use your time and energy with efficiency and in a manner that mirrors the marketing of products and services. We'll cover many examples of this throughout the book for it is one of many common threads you need.

One example that will give you a taste of what I mean is in the résumé process. You will see when you read Chapter 9 that using a simple, chronological résumé is much less effective than using a marketing-oriented instrument. This type of instrument uses a specific design to focus on a particular job target and places the elements of skill and qualifications in the first few lines of a résumé where they can have the greatest impact.

> *...if you get into a mindset of emotional detachment like you would a business project, you can avoid potential stress and remain much more objective.*

Another example is in the marketing plan section where it is absolutely critical that you dedicate your time to efforts that give you the biggest bang for the buck, not just do what is easy. These are only a sampling of the marketing principles that will be discussed here.

Bottom line: you always need to be thinking of ways to market yourself; that is, ways to stand out from the pack and make yourself known to the decision-makers.

Strategic Thinking Concepts

This is another area where the searcher can separate themselves from the typical crowd. Strategic Thinking is about using tactical processes and actions different from and superior to traditional views regarding job search. Businesses often strategize, plan, and prepare for events throughout the life of a project. Likewise, in the Career Game Championships you are going to use strategic thinking throughout the processes and activities.

One prime example of this is applying the information in the interviewing chapters so you have ready answers to difficult interview questions, thereby presenting yourself and your skills in ways far different than your competition. By employing this strategy you will know how to approach this often nerve-wracking activity and not just "get through" it, but instead control and conquer it. That is only one, very empowering tactical concept that gives you a tremendous edge in this process, and is another valuable thread that we discuss many times throughout this book.

For every action you need to perform in your search process I provide information to explain and demonstrate specific strategic thinking and tactical advantages that you can use to give yourself advantages over other searchers.

Commitment to the Process

By and large, job search is all about process. Experience has taught me that if a person wants the very best results they must adopt and be committed to the best process available.

> *...you must be committed to not just learning how to be the best, but also to applying the learning and integrating it into every action you take...*

The testimonials I've received over the years and the urging I've gotten to put this process into print tell me that my methods are vastly advanced over most other approaches. However, like accomplished competitors such as Tiger Woods, Michele Kwan, or Lance Armstrong, you must be committed to not just learning *how* to be the best, but also to *applying* the learning and integrating it into every action you take when you are engaged in this effort. Anything less only gets you… less. I am not saying that to get a job you have to be as tenacious as world-class competitors, but by mirroring their commitment you will most certainly get the job you've dreamed about.

The good news is that it is actually simpler than it might appear. Reading about it and gathering what you need to make sure you are completely prepared for your launch is the toughest part. As I mentioned, done correctly, the process will actually cut your search time by about half. But you must be committed to the process, even if your materials and possibly your methods require modification, and especially during any "flat periods." Take the time and do the work up front. In fact, though it seems counterintuitive, if you cut corners your search will actually lengthen.

Innovative Thinking

Right from the introduction of the SOLID method and the Career Transition Model, I'm essentially asking you to have a very open mind and adopt some very innovative ideas. I'm aware that it is a lot of information to digest and much of it is very different than what you've used in previous searches. My colleagues and certainly all my clients with whom I've worked have indicated that I've re-invented career management and made it better, but it requires the searcher—you—to walk with me down a path that is going to be unfamiliar.

If you want to have a different and better result than you have experienced in the past, then you must inevitably come around to being open-minded enough to hear new ideas that will change your situation.

Likewise, if you want your career and job search to be superior to everyone else's, it is important to adopt innovative ideas and concepts that separate you from the multitudes in that vanilla crowd.

Consider that until relatively recently, high jumpers spent their time practicing and perfecting a tried-and-true method—one used throughout the history of the sport—in their attempts to achieve greater heights.

All that changed in the 1960s when a young athlete named Dick Fosbury came on the scene with a technique that at first was scornfully called the "Fosbury Flop." However, the laughing didn't last long. Using his innovative technique, Fosbury *easily* took the gold in the 1968 Olympic Games. From then on, the "Fosbury Flop" set the standard for a nearly unbeatable technique in the high jump; one that remains a favorite of today's high jumpers. With this innovation, Fosbury set

Innovation Comes in All Colors

I recall a client who was referred to me after working with another consultant. She was a former HR manager who felt that she ought to know how to do an effective search, but she was having no luck getting interviews.

After listening to her story I asked if she had a professional copy of her résumé, which she presented.

I announced immediately that I thought I'd uncovered the nature of her difficulty. She was perplexed when I said, "Wrong color."

Her résumé was professional-looking and clearly used quality paper. But the paper color was "wrong" for her field. She questioned my suggestion to change colors, but we agreed she had nothing to lose since she hadn't gotten any interviews at all so far.

She agreed to give it a try. Within a week she was getting interviews and shortly thereafter landed a good job.

himself apart and changed an entire mindset. The innovations I'm advancing here also require a mindset change for most people.

At the same time, I'm a very practical person. My ideas for separating you from the crowd do not venture into the outlandish. For example, I would never suggest that you send out only pink-colored résumés to land the job of your dreams. It would certainly set you apart, but probably isn't an innovation worth pursuing. I will, however, suggest that there are specific paper colors of résumés that have a more favorable impact depending upon who is going to receive it and what type of position you are targeting, as the "Innovation Comes in All Colors" sidebar highlights.

Correct choice of résumé paper is innovative. Doing *all* the activities we cover in the Career Game Championships *all* the time is innovative. The list of innovations for you to implement will increase as we go through the book.

Establishing Career Options and Direction

The next step in the process is to determine your career options so that you can direct your energy in seeking placement in various organizations. While the Myers-Briggs® and Self-Directed Search® assessments provided you with specific job titles to consider, I want to caution you about being too exclusive and seeking only one job title in a particular industry. Instead, use that list as a guide and seek out opportunities *like* those that are recommended, not necessarily the *specific* job titles shown.

I suggest this more general approach because I believe it is more beneficial in both the short and long-term transition. It's too easy to get bogged down by a job title and narrow your options to the point that you severely limit your horizons.

Consider this: there are thousands of job titles and millions of organizations available to the job seeker. You could go to ten different companies and find ten different job titles for the same type of job—or even the *same exact job*. If you limit yourself to "Business Analyst" positions in manufacturing firms, you might miss the perfect opportunity as a "Process Analyst" in a software company, even though the jobs may be virtually identical. By using the list as a guide, you open yourself up to a much broader target range of opportunities for placement. So keep a balance of flexibility and focus in the search process; it will allow you to be more responsive in the market and be able to view and target a variety of positions other than a specific title.

Strategic Career and Job Targeting

The Myers-Briggs and Self-Directed Search exercises described in the "Self Assessment" section of Chapter 5 each should have provided a comprehensive list of job options to consider.

Check the lists and eliminate those positions that do not offer enough compensation or are not viable in the short term because they require significantly higher education levels than you currently possess.

If you're like most people, the remaining list should include some viable job target options that you might not have considered before. Pay particular attention to those options that appear on both assessments.

One important strategy I always recommend is the creation of a "Short List." My rule of thumb for a successful search is to target two or three possible opportunities at the same time. Creating the short list is an important activity. Having too many or too few target options often results in long searches and, on occasion, in searches that are abandoned completely. A single target is often too narrow for a given market; more than three targets may cause you to become unfocused.

This exercise is primarily focused on individuals who are seeking "options" for their career path. However, for those of you who are seeking specific job targets—for example, "I'm a finance guy/woman and I'm looking for that same position"—this process can also serve you well since it forces you to look at other potential job titles that you may have otherwise overlooked.

Balancing Short and Long Term

The language of this book is written from the perspective of a job search performed for immediate transition. However, it will work equally as well for those who are considering long-term transition goals. Where you are today is very likely not where you want to be in five, ten, or twenty years. In addition, today's professionals are aware that the age for retirement is rising and it is not uncommon for people to be working well into their seventies.

As you think ahead to your long-term goals, the path to achieve them may often involve some formal and informal education, as well as relevant experience.

I often have clients who have worked for many years in their field but come to me stating they would like to finish out their working years doing something that is personally rewarding. In many cases, this may require a career overhaul, complete with advanced degree and several small career moves to gain the experience needed to perform competently at the desired destination. Knowing this can help you plan your direction effectively.

To help focus on this short list of jobs, consider the other assessment data components that you worked on. One of the primary components is the "Motivations" section. Examine the larger list of career/job options and pull the jobs that appear to contain the greatest number—hopefully all—of the main motivations you've listed from above. Further scrutiny should also include areas of competency.

Once you've combined the elements of lists of possible jobs—that is, what you are highly motivated to do and which activities you are particularly competent in—you should have come away with a highly focused short list of job targets with which you can begin working.

In addition, you will need some industries to begin targeting. Knowing what kinds of industries to look at is just as crucial to the development of a search campaign as knowing the types of jobs available. Appendix B, "Industry List" contains a list of industries. Select no more than five industries that appeal to or interest you in some way. Don't worry, you can change them as time goes on.

Most industries—not all, but most—have a function that is something like what you do or want to do. The industry may have a variety of titles for those positions, but functionally, there are likely to be many similarities.

> *Most industries have a function that is something like what you do or want to do.*

The 80/100 Rule

So much about the job search is fraught with rejection. I can't see making a habit of volunteering for it by going after jobs that you don't have much of a shot at. Therefore, when you are targeting jobs, especially those that you may find in published job markets, it is important to follow what I call the 80/100 Rule. The rule is simple:

> The most effective way to target jobs so that you have the greatest opportunity to get an offer is to ensure that you embody at least 80% of *all* the requirements of the job and 100% of the *critical* requirements.

The components that are negotiable are those that are tagged as "preferred" or "a plus." For instance, if the advertisement says MBA required, and you don't have one, save your stamp. But, if they say Master's degree preferred it then falls into the 80% side and you can go for it.

Using the Tools

Now that you've selected some potential job targets and a few industries that would be of interest, it is time to work with the career and job transition tools that you need to accomplish your goals. We will be integrating the assessment material into these tools which each have specific applications in the search process and can be applied to the varied needs of the organizations you are targeting.

These tools are:

- Résumés
- Cover Letters
- Your Company "Hot List"

- Marketing Action Plan
- 30 Second Commercial

Very few people effectively perform this part of the preparation process.

These tools are important to the integrated search. Very few people effectively perform this part of the preparation process. It's not hard; it's not that they can't do it, but rather that they don't put in the effort to make it successful.

Résumés, cover letters, a self-commercial, and a marketing plan are seldom developed with self-marketing in mind and are rarely, if ever, put together in a way that represents a well-integrated business research project management plan. Luckily for you, the Career Game Championships is designed to help this process.

The Unpublished Job Market

You may have heard about the "Unpublished Job Market." I reference it throughout this book, and some other career counselors use the term, as well. The process and methods I put forward here are all designed to help you break into the Unpublished Job Market, but most of the time people have no clue what it is. Many think it's some mysterious list of available jobs provided to me by companies that I can produce on command.

This couldn't be further from the truth.

There is, though, a very real Unpublished Job Market. It just isn't a list.

We refer to these markets as "unpublished" because there are no jobs specifically advertised or pre-determined. The jobs are either just being brought forward—possibly in the form of internal postings or press releases—are only a thought in a manager's mind, or don't exist at all. It is this last category that is ripe for the picking, and one that I will show you how to use to your best advantage. This chapter serves as a bit of a preview to a number of concepts I'll cover in much more depth later. But I believe that it's important for you to understand the Unpublished Job Market early in the process, because it is at the heart of a fully-realized job search. It provides the opportunity to design your dream job while having little to no competition for the position. It is, quite simply, one of the best ways for you to uncover—or develop—your "right" job.

When dealing with the unpublished market, it is important to realize that *you aren't looking for a job...* at least not yet. Instead, you are looking for a company that is a good fit. On the face of it, this seems like a radical concept, but as I'll show you in later chapters, it's not as crazy as it might seem.

As you might expect from such a non-traditional idea, the focus on the Unpublished Job Market requires you to think differently about your job search. Instead of relying on ads and published listings for leads into jobs—jobs that, by the way, usually already have a predetermined set of criteria; the quintessential job-in-a-box—you rely on your own research and resources to uncover needs within an organization that you can fill with your own unique combination of skills, motivations, and experience.

> *There are actually three unpublished markets available to the job searcher.*

Because the job description hasn't been completely formed, you have the opportunity to take the company's need and mold a job around it. This is an extremely powerful way to ensure that the job you land is the right job for you, because you have a large part in creating it!

Understanding the Unpublished Job Market

Most people are so used to the traditional methods of job search, they have never even considered that such a market could exist. This is a bonus for you, because you are about to understand this market, and by the time you finish this book you will know how to use it to your advantage to open doors. Done correctly, many of these doors can be opened with absolutely no competition at all.

There are actually three unpublished markets available to the job searcher.

1. Organizations—at least the good ones—always plan for their future. Most organizations that are in growth mode plan well in advance—sometimes a year—of actually starting the hiring process. Needs and possible job positions are identified, but they are not published in job listings until they are fully signed-off and the authorization for publication is made. Until then, even though the need exists, the job requisitions sit on a hiring manager's desk, and they remain unfilled *unless* someone comes in and demonstrates they could easily fill the slot that is about to become open.

2. Organizations that are not in a formal growth mode can still offer great opportunities. Many companies or departments within companies have a budget line item with a dollar figure attached, but with no name or position title associated with it. These dollars are earmarked for future hires that have not yet been identified. By following the techniques in this book, you can easily carve out a slice of that money for your own position. This is because in many instances, a need within the organization has been identified but a specific job description has not been drafted. The job and its requirements reside solely in the mind of the hiring manager, who is probably considering the right attributes for the person who can solve their particular problem or problems. If you can convince the hiring manager

that your skills match their needs, you have a good chance of creating a position with that company.

3. Executive, senior- level, and "C-Suite" positions are seldom in print and "on the table" waiting for someone to fill the slot. Usually, positions at this level are developed around a candidate once they have appropriately impressed the decision makers. You may think that counts you out, but I have some great news for you. An important aspect of The Career

> *Executive, senior- level, and "C-Suite" positions are seldom in print and "on the table" waiting for someone to fill the slot.*

Game Championships is Resource Development. We will cover this in depth in Chapter 14, "Resource Development". The techniques we discuss will give you the key to developing a broad resource network in a manner that is easier and less stressful than what you've likely encountered in the past. This is also the key to these upper-level positions, and to the Unpublished Job Market itself.

Discovering the Unpublished Job Market

So how do you find out about the opportunities in this market if they are unpublished?

One way is to keep informed about what is happening in the businesses in your desired area. As part of their own marketing plan, corporations will often publicize their growth activities. If an organization's plans for the future include increasing their headcount, then that information will often be included in trade magazine and news articles. It won't be in the form of a job listing, but more likely in the form of a statement along the lines of "This move is expected to create x positions." Although most job searchers overlook this very valuable nugget of information, you should take advantage of this free publicity as an invitation to use the processes we cover here.

By seizing on the opportunity, one of those "x positions" can be yours if you persevere and network your way around to the "side door" as it were. In this scenario, there is no one to compete against and you have a golden opportunity to sample the market and pick for yourself the kind of organization you would like to work for. The job that you are searching for, and that you set aside as I suggest, falls into your lap when the time is right.

Another way is by simply talking to people. Not by asking if people know of any available jobs, but simply by keeping your ears open and having general conversations with business associates and colleagues about what's happening in companies that they know of.

People often have valuable information that they've picked up just through conversations with *their* colleagues and associates.

Articles, interviews, television news spots, even advertising can all be viable roads into the Unpublished Job Market. It only takes a little imagination to begin to identify many subtle messages that you've probably previously overlooked that provide clues to an organization's plans and needs.

Leveraging the Unpublished Job Market

Now for the important question. Once you discover a possible unpublished lead, how do you land it?

In the process' simplest form, all you need to do is have a conversation with a hiring-level individual in a target organization and let them know what you can do for them as it specifically relates to their needs—which, of course, you've discovered as a result of your excellent research. The onus is on you to convince the person that you would be a great addition to the organization. Obviously, this is completely opposite to traditional "front door" interviews garnered through media and Internet ads.

The goal when you do speak with a representative of the company is to determine if you will fit into their organization. Such meetings are often termed *informational interviews*. Here, your résumé and qualifications become the foundation for how you fit into the company. The job search becomes a process of building rapport and much of the job search interviewing travesty goes away. Soon, the unpublished job becomes available and you are the only candidate. There is no doubt that for this process to be successful it is critical to be able to develop the "who" to talk to, but I'll show you how to do that.

To be sure, no one can force you to employ this strategic tactic in gaining access into

The Job Search Fast Lane

The shortest route into a position is when a contact indicates he or she already works at the organization you're targeting. He or she becomes your advocate and forwards your résumé to a strategic employee who calls you. *You* then interview the employee of the target organization—yes, you read that correctly. Often, the hiring individuals like you immediately and you get hired. They will think of ways for you to join them by suggesting that a position may become available soon, or ask if you would be interested in discussing your plans with co-workers. This happens more than most people realize, but it is imperative to get to this point by using your knowledge of the company and industry, ability to impress the company and build good relationships. This is the essence of using the Unpublished Job Market to greatest effect.

organizations. In the end, it is your choice to use it, or not. But once we finish, the tools will all be available to you. The next step in conquering the Unpublished Job Market is yours.

Tools

Tools

Résumés

Without a doubt, the résumé is and will continue to be one of the most important tools for the career and job changer. It is the tool most often used to try and capture the attention of the hiring manager. Traditionally, it has been part of a one-two punch that includes the résumé and the cover letter. But today, with the advent of Internet-based job search engines like Monster.com® and CareerBuilder.com™, the need for cover letters has dropped off, which boosts the importance of marketing and strategic thinking surrounding the résumé. It follows, then, that the résumé is a large piece of the comprehensive self-marketing program that is the job search. It is for this reason that I often refer to résumés— and to a somewhat lesser extent cover letters—as Marketing Instruments.

Typically, people rely on their résumé style to capture that attention and they spend a lot of time trying to find the style that is "just right" for them. There are literally hundreds of résumé styles available—do a quick web search if you don't believe me. Many of those styles are effective, but I've found that searchers often get overwhelmed by the sheer number and variety available and can't select a design that is going to provide concrete results. I think anyone can land a job using any of the traditional formats. The issue I have with these styles is they don't easily capture the attention of a hiring manager—the operative word being *easily*. Remember, our definition of marketing includes being able to easily attract attention.

The résumé is your personal marketing brochure. A winning instrument is of a caliber that demonstrates a focused, polished, well-prepared candidate. A résumé must directly answer any hiring manager's questions about the depth and breadth of your qualifications, and more specifically, how you can increase the bottom line. Candidates who design their instruments using this easy formula will be called for interviews.

It would be impossible to cover everything about résumés in a single chapter. What I will do, though, is give you an overview and suggest some basic and very flexible résumé styles that work in most situations as well as some pointers on best practices for résumés.

Cutting to the Chase

Most everybody knows that hiring managers are very busy and want to "cut to the chase." They appreciate a résumé that tells them very quickly that the applicant has the necessary background to qualify. To determine this, they want to see certain information right away, and this is where most chronology-based résumés start to fall apart.

Hiring managers... appreciate a résumé that tells them quickly that the applicant has the necessary background to qualify.

In the typical résumé format, your skills, motivations, and accomplishments are buried among other bullet items such as projects and tasks spanning your entire career. What we really want to do is draw these out into an easy-to-read format that is going to call attention to this information and make it stand out to the hiring manager.

We are going to go over the specifics of what to include in the résumé later in the chapter, but basically it comes down to a number of main components:

- Basic Structure, Format, and Layout
- Header and Summary Statement
- Key Skills
- Work History and Experience
- Education
- Affiliations, Memberships, and Publications
- Other Marketable Information

Notice that this list does not include an objective statement. This is by design. Objective statements usually look something like, "I'm looking for a place where I can put my talents and skills to use in a team environment." The words change but the themes are relatively consistent. The problem is that none of this is of much use to prospective employers. What they want to know is what you can do for them—remember, the job search is 100% about what you can do for the company. You are much better off including this type of information in the Summary and Skills sections of the résumé. I'll describe these shortly.

I recommend that you include three other critical pieces of information that typical résumés seldom group in a way that allows the information to be found and digested easily.

- A specific job title, if known—usually one that is provided in advertisements—is listed near the top just under the name and address of the résumé sender. This sends the message to the manager immediately that you're a good fit for the position.

- Roughly the first third of the first page contains your core requirements/skills that most closely match those of the company needs.

  - The opening paragraph is usually some form of summary—again, not an objective. This can be expressed in core skills and motivations, for example, "More than 10 years experience in finance, conflict negotiation, interpretation of assessment tools."

  - Related and expanded information can be expressed in the Skills section on the first page of the résumé. This is a section listing many of your core skills—though not the same ones you might include in the Summary section—that you can easily express. They might include, for example, Written and Oral Communications, Attention to Detail, Creativity, Innovation, and Interpersonal Skills.

- A prioritized, current, easy-to-read list of accomplishments, usually laid out using attention-getting bullets.

The information in the bullets above can take on a variety of looks in the résumé. This information is especially powerful if you provide as many quantifiable parameters as you are able. Dollars, percentages, and numbers are important here. Hiring managers want most to know how you can help them, and more specifically, how can you make or save them money. You'll be hard pressed to find a business that exists simply for

Three Words about Embellishing

A recent survey indicates that over half of all job seekers lie or embellish the truth on their résumé.

I have some advice for you on this: don't do it. The repercussions of such mistruths can be severe. Unless your career has been a complete disaster, you should be able to demonstrate your skills and accomplishments in a way that will help you to stand out from the crowd without resorting to lies.

the pure joy of being there. It is key for you to demonstrate that you contributed to the bottom line of other organizations in some way, whether it be through sales, cutting costs, efficiencies and so on. Remember, it is important that you only include items in the summary and skills sections that are truthful and can be demonstrated easily.

My belief is that if these criteria are not met, the real power of an effective job search is diffused almost immediately. Since in most instances the very first exposure you have as a candidate is made when the organization receives your résumé, it is important to ensure that the pertinent information is "in the face" of the hiring manager as much as possible. Refer to the "Specialty Marketing Instruments" section to see what I consider to be marketing-type résumés or self-marketing instruments as I will refer to them.

Résumé Components

There are a number of critical components in designing an effective self-marketing instrument, regardless of the style or layout you use. If you follow the guidelines I'm laying out here and include these components, you're likely to have an excellent résumé that will grab the attention of hiring managers and market yourself properly. As we discuss the components, feel free to refer to the résumé sample pages found in Figure 2 and Figure 3.

Basic Structure, Format and Layout

The overall look and feel is very important. Keep it simple and as easy-to-read as possible. Flourishes intended to catch the eye—lines, borders, graphics, print variety, and unusual fonts—are not as marketable as you might think. Avoid these distractions. Simple, clean résumés that are easy on the eyes are more effective as marketing instruments.

JOHN Q. PUBLIC

116 Great Street
Anyplace, MA 01110

Phone: (900) 398-7007
JQP@ultra.com

CAREER CONSULTANT

Summary: Advanced degree with more than 25 years experience in career development and design and delivery of training programs in academic, manufacturing, and retail environments. Specific expertise in succession planning and motivation of individuals in transition. Deliverables include Job Search Team Approach, Career Portfolio Design and Development, and Life/Work Assessment.

SKILLS

- Life/Work Counseling
- Training
- Motivational Speaking
- Leadership
- Platform Skills
- Alumni Relations
- Written & Oral Communication

ACCOMPLISHMENTS and EXPERIENCE

Senior Career Consultant   1997 to Present
XXXXXXXXXXXXXXXXXXXXXXXXX, Westboro, MA

- **Provided** career transition consulting services to non-exempt through senior executives in both domestic and international communities.
- **Designed** and implemented numerous "Job Search Strategic Planning" modules focused on the needs of the individual identified as *"dual transition,"* e.g. relocation and in career change.
- **Trained** and instructed three associate consultants in use of career transition assessment tools and various strategic market-driven job search tools.
- **Maintained** exceptional client services through accumulation of stellar client success stories, e.g. one client = **nine** resumes, resulting in **five** interviews yielding **four** job offers.
- **Provided** guidance in self-assessments that assisted individuals in examining their skills, interests, and values.
- **Instructed** participants in development of market-driven resumes and cover letters that resulted in an increase in interviews of up to 20%.
- **Managed** case load of 55 individuals. Most were placed within 3-4 months of start date.

Continuing Education Instructor (Part Time)   1997 to Present
XXXXXXXX, MA

- **Instructor** of Academic Planning Seminars and Graduate Studies Program Seminars designed to assist adult learners in academic planning toward effective career development.
- **Research** consultant for Career Services Center project for the College.
- **Maintained** student advisement load of more than 50 learners.
- **Designed** and developed five focus courses including Effective Oral Presentations, Diversity in the Workplace, Career Counseling: Theory and Practice, Effective Oral Presentations, Assessing Diversity Development, and Designing Career Portfolios.

Figure 2: Sample Résumé #1: Traditional Self Marketing Instrument (Page 1)

JOHN Q. PUBLIC   P - 2

Independent Contractor and Training Consultant, Foxboro, MA   1986 to 1994
- **Project** Management for small and large companies and personal business.
- **Provided** management, training, and operations expertise for 500+ retail outlets.
- **Managed** major home/trade show operations.

Senior Training Specialist - Personnel Department   1976 to 1986
XXXXXXXXXXX, MA
- **Delivered** numerous career management and human development training programs
- **Facilitated** group training focusing on self-assessment and career development.

PUBLICATIONS
- "Evaluation of a Holistic Career Portfolio as a Job and Career Transition Tool," The Union
  Institute, Cincinnati, OH, 1997. (Focused on the workforce in transition).
- "Five Easy Steps to a Gold Medal-Winning Resume", Job Smart News Magazine, 12/4/96.
- "Portfolios Take Resumes to a New Level", Job Smart News Magazine, 5/19/96.

EDUCATION

Ph.D. - Sociology, The Union Institute, Cincinnati, OH   1997
M.Ed. - Integrated Studies and Adult Assessment, Cambridge College, Cambridge, MA   1995

COMPUTER SKILLS

- Micro Soft Word '97   • Access   • Internet

AFFILIATIONS

- International Association of Career Management Professionals (IACMP)
- Boston Human Resource Association (BHRA)

Figure 3: Sample Résumé #1: Traditional Self Marketing Instrument (Page 2)

Be sure that you have one-inch margins on *all* sides. Always select a visually-pleasing font style such as Times New Roman, Arial, or Helvetica and an easy to read font size—usually 12. You may think that 12 point font is too large, but with the style of résumé presentation I'm advocating here, you will be able to fit all of your pertinent information.

Your name—but not your address—and each of the highlighted section headers present better when they are in a larger font size. I suggest 14 point, all caps, and bold. Avoid inconsistencies such as mixed fonts or formats, unintentional inconsistency in font sizes and other distracting attributes such as multiple indents.

Résumés should never exceed two pages. Conventional wisdom says that the résumé shouldn't exceed a single page; I disagree. One page is acceptable as long as it does not leave out critical material that would be helpful in marketing yourself but often a single page is too limiting. Also, make

> *Conventional wisdom says that the résumé shouldn't exceed a single page; I disagree.*

sure that you put your name and page numbers on anything that is more than a single page.

Use only top-quality stationery. Twenty-four pound weight cream, beige, ice blue, or light gray tend to be the most popular. Pure white is certainly appropriate, but not always a favorite choice for most exempt-level searchers; the major exception is in the medical profession, where white *is* preferred. Interesting to note is that cream and beige seem to be more effective in business and humanistic roles such as finance, marketing, and human resources, while ice blue or light gray seem to be successful in engineering, sciences, and technical applications. For non-exempt or hourly wage searchers white is almost always the color of choice.

Now that you have the basic foundation of building an effective self-marketing instrument, you can begin to go through the various stages of including materials that have the capacity for capturing the attention of those who have the power to either eliminate you from the competition or decide you are competent enough to be brought in for an interview.

Instrument Header and Summary Statement

Include a header with your name, address, phone number, and e-mail address centered at the top of page one. Your address can be split to the left and right margins for a balanced look. This may also provide more room. Some professionals, such as psychologists and lawyers, place their field license numbers under the header. If you don't have an e-mail address, *get one*. Marketable professionals demonstrate that they are computer savvy and up-to-date with technology. There are many free e-mail services available.

Below the instrument header you should place a well-developed "Summary" statement. The summary statement is a succinct paragraph in direct response to the question, "tell me a little about yourself," and is the foundation for the entire document. It should be a paragraph of four to five lines that precisely states your degree and possibly your major if they apply to the position, number of years of experience, field area(s) you are targeting, and your specific areas of expertise.

> **Use the Past Tense**
>
> Make sure that the entire résumé is in the past tense. I have seen many résumés that mix tenses, with the summary and most current position bullets in the present tense and the rest of the résumé in the past tense. Not only does this mix come off somewhat stilted, I have found it causes a variety of errors and puts subjective perception to question.
>
> Quite simply, if the ink is dry then it was accomplished yesterday. That makes it past tense. Stick with it.

It is important to include what you are passionate about. Examples might be organizing, strategic planning, business development, and so on. This section often contains industry-specific buzzwords that target organizations are looking for and you should use the specific language they have used in their advertisement.

If you are targeting other positions outside your field, then use verbiage appropriate to the field and create other versions of the instrument so as not to confuse the hiring organization as to the types of positions you are seeking. That's right, you should have multiple résumés; "one size fits all" résumés have long been obsolete and represent a marketing *faux pas*.

Key Skills

This section, placed immediately under the Summary, should include the key attributes that qualify you for the job and most directly support the summary by answering the hiring manager's question of "what do you bring to the table for this position?"

These skills should be in the form of short statements or words in a horizontal bullet format that present your most significant talents in the field such as management skills, attention to detail, research, oral and written communications, negotiation, and conflict resolution. Other job qualifiers may be listed that relate to the advertised qualification requirements such as training and development expertise, marketing, and business analysis. Choose statements or words most necessary for the targeted job.

It is very important that this section *not* exceed three lines of type. Remember that listed skills must factually represent your high-level skill base.

The Summary and Key Skills sections should be framed in a way that the busy reader can scan these sections in less than thirty seconds. Numerous researchers have verified this to be the maximum amount of time prospective employers will spend to determine if you have qualified for an interview presentation.

You'll note in the sample shown in Figure 2 that these two sections are succinct and require very little real estate, yet they present a wealth of useful, pertinent information for the hiring manager.

Work History, Accomplishments, and Experience

This section is often referred to as the body of the résumé and describes your accomplishments *as they relate to the target function or job*. Avoid the page and a half of duty descriptions at previous jobs or chronology of your work history. Yes, they are part of your personal work make-up, but they have much less marketing impact than bullets noting responsibilities and results-oriented accomplishments specifically related to the target position. Furthermore, it is important to hiring managers that they not have to read through dense narratives for the information.

Information in this area must tell the decision-maker where you worked, dates you worked there, job title, and most importantly, accomplishment statements from those positions that express why you are the best candidate for *this* position. Sentences should be one to two lines—occasionally three, but only if you have a great reason. Notice that the first word of each bullet is bold for emphasis and that the

...words like "managed," "produced," "maintained," "planned," and "enhanced" are expected to be found here...

highlighted words are action oriented. Lead words like "managed," "produced," "maintained," "planned," and "enhanced" are expected to be found here at the opening of the bullet, followed by concise statements describing the depth and breadth of your specific experience.

Hiring managers will be looking for words like "increased" and "achieved" followed closely by numbers and dollars to help them determine your level of achievements. If you are a manager yourself, organizations will be looking for how many people you "managed" or "trained," and how complex your position was. If you were responsible for finance, human resources, profit and loss, purchasing, or another group, this is critical information to include, followed closely by any dollars, percents, or numbers you can provide.

This section often runs over into the second page of the instrument. Experience dictates the overall length. Specific experience may provide only enough material to fill parts of the second page. If this is the case, try to avoid having only a couple of lines on the second page. Either add material to get it to about a quarter of a page or shorten the instrument so it becomes one page.

One last thing: I recommend that professionals include accomplishments and work history going back about 15 years. History beyond that often represents obsolete technology.

Education

This area should list your education credentials in reverse chronological order, such as Master's degree, then Bachelors degree and so on. After listing your degrees, you should include certifications and other specialty coursework that show relevance to your specific job focus. GPAs, college honors, and other academic activities will have little relevance for most professionals and I usually recommend including them only if you have plenty of room and/or some specific application suggests inclusion.

Affiliations, Memberships, and Publications

These résumé attributes should include all professional organizations or affiliations, publications you may have authored, State Bar Admissions, organizational memberships, and community service activities that are appropriate to the field and also target the job focus. These are important enough to have their own heading and appropriate listing in the résumé.

Other Marketable Information

Other marketable components include items such as court admissions, languages, and computer skills, if applicable. Be sure to include computer skills such as Microsoft® Word, Excel® spreadsheet software, PowerPoint® presentation graphics program, and any others if they are appropriate since these are the industry-standard software in use today. Again, it is usually important to demonstrate the versatility, depth, and breadth of individual performance competency in order to be viewed as among the top job contenders.

Checking for Inconsistencies and Errors

The three most common errors when creating a résumé are grammatical errors, typographical errors, and inconsistencies in formatting. While word processor spell-checking tools are very effective, they are by no means perfect. After using the automated spell checker, *always* double check the text yourself. This includes printing the résumé and checking it on paper. Studies have shown that the human eye is more likely to catch problems and errors on paper then by scanning on a computer screen.

To help reduce the chances that errors slip through, I suggest you make sure that at least three other pairs of eyes—preferably detail-oriented people who are very good at written English—scan your marketing instrument *before* it ever goes out. Inconsistencies such as different sized dashes in the dates, different fonts sizes when they are all supposed to be the same, different fonts in the text, and inconsistent left and right margins/tabs are very easy to miss. The additional checks can be most helpful.

A LIttle Test

There are 8 errors in Sample #1 shown in Figure 2 and Figure 3 starting on page 73. Test your ability to spot them.

The errors I intentionally introduced into Sample #1 are representative of those that I find most often in résumés. I have even occasionally found some of these on professionally-prepared résumés.

The answers can be found on the page 97.

Packaging

The marketing instrument is complete when you package it in a way that eliminates the competition and leaves you standing among the finalists in the job search competition. The packaging step includes targeting the right positions, tailoring the résumé appropriately, and following through.

- Targeting—spend your energy going after jobs that you can match with your skills or experience.
- Tailoring—pinpoint the wording of the résumé to meet the requirements of the job being targeted.
- Following through—follow-up once the professional résumé has been sent is as critical as the effort itself. Top professionals have generally gained the winning edge in completing their job search activity with excellence in the following through department. After a week or so, you must call the firm or company and verify that they have received your résumé and ask where they are in the selection process.

Specialty Marketing Instruments

You have already seen a traditional style résumé in Figure 2 and Figure 3. In addition, there are a number of specialty marketing instruments that may be of use. Each variation has its own unique use and can be used when a specific focus is needed.

The particular models that follow are often referred to as "brochure résumés" and are designed with that marketing concept in mind; clear, easy to read, they get to the point in a hurry, and are succinct.

> *Typical résumés tend to look just like scores of others that come in the door.*

First, I'd like you to consider that they actually are *not* typical résumé designs. You may have already gathered that they don't look much like others you have seen. These shy away from the chronology-method that I mentioned earlier. Again, a blow-by-blow retelling of your career doesn't do much to entice hiring managers to bring you in for an interview. Typical résumés tend to look just like scores of others that come in the door. These will help you stand out.

I've broken the different styles out by the different variations. I'll describe them individually.

The Functional Marketing Instrument

One of the most common variations on a self-marketing instrument is the functional version. Sample #2, shown in Figure 4 and Figure 5, is an excellent example of this design. This design is particularly effective for professionals who are making career changes, for example, Manufacturing Operations Manager to Training and Development Coordinator. This design allows the candidate to present pertinent bullets and accomplishments that will resonate most with future employers who are looking for individuals in those fields.

JOHN Q. PUBLIC

116 Great Street
Anyplace, MA 01110

Phone: (911) 358-7007
JQP@ultra.com

CAREER CONSULTANT

Summary: (max 5 lines) Advanced degree with more than 25 years experience in career development and design and delivery of training programs in academic, manufacturing, and retail environments. Specific expertise in succession planning and motivation of individuals in transition. Deliverables include Job Search Team Approach, Career Portfolio Design and Development, and Life/Work Assessment.

SKILLS

- Life/Work Counseling   • Training   • Motivational Speaking   • Leadership
- Platform Skills   • Alumni Relations   • Written & Oral Communication

ACCOMPLISHMENTS and EXPERIENCE

Management and Business Development

- **Provided** career transition consulting services to non-exempt through senior executives in both domestic and international communities.
- **Maintained** exceptional client services through accumulation of stellar client success stories, e.g. one client = **nine** resumes, resulting in **five** interviews yielding **four** job offers.
- **Managed** case load of 55 individuals. Most were placed within 3-4 months of start date.
- **Procured** and provided job leads to qualified candidates. 100-200 current reqs. per week.
- **Research** consultant for Career Services Center project for the College.
- **Developed** five focus courses including Effective Oral Presentations, Diversity in the Workplace, Career Counseling: Theory and Practice, Effective Oral Presentations, Assessing Diversity Development, and Designing Career Portfolios.
- **Project** Management for small and large companies and personal business.
- **Provided** management, training, and operations expertise for 500+ retail outlets.
- **Managed** major home/trade show operations.

Training and Development

- **Designed** and implemented numerous "Job Search Strategic Planning" modules focused on the needs of the individual identified as "*dual transition,*" e.g. relocation and in career change.
- **Trained** and instructed three associate consultants in use of career transition assessment tools and various strategic market-driven job search tools.
- **Provided** guidance in self-assessments that assisted individuals in examining their skills, interests, and values.
- **Instructed** participants in development of market-driven resumes and cover letters that resulted in an increase in interviews of up to 20%.

Figure 4: Sample Résumé #2: Functional Self Marketing Instrument (Page 1)

JOHN Q. PUBLIC   P - 2

ACCOMPLISHMENTS and EXPERIENCE (Continued)

- **Conducted** network and recruiter seminars to help individuals in job search.
- **Designed** and developed target company contact database: small to Fortune 100 companies.
- **Instructor** of Academic Planning Seminars and Graduate Studies Program Seminars designed to assist adult learners in academic planning toward effective career development.
- **Maintained** student advisement load of more than 50 learners.
- **Delivered** numerous career management and human development training programs.
- **Facilitated** group training focusing on self-assessment and career development.

PROFESSIONAL EXPERIENCE
Senior Career Consultant   1997 to Present
XXXXXXXXXXXXXXXXXXXXXXXX, Westboro, MA

Continuing Education Instructor   (Part Time)   1997 to Present
XXXXXXXX, MA

Consultant/Trainer/Career Counselor, (Westborough, MA site)   1994 to 1997
XXXXXXXXXXXXX, Chicago, IL.

Independent Contractor and Training Consultant, Foxboro, MA   1986 to 1994

Senior Training Specialist - Personnel Department   1976 to 1986
XXXXXXXXXXX, MA

PUBLICATIONS
- "Evaluation of a Holistic Career Portfolio as a Job and Career Transition Tool," The Union Institute, Cincinnati, OH, 1997. (Focused on the workforce in transition).
- "Five Easy Steps to a Gold Medal-Winning Resume", Job Smart News Magazine, 12/4/96.
- "Portfolios Take Resumes to a New Level", Job Smart News Magazine, 5/19/96.

EDUCATION
Ph.D. - Sociology, The Union Institute, Cincinnati, OH   1997
M.Ed. - Integrated Studies and Adult Assessment, Cambridge College, Cambridge, MA   1995

COMPUTER SKILLS
- Microsoft Word '97   • Access   • Internet

AFFILIATIONS
- International Association of Career Management Professionals (IACMP)
- Boston Human Resource Association (BHRA)

Figure 5: Sample Résumé #2: Functional Self Marketing Instrument (Page 2)

The Scannable Instrument

The scannable instrument design is used primarily in situations where an electronic "text" version résumé is required by the target organization because they determine candidacy based upon a computerized scan of the document.

Sample #3, shown in Figure 6 and Figure 7, is an example of instrument #1 in a scannable version. You can see from the example that it is lacking from the eye appeal standpoint but it isn't meant to be pretty.

In this case the font needs to be Arial or Helvetica. For this instrument there is no bolding, centering, tabbing, italics, or anything to distinguish one point over another. Periods and commas are allowed. Capital letters and line spacing are essentially the only way to delineate a header or distinguish one part of the résumé over another.

This is also the one time where the page count may exceed two. It is common for pages of scannable self-marketing instruments to reach as many as five.

It is absolutely essential when using this version to make sure you have captured exactly the "buzz words" used by the target company when applying for a position. Close or similar language work against you. Scanners have no tolerance for "close."

The Technical Instrument

Sample instrument #4, shown in Figure 8 and Figure 9, demonstrates another common version for people who are largely technical. The primary difference here is in the "Technical Skills" section near the top of the first page. The technical candidate should separate out the specific areas of expertise, for example, programming languages, platforms, systems, etc., and horizontally list (string) their appropriate information. Another attribute of the technical version is that the "Education" section should also contain all the various certifications obtained.

JOHN Q. PUBLIC
116 Great Street
Anyplace, MA 01110
Phone: (900) 398-7007
JQP@ultra.com

JOB TARGET: CAREER CONSULTANT

Summary: Advanced degree with more than 25 years experience in career development and design and delivery of training programs in academic, manufacturing, and retail environments. Specific expertise in succession planning and motivation of individuals in transition. Deliverables include Job Search Team Approach, Career Portfolio Design and Development, and Life/Work Assessment.

SKILLS
Life/Work Counseling, Training, Motivational Speaking, Leadership, Platform Skills
Alumni Relations, Written & Oral Communication

ACCOMPLISHMENTS and EXPERIENCE
Senior Career Consultant, 1997 to Present
XXXXXXXXXXXXXXXXXXXXXXXX, Westboro, MA
- Provided career transition consulting services to non-exempt through senior executives in both domestic and international communities.
- Designed and implemented numerous "Job Search Strategic Planning" modules focused on the needs of the individual identified as "dual transition," e.g. relocation and in career change.
- Trained and instructed three associate consultants in use of career transition assessment tools and various strategic market-driven job search tools.
- Maintained exceptional client services through accumulation of stellar client success stories, e.g. one client = nine resumes, resulting in five interviews yielding four job offers.
- Provided guidance in self-assessments that assisted individuals in examining their skills, interests, and values.
- Instructed participants in development of market-driven resumes and cover letters that resulted in an increase in interviews of up to 20%.
- Managed case load of 55 individuals. Most were placed within 3-4 months of start date.

Continuing Education Instructor (Part Time), 1997 to Present
XXXXXXXX, MA
- Instructed Academic Planning Seminars and Graduate Studies Program Seminars designed to assist adult learners in academic planning toward effective career development.
- Research consultant for Career Services Center project for the College.

Figure 6: Sample Résumé #3: Scannable Self Marketing Instrument (Page 1)

JOHN Q. PUBLIC, PAGE - 2

- Maintained student advisement load of more than 50 learners.
- Designed and developed five focus courses including Effective Oral Presentations, Diversity in the Workplace, Career Counseling: Theory and Practice, Effective Oral Presentations, Assessing Diversity Development, and Designing Career Portfolios.

Independent Contractor and Training Consultant, Foxboro, MA, 1986 to 1994
- Project Management for small and large companies and personal business.
- Provided management, training, and operations expertise for 500+ retail outlets.
- Managed major home/trade show operations.

Senior Training Specialist - Personnel Department , 1976 to 1986
XXXXXXXXXXX, MA
- Delivered numerous career management and human development training programs.
- Facilitated group training focusing on self-assessment and career development.

PUBLICATIONS
- "Evaluation of a Holistic Career Portfolio as a Job and Career Transition Tool," The Union Institute, Cincinnati, OH, 1997. (Focused on the workforce in transition).
- "Five Easy Steps to a Gold Medal-Winning Resume", Job Smart News Magazine, 12/4/96.
- "Portfolios Take Resumes to a New Level", Job Smart News Magazine, 5/19/96.

EDUCATION
Ph.D. - Sociology, The Union Institute, Cincinnati, OH, 1997
M.Ed. - Integrated Studies and Adult Assessment, Cambridge College, Cambridge, MA, 1995

COMPUTER SKILLS
Microsoft Word '97, Access, Internet

AFFILIATIONS
International Association of Career Management Professionals (IACMP)
Boston Human Resource Association (BHRA)

Figure 7: Sample Résumé #3: Scannable Self Marketing Instrument (Page 2)

JOHN Q. PUBLIC

116 Great Street   Phone: (911) 358-7007
Anyplace, MA 01110   JQP@ultra.com

JOB TITLE If known, goes here, otherwise leave blank

Summary: Master's degree with 15 years IT executive and operations management experience in technical environments. Expertise in strategic planning and implementation, business development, and training and development. Broad-based technical skills with an acumen toward team building excellence and superior project management.

SKILLS

- Written and Oral communication   • Teambuilding   • Troubleshooting   • All-phase testing
- Complex problem Solving   • Customer Service   • Quality Assurance

TECHNICAL SUMMARY

Programming Languages: InterDev 6.0, ASP, VBScript, JavaScript, HTML, CSS, Visual Basic 3.0-6.0; Delphi 2.0; AutoLISP
Databases: Oracle 8.0.; MS-SQL 6.5, 7, 2000; Access 2.0- 2000; Paradox 4.5- 8; SQL AnyWhere; Interbase 4.2, 5.0; Sybase 11.
Report Writers: ReportSmith 3.0, Crystal Report 5.0 – 8.0.
CASE Tools: InfoModeler, S-Designor
Hardware: IBM compatible computers, printers, scanners, modems.
Operating Systems: MS-DOS 4, 5, 6.xx; Windows 3.x;Windows 9.x, Windows NT; Windows 2000, OS/2 Warp; Novell DOS 7; System 7., Novell
Internet Servers: IIS, iPlanet
Software Applications: Norton Utilities, AntiVirus, Microsoft Word, Excel, Improv, Adobe PhotoShop 5.5., Lotus Notes, Microsoft FrontPage, Internet Explorer, Netscape Browser, Oracle.

SELECTED ACCOMPLISHMENTS and WORK EXPERIENCE

Senior Programmer/Analyst   1997 to 2004
Anyplace, Inc., Boston, MA

- **Developed** the Firm's WEB related sites: Internet, Intranet sites, Extranets.
- **Designed, developed, maintained, and enhanced** Internet and Client-Server based applications using one or more of the development tool sets.
- **Developed** functional specifications, designing databases, prototyping for users, security setup, unit testing, and training/support of end-users.
- **Executed above projects** using the following technologies: VBScript, MS-Access 97, 2000, ASP, HTML, DHTML, CSS, JavaScript, , Informix, and SQL 6.5, 7.0, 2000.

Figure 8: Sample Résumé #4: Technical Self Marketing Instrument (Page 1)

JOHN Q. PUBLIC   **Page 2**

Project Leader/Senior Analyst   1992 to 1997
Another Place, Worcester, MA
➢ **Managed** information technology group, 9 people full-time and contractors, that consisted of
  three sections: Development, Q/A and UAT Testing, LAN Management.
➢ **Managed Projects**: "Balance exception," "Report," "Loan," "AW Tracking", update of
  "Inquiry Tracking Device" , and "Y2K" conversion. Tools and databases used in project
  were: Visual Basic 5.0, Paradox 7.0, Delphi 2.0, MS Access 97, Interbase 5.0.
➢ **Designed and developed** reports for: "Data Enrichment and Query" application. Reports
  were written in Crystal Reports 5.0, 6.0 against Sybase 11 database.
➢ **Developed** departmental WEB site on Windows NT server, FastTrack Netscape Server.

Technical Trainer/Consultant   1989 to 1992
ABC Corp., Westbridge, MA
➢ **Trained** clients in: MS-DOS 6.xx and Windows 3.1, MS Access.
➢ **Designed and developed** numerous programs.
➢ **Extensive Experience** in training corporate clients and customers.

EDUCATION

Master of Science in Electrical Engineering   1988
Clark University, Framingham, MA

Bachelor of Arts   1980
Umass, Boston, MA

Certificate: Client/Server Development.

Figure 9: Sample Résumé #4: Technical Self Marketing Instrument (Page 2)

The Academic Instrument

Professionals in academia use a version similar to Sample #5, shown in Figure 10 and Figure 11. Often, a Curriculum Vitae (CV) is required that will look similar to the sample but will include extensive white papers, other publications, and course descriptions that have been designed and delivered by the instructor. Essentially, CV's have no limit to their length. I've seen many in excess of fifty pages. That aside, many institutions are asking for the two page type in the sample.

The Legal Instrument

You will see tremendous similarity between the legal Sample #6 shown in Figure 12 and Figure 13 and the academic versions. The education is listed very near the top of the first page. Licensure information such as in which states the candidate may practice are often listed and various courts in which they have tried could also be presented.

Creating Your Instrument

Create your own instrument appropriate to your situations from the models described. Be complete, succinct, and pay careful attention to detail. Once you have completed the original Self-Marketing Instrument Master it should be easy to tailor each document to your needs. I highly recommend that you place the completed instrument in its own folder on your computer. We will discuss the actual marketing of the instrument later in the book.

JOHN Q. PUBLIC

116 Great Street   Phone: (900) 398-7007
Anyplace, MA 01110   JQP@ultra.com

SENIOR INSTRUCTOR

Summary: Advanced degree with more than 20 years experience in career development and design and delivery of training programs in academic, manufacturing, and retail environments. Specific expertise in succession planning and motivation of individuals in transition. Deliverables include Job Search Team Approach, Career Portfolio Design and Development, and Life/Work Assessment.

EDUCATION

Ph.D. - Sociology, The Union Institute, Cincinnati, OH   1997
M.Ed. - Integrated Studies and Adult Assessment, Cambridge College, Cambridge, MA   1995

SKILLS

- Life/Work Counseling   • Training   • Motivational Speaking   • Leadership
    • Platform Skills   • Alumni Relations   • Written & Oral Communication

ACCOMPLISHMENTS and EXPERIENCE

Senior Career Consultant   1997 to Present
XXXXXXXXXXXXXXXXXXXXXXXXX, Westboro, MA
- **Provided** career transition consulting services to non-exempt through senior executives in both domestic and international communities.
- **Designed** and implemented numerous "Job Search Strategic Planning" modules focused on the needs of the individual identified as "*dual transition,*" e.g. relocation and in career change.
- **Trained** and instructed three associate consultants in use of career transition assessment tools and various strategic market-driven job search tools.
- **Maintained** exceptional client services through accumulation of stellar client success stories, e.g. one client = **nine** resumes, resulting in **five** interviews yielding **four** job offers.
- **Provided** guidance in self-assessments that assisted individuals in examining their skills, interests, and values.
- **Instructed** participants in development of market-driven resumes and cover letters that resulted in an increase in interviews of up to 20%.
- **Managed** case load of 55 individuals. Most were placed within 3-4 months of start date.

Continuing Education Instructor   (Part Time)   1997 to Present
XXXXXXXXX, MA
- **Instructor** of Academic Planning Seminars and Graduate Studies Program Seminars designed to assist adult learners in academic planning toward effective career development.

Figure 10: Sample Résumé #5: Academic Self Marketing Instrument (Page 1)

JOHN Q. PUBLIC   P - 2

(Continued)
- **Research** consultant for Career Services Center project for the College.
- **Maintained** student advisement load of more than 50 learners.
- **Designed** and developed five focus courses including Effective Oral Presentations, Diversity in the Workplace, Career Counseling: Theory and Practice, Effective Oral Presentations, Assessing Diversity Development, and Designing Career Portfolios.

Independent Contractor and Training Consultant, Foxboro, MA   1986 to 1994
- **Project** Management for small and large companies and personal business.
- **Provided** management, training, and operations expertise for 500+ retail outlets.
- **Managed** major home/trade show operations.

Senior Training Specialist - Personnel Department   1976 to 1986
XXXXXXXXXXX, MA
- **Delivered** numerous career management and human development training programs.
- **Facilitated** group training focusing on self-assessment and career development.

PUBLICATIONS

- "Evaluation of a Holistic Career Portfolio as a Job and Career Transition Tool," The Union Institute, Cincinnati, OH, 1997. (Focused on the workforce in transition).
- "Five Easy Steps to a Gold Medal-Winning Resume", Job Smart News Magazine, 12/4/96.
- "Portfolios Take Resumes to a New Level", Job Smart News Magazine, 5/19/96.

COMPUTER SKILLS

- Microsoft Word '97   • Access   • Internet

AFFILIATIONS

- International Association of Career Management Professionals (IACMP)
- Boston Human Resource Association (BHRA)

Figure 11: Sample Résumé #5: Academic Self Marketing Instrument (Page 2)

JOHN Q. PUBLIC, ESQ

116 Great Street   Phone: (900) 398-7007
Anyplace, MA 01110   JQP@ultra.com

GENERAL COUNSEL

SUMMARY: Juris Doctor with more than 10 years executive experience as a counsel to focus on expert witness development for clients, law firms and consulting firms involved in complex litigation. Expertise in business development, marketing and strategic planning and plan implementation. Skilled in team development, motivation, project management, concept development.

EDUCATION

Juris Doctor   1996
Tufts School of Law
GPA: 3.78
Cum laude

Bachelor of Science,   1993
University of Massachusetts
Cum laude

Licensed to practice law in Massachusetts (8/16/97) and federal courts (9/10/98).

SKILLS

- Excellent Oral & Written Communication • Self Starter • Problem Solver
- Interpersonal • Creative • Project Management

SELECTED ACCOMPLISHMENTS

Associate Attorney   1992 to Present
Your Own Lawyer Group LLP, Framingham, MA
➢ **Handled** all aspects of litigation from initial pleadings through trial discovery.
➢ **Conducted** written discovery including written interrogatories, production requests and requests for admissions.
➢ **Performed** witness interviews, fact gathering, research and case strategy.
➢ **Designed and developed** depositions and solicited testimony from witnesses and opposing parties using verbal questions.
➢ **Researched and wrote** motions that pertained to cases.
➢ **Negotiated** with opposing counsel and led to alternative dispute resolution mechanisms such as mediation.
➢ **Hired and worked** with experts to assist on particular issues that required expert assistance.
➢ **Prepared** for trials through arbitration preparation, strategy and planning, research, writing, witness preparation, and oral presentation.

Figure 12: Sample Résumé #6: Legal Self Marketing Instrument (Page 1)

JOHN Q. PUBLIC, ESQ.   **Page 2**

<u>CONTINUED</u>
➤ **Performed** as "first chair" position in jury trial, and provided a winning argument.
➤ **Concentrated** in product liability and tort defense, insurance coverage and construction. My clients were primarily commercial.
➤ **Involved** in committees and organizations within and outside of the firm.
➤ **Served** as a coach to associates.
➤ **Participated** in in-house training for first year litigation associates.
➤ **Firm representative** for the 1999 March of Dimes Fund Raising Campaign.

Litigation Assistant   1991 – 1992
Someone Else's Legal Firm, LLP, Boston, MA
➤ **Assisted** attorneys with all facets of litigation and trial preparation.
➤ **Researched** in federal and state courts, as well as local and university libraries.
➤ **Interviewed** witnesses and assisted in document productions.
➤ **Drafted** indices, memoranda and reports on cases.
➤ **Constructed** exhibits and exhibit lists for trial.

Legislative intern   1990
Office of State Representative Joseph Shortsleves, Boston, MA
➤ **Worked** with the Representative and his aide in their efforts to meet constituent's needs.
➤ **Drafted** letters in response to particular issues.

AFFILATIONS AND ASSOCIATIONS

Active member of the Young Lawyer's Committee.
Active Associates Committee member for 3 years.
Solicited funds from within the firm and outside of the firm.

Figure 13: Sample Résumé #6: Legal Self Marketing Instrument (Page 2)

Résumé Challenges

There are a number of issues that can potentially derail what would otherwise be a perfectly good résumé. Two of the biggest are credential issues and chronological gaps in employment. Obviously, the best way to handle these is to not have them at all, but in the event that these issues arise, I have some suggestions to try and address and minimize the effect of them on the job search process.

Credential Issues

Credential issues generally fall into one of two categories: too few, or too many. Depending on your situation, either one might be a problem.

Missing Credentials

Occasionally, I run into high-level managers who work their way up the corporate ladder and find themselves in the position of having huge amounts of experience but no formal degree to put on the résumé. Today, lack of a formal degree is looked upon the same way as not finishing high school was twenty or thirty years ago. Employers see it as a hindrance, regardless of how intelligent or experienced you are. Many corporations use this hole to eliminate the candidate outright.

Professionals in this situation have a major issue that needs to be addressed as quickly as possible. Many people wave this off, saying something along the lines of "I don't have time," or "I'm too old." As someone who was in my early fifties when I earned my degrees, you'll find me somewhat unsympathetic to those who are trying to "get by" and not get the credentials necessary to advance their careers.

> *Today, lack of a formal degree is looked upon the same way as not finishing high school was twenty or thirty years ago.*

I have a suggestion that will help in the short-term, but will not keep the wall from being built if not addressed. I suggest that you research colleges in your area and pick a degree program appropriate for your career direction and at the very least register for a single course toward matriculation of a degree. It shows initiative, professional development, and puts you on a positive path. Having made the initial step you can now put the degree on your résumé "as a work in progress." I usually recommend something like:

Bachelors Degree in Electrical Engineering (Estimated date of completion)   2010
YourBest University, Boston, MA

Technology professionals in particular are expected to keep current with their credentials. Most will need to attend educational courses, seminars, certifications, or pursue further degrees nearly their whole life. Other career professionals may not need to follow this path, but appropriate credentials are very important to be competitive.

Job searches without the necessary credentials are like trying to win a game of chess without the queen. It's not impossible, but it makes the road to a successful outcome a whole lot more difficult. Do what you need to do.

Too Many Credentials

Sometimes when a professional is making a career transition, the credentials that they have earned could impede the effort. For example, in some cases having a Ph.D. for a target job could eliminate you as being "over-qualified." In these cases, I have found it to be successful for candidates to replace the specific degree mentioned in the summary with simply "Advanced Degree."

As a person with a doctorate, this is not something I like to address, but in some cases it might be necessary to "dumb down" the instrument and eliminate the degree from the résumé altogether. I consider this to be a radical part of "tailoring" a résumé and crafting it into a self-marketing instrument.

Why would you need to do this? Sometimes a person just needs to get a job and bring in some cash. In other cases they may be making a radical transition because they have decided they don't want to continue in a career that has become "toxic" to them.

A Tailoring Example

I recall an instance when a person came to me after paying a hefty price to have a professional résumé writer craft hers. However, she was not getting any interviews.

The résumé looked good, but as I reached the bottom I noted that she had—justifiably—put her almost-completed MBA in the Education section. At that time, she was focusing on completing the MBA and was looking for a a lower-paying finance position. Once the MBA was completed she would move ahead with her long-term career plans.

From a marketing perspective, her strategy seemed clear to me, but the MBA would be a red flag to potential employers for a position of the level she was seeking. I recommended that—for the moment—she remove the credential from her résumé. As a result she landed a good job within a couple of weeks.

Gaps In The Résumé

Another challenge you may face is the chronological gap. Fluctuations in the job market and rapid shifts in the economy may cause reductions in job availability and as a result, you may find large time gaps appearing in your résumé. While it might seem acceptable to give reasons for such holes, from a marketing perspective it is always better not to have anything to explain.

My suggestion is to fill the gap with *something*. Never make anything up, but you can be creative about the items that you include. Temporary or short-term contracts may be one option, but in other instances you may need to consider and document various pro-bono, volunteer, or "freebie"

> *...from a marketing perspective it is always better not to have anything to explain.*

projects you might have done. These projects might have only taken minutes over a whole week, but can still constitute a bullet point on the instrument. I have usually suggested that these be placed under the job title of "Smith's Consulting Services."

As a rule of thumb, if the gap is under six months it isn't much of a problem and may not need to be addressed. Once it exceeds that time frame it is probably time to start documenting possible bullet points. Of course, the truly proactive searcher "sniffs" out activities to put on their résumé right from the start.

There are situations, though, when there are perfectly valid reasons besides the inability to get hired that keep people out of the workforce for extended periods. These include those times where a woman or man has been a stay-at-home parent, have been sidelined by extended illness, and so on.

In these cases, when the time comes to enter or return to the workforce, I recommend registering for some specific coursework as it relates to your passion. In addition, register at numerous temporary agencies to not only try and get a foothold in a company, but also to begin building applicable work experience. If you have previous work experience, document that. If you do a good job of documenting the combination of your passions and some work experience, and follow the resource development process as described in Chapter 14, "Resource Development", you should find yourself in interesting positions after only a short amount of time. A little more patience may be needed here as opposed to the scenario where the searcher has been continuously employed, but this process will yield results. The alternative for those who haven't had such a program as the Career Game Championships available to them is that they most often fall into whatever they can get.

They usually also need to get multiple jobs to sustain them, which leaves them feeling more like slave labor than someone who is in charge of their options. Using this method should alleviate that entirely.

Personal Information

Remember, never volunteer personal information. You are not required to include race, creed, gender or age information on your interview, and in the United States and many other countries it is illegal to be disqualified because of it. Even so, never volunteer prejudicial information that could disqualify you as a candidate. If you feel that you must address them, always put it in a positive frame that speaks to being available for work, family support, and full support of this new position.

I've also seen individuals put spousal and family information on their résumés. This is absolutely taboo. I don't even recommend including hobbies on the résumé. You never know what non-work related information may bias a hiring manager or other interviewer.

Pyramid Résumé Design

The résumé layouts that I describe are designed in a very specific way. I've laid out the information so that the components are listed in order of their importance as they relate to a particular job target. This lends itself to a subliminal pyramid "shape" and is not accidental. The pyramid is a symbol of strength; therefore, the marketing instrument, at a conceptual level, should also come from a position of strength. The subliminal pyramid design achieves this.

YOU
(Name, Address, Phone, Fax if available, and E-mail)

JOB TARGET
(Can be written or subconscious)

SUMMARY STATEMENT
(Credentials, years of experience, what field, and expertise)

SKILLS, AS THEY APPLY TO THE JOB TARGET
(What you are skilled at that demonstrates ability to perform job target)

**RÉSUMÉ BODY – Quantitatively based accomplishments
as they relate to the job target.**
(Action word statements with $, #, and or % that indicate value added to organization)

EDUCATION AND CERTIFICATIONS
(Demonstrates motivation to keep pace with job target foundation)

PROFESSIONAL ORGANIZATIONS and AFFILIATIONS
(Demonstrates motivation to associate with other professionals' ideas who are in the field)

A hiring manager is not likely to "see" the pyramid design, but subliminally it is there. Since you cannot be physically present to emphasize or demonstrate your ability to be the best candidate when the résumé is read, it is important that the instrument do the job for you. Thus, using very powerful subconscious attributes in the flow of information in the layout has a strong impact when presented in this way.

Of course, there may be exceptions when the type of organization to which you are applying requires a different order of importance. Technical, academic, and legal résumés are examples of such exceptions. But the original concept remains intact.

Errors in Sample #1

Earlier in the chapter I mentioned that there were eight errors in Sample #1, the traditional marketing instrument shown in Figure 2 and Figure 3 and challenged you to find them. Here are the answers.

1. Extra space in the second "1997 to Present" date entry.
2. Spacing between bullets in the Skills section is not consistent.
3. Bullets in "Senior Career Consultant" section are not consistently indented.
4. Inconsistent font size in the second bullet on page #2 "Provided Management…" The font size is smaller than normal.
5. Missing period at end of sentence in "Delivered numerous…" bullet.

6. Date entry 1976 to 1986 is ragged—not to far right margin.

7. Missing space between the Publications heading and the text section.

8. Typo in "Microsoft" under the Computer Skills section.

These errors might seem very finicky, and in fact they are, but in a medium where presentation is all-important, they could mean the difference between getting a call and a silent phone.

If you found them all, congratulations, but that still means you should have your own materials checked by others. If you didn't find them all, then that is all the more evidence that it is critical to have others check your work.

We'll now move on to another important self-marketing tool—the cover letter. This tool combined with a great résumé can provide the one-two punch you need to get in the door. I'll show you how to get the most out of the cover letter and make sure it complements and mirrors the résumé.

Cover Letters

In years past, it went without saying that once the résumé was complete it was absolutely necessary to support it with a matching marketing-oriented cover letter; inclusion of a cover letter was as essential as handing out business cards. The thinking was that the cover letter was the very first thing any future employer saw from a candidate and that the first impression was critical. In this new century, the use and application of self-marketing tools has changed a bit. As I mentioned in Chapter 9, job search engines like Monster.com® and CareerBuilder.com™ have reduced the need for cover letters.

This doesn't mean that there isn't a place in today's job search for the cover letter. It just means that for opportunities gleaned from the Internet-search sites, they often aren't needed. However, magazines, newspaper job ads, blind ads, some company web site job ads, and company targets within the unpublished markets represent areas where cover letters are still important, often crucially so. Here the classic thinking applies: what good is a killer résumé if it never gets read? Occasionally, even Internet ads require a cover letter to be sent with the résumé. When those times arise, you are once again faced with the cover letter being the very first thing any future employer sees and you should be prepared by having one before you need it.

In the typical job search, the cover letter is used merely as an introduction to the résumé with no attention to self-marketing. Usually something like "I am responding to the ad placed in last Sunday's *Weekly Post*. As you'll see in my resume (sic) my qualifications are a good match..." This results in a very bland introduction to the searcher when a few well-placed marketing tools would draw out the information that the hiring manager is looking for—remember, they want to cut to the chase and you want to get noticed.

This chapter will assist you in drafting the basic elements to cover letters that are most likely to be needed.

Basic Structure, Format and Layout

Like the résumé, the overall look and feel of the cover letter is very important. Again, keep it simple and as easy to read as possible. Use one-inch margins on all sides. For consistency, use the same font and paper as the résumé. Use the same font size if possible.

> *Like the résumé, the overall look and feel of the cover letter is very important.*

Generally, the cover letter goes with and precedes the résumé as a single, unattached page. Cover letters should never exceed a single page. Make sure to include your name and address in a traditional address box at the top left of the page, then move into the body of the letter. Here, relating your specific qualifications to the job requirements as they have listed them is an easily-readable form is most important. The reuse of language from their advertisement—not approximate words—is essential. Samples that can be customized to your situation are discussed later in this chapter. Avoid the temptation to cut and paste information verbatim from the résumé to the cover letter, but be sure to leverage marketing concepts like those used in the summary paragraph at the top of the résumé. You should also make sure that the list of Key Skills that you included in your résumé are mirrored in the cover letter.

Here again, spelling and grammar are extremely important in the cover letter. Like the résumé, make sure that a detail-oriented person looks over a hard copy of your cover letter before sending it.

Cover Letter Variations

Following are some cover letter designs that will be helpful to you as you move forward in your job search. This information will help you design an effective cover letter that is very flexible, comprehensive, and easy to read.

Use cover letters #1 and #2, shown in Figure 14 and Figure 15 respectively, when responding to ads from the newspaper or internet. They are specifically designed for the purpose of marketing yourself. In my experience, job searchers have used both with great success. The primary difference is the presentation of the material.

For practice, find an ad in the newspaper or on an Internet site where you are a match for the required tasks and design a cover letter using one of these two models.

Cover letter #3, shown in Figure 16, is the letter most used for targeting recruiters or headhunters. It is similar in design to letter #1 except there are no advertisement criteria to follow. Here you must select three or four bullet points describing activities that you both truly enjoy and can demonstrate significant competency.

Cover letter #4, shown in Figure 17, is used to make direct contact with an organization that you want to target. Essentially it is a "blind" letter, affording you the opportunity to contact organizations you want to work for, but where you have no job ad to respond to.

Each letter you send should be customized in some way to the company and position in question.

You should spend some time preparing templates of each type. Use the samples in Figure 14 through Figure 17 for ideas and format. Once completed, you will have three "templates" of cover letters to use in your search. I say templates because it is important to remember that you don't want to send the same letter to every organization, simply swapping out the names. That practice lends itself to stagnation and goes against my principle of constant quality assurance that we'll discuss in depth later in the book. Each letter you send should be customized in some way to the company and position in question.

(Your Name and
Address Goes Here)

Date:

P. B. Jones, Vice President Human Resources
Dicy Computer, Inc.
901 Your The Drive
Anywhere, New York 01234

Dear Mr. Jones:

Your advertisement for Training Coordinator in the Worcester Times specifies the following requirements:

1. *"...responsible for the coordination, development and implementation of training programs for our staff and customers, 5-6 years experience." (substitute actual ad wording)*

I have the required years of experience in designing and delivering training programs which our customers say have helped them greatly. (substitute your wording)

2. *"...perform needs assessment, define training objectives and design..."*

My training experience combined with my human resource background in program design has helped me to pinpoint needs of organizations and then package the material so it is appropriately delivered and integrated.

3. *"...related training experience with excellent communication skills."*

My training experience has been with numerous companies. Please review the enclosed resume.

Dicy Computer is a company that would provide the type of potential for growth upon which a strong training program could provide. At a personal meeting, I would like to discuss with you how I could make an immediate contribution to your organization.

Sincerely,

Rhoda A. Dendron

Enclosure

Figure 14: Sample Cover Letter #1: Advertised Positions

(Your Name and
Address Goes Here)

Date:

Judas B. Ritch, President and CEO
WEMAKE Gold, Inc.
123 Fake Street
Manyapples, ID 00011

Dear Mr. Ritch

As a professional with five years of experience in marketing, research, sales, and management, I am
Responding to the Marketing Manager position I saw in the New York Times on January 02, 2002.

I believe my extensive experience suggests I am an ideal candidate to market IBM, as the following
demonstrates.

Your Requirements	**My Qualifications**
Experience developing markets	Extensive experience developing markets from concept to implementation to evaluation.
Effective research skills	Several years market research working directly and in a management and analytical capacity.
Coordinate promotional and advertising campaigns	Developed and coordinated advertising and promotional campaigns. Developed concepts and coordinated all resources.
Knowledge of computer industry	Extensive knowledge of computers through positions held.

As requested, I have enclosed my resume to further detail my qualifications and accomplishments. At a
personal meeting I would like to demonstrate how I could make an immediate contribution to your
organization.

Sincerely,

B. Wiley Kiote
Enclosure

Figure 15: Sample Cover Letter #2 The "T" Letter

(Your Name and
Address Goes Here)

Date:

Iam Infamoss, Director
Getemoffme, Inc.
Iwent Twofer Street
Miami, FL 02355

Dear _____:

Your firm has been recommended to me as one which may be able to offer career opportunities at both the right level and within the right type of industry. As a successful Operations Manager, I have been responsible for the operations of many companies including domestic and international subsidiaries, and their product lines. I would like to build on this experience with my next company.

I believe most corporations need strong operations management. Skills which could be of immediate benefit to a client of yours would include:

- **Reporting systems**. Consistently improve at all levels so quality, accuracy, and speed of information meet corporate expectations.

- **Production Management**. Provided leadership in multiple production areas improving productivity, enhancing efficiency, and cutting costs.

- **Profitability.** Through successful operations leadership and exceeding company goals, and increased profitability from 10% to over 125% yearly.

Additional accomplishments are described on the attached resume.

Although I am specifically interested in Operations Management, I realize that you may not be conducting a search for this title at this point. Regardless, I would welcome your advice and recommendations about companies with developing needs. At a personal meeting, I would like to discuss with you how I could make an immediate contribution to your clients.

Sincerely,

Oliver Twist

Enclosure

Figure 16: Sample Cover Letter #3: Executive Recruiter or Headhunter

(Your Name and
Address Goes Here)

Date:

Ryan Toss, VP Operations
Any Corporation
660 High Street
Corpus Christie, TX 09876

Dear Mr. Toss:

We both manage companies that thrive on sound operations management. As a successful manager, I have been responsible for multiple production operations during a rapid growth ($10 million to over $1 billion in increased revenue).

Using my experience to lead departments to become more effective, efficient, and therefore productive has been particularly exciting. Not only am I able to make revenue gains, I could also bring the following experience to your organization:

- Analysis of production operations from diverse industries to development of efficient operations help me deliver the most effective results.

- Knowledge of the Corpus Christie community through prior employment at a Big 4 business firm in the area.

- Sole responsibility for production management for a German parent company.

At a personal meeting I would enjoy the opportunity to talk with you in greater depth about some of the ways I could make direct contributions to your organization.

With best regards:

Lit L. Emporer

Enclosure

Figure 17: Sample Cover Letter #4: Company Target (Blind) Cover Letter

11

Company Lists and Other Strategic Materials

In the traditional job search, résumés and cover letters typically make up the entire toolset used by job searchers but in reality they are only two pieces of a far more comprehensive pie.

In this chapter, we'll look at some more strategic materials before we move into the discussion of an action plan to put these written tools into practice. We'll also discuss the creation of a critical verbal tool that is going to streamline an important part of the process and be invaluable throughout your search.

Company Lists

As you prepare for your job search, you should be thinking about companies that interest you. They can interest you for any number of reasons: perhaps you've heard good press about them; perhaps you know that they have an excellent work culture; maybe they have great compensation and benefit plans. Whatever the reason, if the company piques your interest and you think there's a chance you might like to work for them, you should keep them on a list.

As you go through your search, however, that list can grow to become very large and possibly unwieldy for day-to-day use. Therefore, to conduct a well-managed search, I recommend that you break up your list. In this chapter, we'll be discussing three levels or lists to use in your search. You may think it is cumbersome to maintain three lists, but in reality, by breaking them up you'll find that it is much easier to manage the process.

The three list types we'll discuss are:

- **Master List**—This list is usually very large. It is intended to be a repository for all of the companies that you turn up during your search. Usually you will have a number of companies for which you have little to no data.
- **Target List**—A subset of 30-50 companies from the Master List that interest you. This becomes a manageable list from which to work.
- **Hot List**—A subset of the Target List. These are the dozen companies that currently are your highest priorities for research at any given time. This list should never exceed twelve. These get put on your Hot List sheet to use as a discussion point when speaking with people.

The creation of your Hot List is an iterative process and requires some thought and research beyond simply listing the ten to twelve companies that first pop into your mind. For every company you know by name, there are probably three or four others like it that you have never heard of.

Creating a Hot List

As I mentioned, creating the Hot List is an iterative process. The Target List and Hot List are intended to be dynamic, so don't be surprised or alarmed if you find yourself making changes. As you go through your search you should be moving companies on and off as you gather more information.

The process for getting from the Master List to the Hot List is generally this:

- Think about different industries that might interest you.
- Choose up to ten company types from those industries.
- Think of companies that fit into those industry types.
- Add any company that you think you might be interested in working for into the Master List.
- Select 30 to 50 organizations from the Master List and put them into a Target List.
- From the Target List, select about a dozen companies you want to focus on and place them into your Hot List.
- Modify and revise the lists as needed.

This method keeps everything organized and provides a means to track all of the companies you have heard about without causing yourself major confusion.

Industries and Company Types

While you may think it is best to jump right into identifying the ten to twelve companies that you want on your Hot List, I caution you against it. Instead, take a step back before getting into specific companies and think about different *industries* that might interest you. While up until now you may have worked only in a single industry, you need to think on a broader scale. There may be opportunities for you in industries far different from those in which you have experience.

In Appendix B, "Industry List" I've provided a large list of industries and company types within those industries. Go through the list and choose a few industries and up to ten company *types*. Your personal preferences will dictate the types of companies that interest you within each industry. Remember, don't limit yourself too much and don't feel limited by the industries and company types listed; there could be many others at your disposal that are not shown on the list.

> *...take a step back before getting into specific companies and think about different industries that might interest you.*

Selecting Companies for the Master List

Once you have selected your company types, list the companies you've been thinking of that you might be interested in working for. Then expand your list by adding other companies that fall into your selected company types. You should list as many as you can think of; don't be selective. The only companies that you shouldn't add to the list are those that you are sure you have no interest in working for.

This list becomes your Master List—the complete list of companies that come up during your search process. This list is intended to be a repository for companies and related information regardless of the amount of data you have on a company or your actual interest in the company. The reason you don't want to be too selective is that you will end up moving those that interest you most onto your Target List, and potentially the Hot List.

If the list starts out smaller than you'd like, don't panic. Just keep your eyes and ears open and as you talk to people in your search, companies will get added. When you hear of a company that you think may interest you, add it to your list.

If you know the names of any contacts in a particular company, include that information with the company name. Include address, phone number, and web address if you know it. If not, consider doing some research to get that information. In today's Web-enabled world, it is a rare thing for a company—large or small—not to have a web site. And the vast majority include—at the very least—address and phone number information on their site.

Crafting the Target List and Hot List

From your Master List extract a manageable subset of 30 to 50 organizations that interest you. This is your Target List—those organizations that you are currently giving attention. Then, from those potential targets, create your Hot List by culling out about a dozen companies that *most* appeal to you. These should go on a piece of paper with some space for writing in between. See Figure 18.

Bringing the list down to ten or twelve serves two purposes. First, it brings focus to your targets so that your efforts aren't all over the map. Second, since you'll be using your Hot List when you begin to talk to people, focusing the list to about a dozen prospects makes the list more digestible to the person with whom you're speaking. In fact, the Hot List is much less about a tool for yourself than it is a method to trigger information about the companies on the list—or similar companies—that the person knows. We'll cover the process of using your Hot List when meeting people more in Chapter 14, "Resource Development".

> *For most of my clients, the vast majority of the companies that they originally listed during this exercise disappeared as information about exciting new prospects was brought to light.*

As you have those discussions, you'll find that you'll gain more information about the companies on your list—and possibly more important the companies *not* on your list—and you will find that your level of interest about certain companies changes. When this happens, update your lists accordingly. I recommend you leave spaces in between the company names so that you can easily add information to the list based on the conversations you have.

For most of my clients, the vast majority of the companies that they originally listed during this exercise disappeared as information about exciting new prospects was brought to light. Remember, all companies and information go on your Master List, and companies will be added to and removed from the other lists as your information gets constantly updated. Because of the dynamic nature of these lists, I recommend using a spreadsheet or database for this exercise if at all possible.

TARGET COMPANY HOT LIST

Company	Contact	Research Information

1) XYZ, Inc. Hudson, NY

2) HowNOW Corporation, Albany, NY

3) SquankCo, Springfield, MA

4) ALPHAZ, Wilmington MA

5) Soaring Falcon Document Technologies, Burlington, MA

6) GigaGraph Incorporated, Waltham, MA

7) RealWire, Cambridge MA

8) Majic Technology, Worcester MA

9) Duke Enterprises, Springfield, MA

10) Gagarin Aerospace, Dallas, TX

11) WistaTech, Worcester, MA

Figure 18: Sample Target Company Hot List

If you find the Hot List dropping below ten, draw from the balance of the thirty or so companies on the Target List to ensure the Hot List always stays at the desired level of ten to twelve. My experience, however, is that those who closely follow the program find themselves trying to keep the list from getting too *big*. When that happens, take something off the Hot List that doesn't seem to be developing as well as the others and put it back into the Target List for when, and if, it needs to be re-entered.

Finding Companies to Add

There are many ways of finding companies to add to your list, and this is an area where the Internet can be of great benefit to you. Use these suggestions—and any others you think of—to develop your pool of companies.

The Business-to-Business directory is a good way to discover many organizations located in your area. Another great way is to Google the information. Literally hundreds of companies can be found in this way, so of course you'll need to weed out the ones you do not want and select the ones that interest you. Yet another resource is to visit your local Chamber of Commerce. They have resources for locating companies in your area.

Business contacts, friends, and family are also likely to have information about organizations you aren't familiar with.

Business contacts, friends, and family are also likely to have information about organizations you aren't familiar with. They can easily provide you with names to add to the list. All business contacts are useful, but think specifically of people who you know who are in sales. By the nature of their role and their exposure to many people in many organizations, they may be able to provide significant input to your list about companies and contacts that could be valuable to your search—even if the news is not favorable. This information could help you avoid spending time researching a dead end.

Newspaper job listings often represent opportunities other than the jobs advertised. Using job postings as a source of companies instead of specific positions may help you get an inside track on other opportunities before the job gets published.

Other Strategic Materials

In addition to the self-marketing instruments we've discussed, you will need additional materials to conduct an effective campaign. It is important to be sure that you have these items prepared *before* launching your marketing campaign. To have them at your fingertips upon request strengthens your professional appearance.

Reference List

It is a rare thing not to be asked for references when discussing employment. Therefore, it is always useful to have a prepared list of references available.

The reference list should contain between four and six people who can speak well of you. Use paper that matches your résumé and cover letter. List the names, position titles, addresses, contact numbers—phone, cell, and fax—and, if possible, e-mail addresses of each of the selected individuals who are willing to have a conversation with a prospective employer about your competency and professionalism. It is also acceptable to include their relationship with you, for example, colleague, manager, and so on. The best presentation is to have the list printed on the left margin. Don't forget to include your name and address on the header. Avoid descriptive text of any kind. Keep it simple.

Take the time to be sure that each of your references will actually speak about you the way you would like them to. My experience tells me that roughly 25% of the time one or more references speak poorly about a candidate. The result is a candidate ends up not having a clue as to why they did not get the offer when it seemed "in the bag." Sometimes the "torpedo" was inadvertent, but sometimes it was very deliberate.

> *Take the time to be sure that each of your references will actually speak about you the way you would like them to.*

To avoid this embarrassing and very costly situation I recommend that you ask a trusted person—someone who is not going to appear on the reference list such as a family member or a close friend—and ask them to do a mock reference check. Have them ask poignant questions of your listed people and see how they present. If you find one that is suspect, inadvertent or not, get a substitute immediately.

Letters of Reference

The Reference List discussed in the last section is different from a Letter of Reference. This resource is an individualized letter from a specific person usually addressed to "To Whom It May Concern" that essentially discusses your work record at a specific position or their professional relationship with you. This letter is sometimes used as a portfolio device and some employers—although usually not many—may ask to see such letters. These are very good to have if you are able to get them. Make sure that you make copies of the original and take only the copies with you to interviews or with you on the campaign trail.

Resource List

I won't spend a lot of time on this here because we are going to discuss it in depth in Chapter 14, "Resource Development". But, in a nutshell, this is a list of as many people who you know who can be of assistance to you in your transition process. Like your company lists, don't limit this list to those you think are important. *Everyone* is important in this process. Don't worry about formality, just start making a list; it's a work-in-progress and will grow as time goes on.

Writing Sample

For positions where writing is an important aspect of the position—Attorneys, Public Relations, Senior Executives, Academics, and in some cases Engineers—many employers require writing samples. If you fit into this category, now is the time to prepare one.

The sample is usually one to two pages of your free writing style. This should be an essay or a part of a larger written work, not a form you designed nor a business letter you've written. Choose a topic that is considered non-controversial. The writing sample is used to determine your competency regarding writing structure, logical thinking, and command of grammar fundamentals—you don't want to be disqualified based on your chosen subject matter. If you decide to use a document that is already written, it might need some re-vamping or sanitizing to be appropriate. Be prepared, and do this before you launch.

Strategic and Self-Marketing Action Planning

Strategic and Self-Marketing Action Planning is the most comprehensive and involved component to any effective job search. Essentially, it holds everything together. You can have excellent marketing materials, good contacts, and so on, but if you don't have an effective plan you can sabotage your hard work and spend a lot of time going nowhere.

If you have an action plan, stick to the marketing protocols, and are disciplined, you are likely to have a much easier time getting a new position than if you just jump in. If the search is not structured, framed, organized, or managed as it ought to be, the result can be frustrating. In fact, it is a rare individual who is in control of their job/career change. This often happens because many people have not educated themselves regarding an effective search process. They often do not want to be in a career transition in the first place and they certainly don't want to have to actually manage it. However, with management and a plan you will have control over your search, and I can assure you that makes all the difference.

There are a number of things you must consider as part of your Strategic and Self-Marketing Action Plan.

- Channel Management
- Process Management
- Time Management
  - Weekly Time Allocation
  - Financial Time Frame
- Campaign Management
  - Interview rate
  - Résumé Output Rate?
- Follow-up

I am going to go through each of the major activities used in conducting an effective search and discuss methods of approach through a strategic lens. Upon completion of this material you should have an excellent idea about how to put together a campaign that is vastly different from any of your competitors.

Channel Management

To begin the development of an effective Self-Marketing Action Plan you first need to accept that it must be treated as a business project. Further, I believe it is important to think from a marketing perspective. Like marketing a product, your job search on one level is a numbers game, yet on another it is highly targeted and specific.

> *Like marketing a product, your job search on one level is a numbers game, yet on another it is be highly targeted and specific.*

When effective marketing people begin to think about marketing any product, they examine various "channels" that could be instrumental in a successful campaign. For products, the channels may include telemarketing, multi-level marketing, multi-media, TV, or E-Commerce. The channels chosen depend on the intended audience and the product. The same holds true for marketing the self. Here, the channels include:

- Newspapers and Internet
- Recruiters
- Contract Agencies and Temporary Agencies
- Trade or Business Magazines
- Proposal Marketing
- Resource Development

Each of these represents an avenue that could lead to obtaining a great position inside a company of your choice. But unlike marketing a product, when marketing yourself you can't pick and choose channels; you must engage in all of the avenues. This is usually a huge change for many searchers since very few have ever done that in previous searches.

Newspapers and Internet

Without a doubt this method seems like the easiest way to go after a new position. It is easy if your only consideration is that you don't have to work very hard to ferret out positions to apply for. However, what you may not know is this method is the weakest link in the search chain. The reality is your greatest competition resides in this group, easily half of the positions posted in this area are bogus, and for all intents and purposes, it represents a "job in a box" that generally keeps you in the same kinds of positions you are accustomed to and may place you back in another victim role. These types of positions will, in most situations, not provide career resiliency.

All that said, it does remain an option that can yield opportunities approximately 5% to 10% of the time and from that perspective, rates a shot at positions that appear to be good targets. My suggestion is to spend *only* about 5-10% of your available search time using this method.

...what you may not know is this method — using newspapers and the Internet — is the weakest link in the search chain.

It will be important to make sure that *if* you are submitting résumés to target jobs gleaned from newspapers and the Internet that you tailor the cover letter and résumé to specifically target the needs of the organization as you see them in their advertisements.

If you are going to use this method, be sure that you send in as many résumés as you can to the same position. Essentially, attempt to "paper the walls" of the target company with your marketing materials. This is what is referred to as "exposure" and is much more effective than simply sending in one résumé and hoping to get a hit with that single shot. Follow the "five résumé marketing blitz" I discuss in "Quality Assurance and Marketing Instruments" on page 229 in Chapter 20, "Process Metrics and Quality".

Although this is the weakest part of the search process I have seen many searchers who have followed my suggestions and moved way ahead of the competitive pack as a result. The above tactics can make a huge difference in the results.

Recruiters

Recruiters, or headhunters as they are sometimes called, can be helpful to the job searcher. Statistically, the hit rate on using recruiting firms is also between 5% and 10%. Most recruiters are paid by the companies who retain their services and make their money through contingency or retained processes. They only get paid when the company hires the selected candidate. Many companies find that recruiters do a good job of "screening" candidates and often send only the most qualified people to interview.

Certainly, the advantage of using recruiter firms is that if you qualify for a target position they will slide you right into an interview and will often coach you in advance as to what to expect. The down side to recruiters is they work within a blizzard of résumés and you will typically only be called if you happen to get your résumé in at the time they have a job opening that matches your skills. From that standpoint I recommend that you apply, but realize that using recruiting firms is probably a "one shot" opportunity. Again, since the hit rate is so low you should avoid spending much time working in this arena; time spent should be proportional to opportunity: 5-10%.

> *...realize that using recruiter firms is probably a "one shot" opportunity.*

I suggest you find as many recruiters in your geographic target area as you are able and send cover letters and résumés to each and every one. After about a week, follow-up with a call and make sure that they received it and *ask* for a time to come in and discuss your qualifications. By and large most of them will decline the offer, but you may get one or two of them that will say they happen to have a position for which you might qualify.

Once you've gone through this exercise, though, I suggest that you go back to more productive search processes. Continue activities with this approach only if a recruiting firm continues to show specific interest in you by providing leads to target jobs and organizations. Otherwise, move on to other search activities.

Contract Agencies and Temporary Agencies

Here is a group of different kinds of agencies that may be very helpful to you in your search. This will be especially true if you are short on financial reserves and/or if the time gap in your résumé since you left your last place of employment is growing. Remember, up to about six months is not much of a problem, but after that pay particular attention to not letting it get any larger. After six months of gap time it is appropriate to find a fill-in position before things get out of hand and you end up having to explain things.

Major agencies to consider are Contract and Consulting Houses and Temporary Agencies. Contract and Consulting Houses are organizations who have a cadre of specifically-skilled individuals such as yourself who may be sent out to the corporate world on short- and long-term projects. These jobs usually pay well, sometimes have benefits, and while they usually run for finite periods, they can, in many instances, turn into full-time jobs at the work site.

Temporary Agencies are similar to Contract/ Consulting firms. They also gather a huge cadre of skilled talent who go out to work sites on short- and long-term assignments. These companies also have some benefits, but do not pay as well as consulting and contract firms.

They may provide temporary for-hire services from entry level through executive levels and in most instances pay by the hour. They can be a great way of getting into organizations so they can see you perform.

Contract/Consulting Houses and Temporary Agencies are your best bet for an alternative search plan approach; that is, if you need to fill some gaps or facilitate a quick placement. You should realize, however, that the rate for landing a full-time job from using temp agencies is less than 5%. It is best to allocate your time accordingly, meaning only an hour or two per week or less than 5% of your total job search time should be expended on this method of finding opportunities.

Trade or Business Magazines

From a strategic standpoint, trade or business magazines are an area of self-marketing that few people leverage as a resource for their job search. As we discussed in Chapter 8, "The Unpublished Job Market", trade magazines, business magazines, business journals, and the business sections of newspapers very often publish company public relations articles, often referred to as press releases. These are fantastic resources for finding positions before they become "jobs in a box." Companies print these articles because it gives them good press, but for you they are usually a good sign that the company will be hiring soon. There are many instances where these press releases disclose what kinds of jobs the organization will be looking to fill, approximately when they expect them to come available, and sometimes, who is in charge of the activity.

Once you've identified a potential opportunity using this method, keeping your eyes on their website for recently open positions is one way to use this method to identify jobs. Another way is to simply begin sending "cold" letters to staff-level individuals in the company and let them know that you had noticed their recent increase in activity and you

> *Trade and Business Magazines are fantastic resources for finding positions before they become "jobs in a box."*

have appropriate skills that they could likely use when the time is right.

The Unpublished Markets

Again, the Unpublished Markets discussed in Chapter 8 represent an interesting and unusual approach to job search. As part of their own marketing plan, corporations will often publicize their growth activities. Organizations will always plan for their future and if those plans include increasing their headcount, then that information very often will be included in trade magazine and news articles. The job searcher should take advantage of this "free" publicity.

Resource Development

As I've discussed, you may have become aware that Resource Development actually has it own embedded marketing methods. You can develop your network to identify who knows organizations and individuals within them. In addition, when you apply for positions through advertising or Internet, networks can be very effective in helping you to gain an edge.

Although Resource Development may be time-intensive and difficult for many people to do, it becomes much easier on the other end with regard to the interviews. When you approach a person to develop them as a contact lead, approximately one in three individuals will provide valuable information or another contact person to work with. This is about three times better than the yield a person could expect using the old "traditional" networking method.

When you use resource development concepts in conjunction with the Strategic Marketing Action Plan, the process gets results that most searchers only dream about.

How I manage to get these much more dramatic results and how to use this all-important method will be discussed in detail in Chapter 14, "Resource Development". When you use Resource Development concepts in conjunction with the Strategic Marketing Action Plan, the process gets results that most searchers only dream about. I recommend you spend 80% or more of your time on this area of the job search. This is because, for executive-level individuals, more than 90% of the jobs are obtained in this way. Many clients have said that it is the *only* method they have ever used to secure a job.

Process Management

Again, to be effective you *must* treat your Self-Marketing Project—that is your job search—as a short-term business project. It must be as disciplined and as thorough as any business project might be, with careful measurements about the effectiveness of each component and each piece of the project. You must understand that your project needs to be carefully and diligently managed. This point is absolutely crucial to the success of your campaign. If you don't manage the project, it will manage you. I cannot emphasize this point enough. I have known many people who are very good at multi-tasking that found conducting an effective search campaign to be a bit challenging. But I will discuss how to make this easier than it appears. It's sort of like eating an elephant, one bite at a time.

Managing the project is a major strategic attribute that separates you from the average job searcher. Most people create a résumé, send it out to a few places, and wait to see what happens. They usually contact a few close friends to find out if they know of any jobs. But, by and large, most people assume a "hat-in-hand" approach to finding a job, meaning they look in a haphazard way for whatever they can find.

My approach, on the other hand, allows you to take control. It is one where you selectively examine organizations to determine which may be the best fit for you, then target them to see which ones come forward and make an offer.

> *...managing the project is a major strategic attribute that separates you from the average job searcher.*

There are many considerations that can severely impact a job or career change campaign. The following sections discuss these considerations and assist you in developing a more realistic and effective job/career change campaign.

Time Management

Prior to putting together the components of an effective strategic marketing action plan, we must think about time management. As in any business project, the planner must consider what the deadline is. While you may have an idea about when you'd like or need to be in a new position, we must first establish a weekly plan that will get you there when you need to be.

Weekly Time Allocation

It is important to establish how much time in any given week you plan to devote to the search campaign. Your decision as to a practical amount of time will be applied directly into the self-marketing plan. For the most part, a full time search requires 20-30 hours of planned and organized effort per week. Acceptable time frames fall within 10-20 hours. Fewer than 10 hours per week will likely cause the target time frame to stretch. You need to consider the amount of time consumed if you already are in a position as well as family commitments, social commitments, volunteer commitments, and so on. It may be important to your plan to put some of these things on hold for a short time if you expect to reach your target. Of course, some things will not have that flexibility.

Nearly every person I've ever worked with previously spent the lion's share of their search time looking in the local newspaper or surfing the Internet for positions.

I suggest that a person also plan for some amount of down time to re-energize. Once the commitment time has been established we can begin to see how it directly applies to the Self-Marketing Action Plan.

Once you have established the average amount of time you can realistically commit to the process you can then determine *how* your time will be allocated. This is the first critical difference in having an effective versus an ineffective campaign. Nearly every person I've ever worked with previously spent the lion's share of their search time looking in the local newspaper or surfing the Internet for positions. In the Career Game Championships that will shift to far more productive activities.

Financial Time Frame

For most people, it is important to determine how long your existing finances can sustain you and your family, usually in terms of weeks. If you are still working this answer tends to be more open-ended, but if you are not working this number is usually considerably less and, therefore, more critical. This calculation will, of course, be different for everyone and be based on the current financial resources available, ongoing income, and expenses. Fill in that answer below. Next, subtract four to six weeks from that number. The purpose for having this number is because a good plan also has a safety net to implement an alternate or emergency plan. An emergency plan might be to take on a contract, temporary, or other kinds of filler jobs to hold you over until you land a more appropriate position. Of course, you should be checking into these alternative opportunities concurrent with conducting your normal job/career search so that you aren't forced into a panic situation where you must research and investigate such alternatives at the last minute.

Now calculate the final emergency implementation date.

Current Date:	_____
# weeks I can last with what I have:	_____ weeks
Safety Net:	- 4-6 weeks
Emergency Plan Implementation Date:	_____

Campaign Management

Now that you have calculated the number of weeks you can last, we need to start thinking about some specific campaign management in terms of output.

Interview Rate

Let's add another dynamic in the information. It is generally known that a person usually interviews many times before getting an offer. What is not generally known is the average number of times this usually occurs before a person actually lands a job.

My own experience coupled with information from many experts in the industry indicates that in a successful career change campaign, a person engages in approximately 15 to 30 interviews or discussions (including informational) with decision-makers. People who are staying in the same field and industry may require fewer interviews to transition successfully unless the industry is in decline.

> *...a person engages in approximately 15 to 30 interviews or discussions... in a successful career change campaign.*

You can now use that information to make another calculation. Say you plan on your search taking about thirty weeks based on our first calculation. Because we know you will need 15 to 30 interviews over the course of your campaign, then we know that for every week you are in career change mode you need to be sitting and speaking with roughly one decision maker per week.

Interviews / # of weeks of Campaign = # hiring managers to be seen each week:

15 to 30 Interviews / 30 weeks = ~1 manager seen each week

If, after you are launched and you have been searching for a few weeks, you have not been able to maintain a track record of one or more interviews per week, then it is time to make an adjustment to the numbers in the plan. This is no different that if you were managing a project and, due to new information, you found that the deadline wasn't realistic.

The adjustment can come from a variety of places. You can find a way to increase the time target beyond the number of weeks you originally planned, you can "ramp up" your efforts, or you can change the strategy by using another approach such as the proposal method described in Chapter 15. However, the worst thing you can do is *not* pay attention to this.

Résumé Output Rate

Now that you know how many interviews you are going to need per week, you can translate that into the number of résumés you're going to have to produce each week to meet that number. The industry standard is that 10-15 targeted résumés normally yield at least one interview. The operative word being "targeted." Sending out a bunch of résumés that are of the "vanilla flavor" variety is virtually a waste of time.

> *...effective searchers have told me that they spent anywhere from thirty to sixty minutes of effort on each résumé...*

As an aside, effective searchers have told me that they spent anywhere from thirty to sixty minutes of effort on *each* résumé, fine tuning it so that it speaks clearly and specifically to the needs of the company. I have known many people to get a better return on that investment, but it is a good average number with which to work.

The formula is simple. You need to be sending out enough résumés to produce the desired number of interviews that in turn produce the necessary number of job offers to land you the job within the planned time frame.

NOTE: The résumé "pipeline" takes about four to six weeks to begin generating desired results. That has been taken into consideration for this exercise. In business projects this would be known as "lead time."

10-15 targeted résumés per week = ~1 interview per week
~1 interview per week = 1-2 offers in 15-30 week period
1-2 offers in 15-30 week period = job landing in 15-30 week period.

You should run a few scenarios of your own and see what happens. For example, if you cut the résumé output number by half, it would likely decrease the number of interviews and offers by half, and potentially double the length of time it takes to land a job. The reverse is also true. If you increase the activity and output, the yield and results will occur more quickly. The above formula assumes that one in five interviews are traditional interviews and the balance are informational type.

Plan for Any Breaks

If for whatever reason, you impede the pipeline flow by taking a vacation—or simply taking a long break for a few days or weeks—past experience indicates that getting the project going again is almost like starting over. Therefore you need to plan those events into your search project. Once the pipeline is developed and you have launched your campaign, priming the pump again, as it were, will take more time.

It is important to examine where the résumés are going and how to control the recipients. As I mentioned before, many searchers like to use the Internet now more than ever before because it's easy and accessible. The down side as we've discussed is that the information is accessible to everybody else, and as a result represents your greatest competition. Excessive use of the internet job sites, that is more than 5-10% of your time, is *not* managing a successful job/career change project at peak performance or efficiency. However, that is not to say that this avenue should be ignored, just that an appropriate amount of time is devoted to the method. Chapter 14, "Resource Development" addresses how to conduct a more productive search campaign.

One other thing: if you are interested about the numbers you've just used in your calculations, know that the above scenarios were derived from the experiences of people who have had the opportunity to perform a career change using this process. This indicates that by and large people using other methods can expect to experience a significantly longer and may expect a more difficult search. My experience has indicated that if this process is followed you will have a very successful and brief campaign. Most of my clients land a new position in fewer than 90 days including prep time. The shortest was 48 hours after the prep time.

Follow-Up

Follow-up is a very important part of an effective job search project campaign. Every single activity will require follow-up in some way. But many job searches "fall through the cracks" due to poor follow through. Some people are very good at it while others find this one of the most challenging areas to control. You should know, though, that follow-up is the area where you have the greatest ability to improve the feeling of control you have over your search. I believe that if you do a good job of follow-up you enhance your control over your job search ten-fold.

You should know, though, that follow-up is the area where you have the greatest ability to improve the feeling of control you have over your search.

Most of the time, follow-up takes place in the form of a simple phone call.

• When you begin to send out résumés to job targets, networks, or recruiters, wait about a week then follow up with an inquiry to determine the status of the situation.

• Once you start to schedule meetings and interviews with organizations, you should also follow up for confirmations.

- Always follow up with your contacts.
- Always follow up after interviews.

Incidentally, contacts are where most people fall down regarding follow-up. Whether friends or constituents, or referrals inside companies, people are busy. You are low on the totem pole of priorities for them and they will be difficult to connect to. You must be persistent or opportunities will disappear.

The most critical follow-up resides in the interview stage. Many—too many—people tend to just wait for that all-important phone call about a job offer. If the hiring team has given you a decision date, and you have not heard back from them, wait a couple of days past the specified date and then call the main contact person.

Many people struggle with this because they don't know what to say or how often to call. My rule of thumb is if you reach them, ask the simple question, "I was just wondering where you are in the selection process?" It is non-confrontational, yet indicates your interest and implies an element of expectance in terms of time-frame. If you are unable to reach them, which is the typical yet frustrating scenario, leave a message one time per week. After that you can *call* daily, but don't leave any more messages until the following week, when you can leave one more message.

Another strategy that has worked well is to call during odd hours such as before normal work hours, just before and just after lunch, or after work hours in the early evening. Many managers are in their offices working during those times because the main part of the day is often dedicated to meetings. The important thing is to avoid leaving multiple messages. There is always the possibility that they have caller ID and they could tell that you've called several times. But if you haven't left repeated messages they will likely not become perturbed. As long as there is still a possibility that the opening is available to you, keep calling and show interest.

If you eventually get to the "no" or rejection, fear not, there are still some things you can do to maximize the situation. From a strategic standpoint there are some very powerful tactics you can use once you get the "no" that can develop into unexpected results. At the very least you could come away with some valuable information.

> *From a strategic standpoint there are some very powerful tactics you can use once you get the "no" that can develop into unexpected results.*

Once you've connected with someone who's told you that you have not been selected for the position, I suggest that you express verbal disappointment, but say that you understand that they had to make a choice. You should then ask the following questions: "How could I have been a stronger candidate? Would you be willing to consider me for any future positions that might be appropriate? Would you be willing to refer me to another organization that could utilize my skills and talents?" This effort will take a bit of backbone on your part, but I highly encourage you to at least give it a try. At this point in the campaign you will have absolutely nothing to lose and potentially have volumes to gain.

In-House Career Management

If your plan is to remain where you are and search for different positions in the company or organization where you currently work, it is an excellent idea to know, based on the information you have just researched, about all the positions throughout the company for which you may qualify. Knowing that information can help you to be career/job resilient in the organization. Job descriptions for every position in the company are usually available from the human resource department and the staff should be happy to share the information with you.

As you continue to research those positions, you can easily determine if some positions require additional, formalized education. Many companies assist employees with tuition or training reimbursement toward such proactive professional development initiatives. Look frequently at the internal postings to determine internal trends. Watching these trends can also give you a leg up in the event that things at the company take a downward turn. For example, if you've noted that the company seems to be going through hard times or puts a hiring freeze in place, take that as an indication that layoffs may be imminent.

If the signs mentioned above are present, the worst thing you can do is hope it doesn't happen to you or feel that you are insulated from such events. In all likelihood, if layoffs are about to occur, your company will *not* give you any obvious advance indications. Security issues, emotional trauma, low morale, reduced productivity, and mass resignations are just some of the reasons why organizations try to keep the layoff process quiet until the plan is implemented and, in that event, you may be instantly placed in the victim role.

To avoid that situation you should have already formulated a plan and have all the appropriate tools ready to use at a moment's notice and have already begun researching other potential organizations as possible targets for future employment. You should already have established a list of industries and types of positions to target. Think proactive. Think strategically about your own situation.

The 30 Second Commercial

"Tell me about yourself."

If I had to make a top ten list of things that are said at interviews, this would top it. Why does it show up so often? Because it's a good entry point for the interviewer. It usually sets the stage for the rest of the interview and it gives the person an opportunity to hear about something that typically isn't on the résumé. For this reason, it is usually the first thing asked at the interview.

My experience shows that most people do not provide a good answer. They fumble through, giving some sort of vague description, thereby missing a prime opportunity. The answer they provide is often a wordy regurgitation of the job history from their résumé, or worse, a non-specific description that has nothing to do with the reason for the interview. Instead of providing the answer that allows them to begin making the connection about who they are and how their skills relate to the organization, they come to the table ill-prepared, and often provide an irrelevant statement. A statement like that almost always fails to provide the interviewer with any real information to match the searcher's skill set with regard to the potential position, and can even cause the interviewer to disengage. It certainly doesn't put the searcher in a position of control during the interview.

So how do *you* answer it? You can either fumble through like the others, missing a golden opportunity, or, knowing that it's almost assured to be asked, you can instead provide an intelligent, well-considered answer that concisely states who you are as a professional and makes a connection between you and a job opportunity. In an interview situation your statement is critical to being effective. A good statement can set the tone for the entire interview. In fact, if you know what to do, it can put you in control immediately.

That critical statement is the "30 Second Commercial."

> *In its simplest terms, the 30 Second Commercial is a succinct, descriptive narrative about yourself and offers exactly what the person is looking for to make a connection between you and a job opportunity.*

In its simplest terms, the 30 Second Commercial is a succinct, descriptive narrative about yourself and offers exactly what the person is looking for to make a connection between you and a job opportunity.

However, the 30 Second Commercial isn't limited only to interview situations. As you begin to talk to people in your search, you'll find that you often need a good way to provide the person you're speaking to with a quick, concise overview of who you are. In these less formal situations, the 30 Second Commercial is critical to setting the stage and making the most of everyone's time.

About the 30 Second Commercial

So, the 30 Second Commercial is your summary. As the name implies, this narrative should only be about thirty seconds long when you speak at moderate, conversational speed. It is geared towards making the connection between your skills and motivations and the position you are speaking about or, in a non-interview setting, giving the listener a good idea of your overall skills.

Why only thirty seconds? After that amount of time, the attention of the person to whom you are speaking will begin to wander.

The 30 Second Commercial should contain your most basic professional attributes as they relate to your search: passions, educational level, type and depth (years) of experience as they pertain to your goals, valuable expertise (knowledge of a function), skills and attributes (highly motivated, high standard of values), and so on.

This is a lot of information to compress into thirty seconds, but to maximize the effect, you must. Tough as it sounds, it can be achieved by including as *little* detail as possible into the 30 Second Commercial itself.

The Value of the 30 Second Commercial

There is great value in creating and using the 30 Second Commercial. In fact, it is useful in at least three portions of your job search:

1. **Search Preparation**—During the early phases of your search, it helps you to create a focus about yourself and helps you capture—in a very succinct way—who you are professionally. The exercise of creating one helps you clarify where you've been, where you are, and where you want to go to.

2. **Resource Development**—The 30 Second Commercial helps you to quickly articulate to resource contacts what you bring to the table and offers the opportunity to express where you wish to go and, hopefully, in what ways the contact may be of help.

3. **Interviewing**—As I mentioned at the start of the chapter, the 30 Second Commercial enables you to answer the question that comes up in nearly 100% of interviews: "Tell me a little about yourself."

Because it is only 30 seconds long—about five lines of typewritten text—it is very tight and efficient. The concise nature of the 30 Second Commercial also often helps to either develop or strengthen your self-marketing tools and offers a window into effective development of cover letters.

Designing Your Commercial

There are a number of elements that you should include in your commercial. The first step is to take some time to jot down some things about yourself that you think you should mention.

Your goal in designing the commercial is to evaluate what it is about your area of expertise that has value in the working world and capture that information in a way that will not cause listeners to lose their concentration. It helps to evaluate not only your skills, but also your passions and different attributes about yourself in the workplace. In essence, you want to identify what is unique about you.

Commercial Elements

To get this information down, think about six areas:

- Passion—What activities are you passionate about in your job/career?
  Including things that you are passionate about is important because it helps you to clue the listener into those job attributes that truly motivate you.
- Education—What is your highest level of completed education?

Level of education is critical not only because it provides information on your education status, but also allows the listener to determine appropriate job level.

- Experience—What are the number of years and your areas of experience and specific expertise?

  Your level of experience also ties into appropriate job level, while your expertise can also provide ideas about specific needs within the company that can be addressed.

- Knowledge—What specific knowledge within your experience and expertise do you bring to the table?

  Many candidates may have the same or similar experience that you do, but no two jobs—or job searchers—are ever completely alike. Therefore, you have specific knowledge that you bring with you from your experiences. This knowledge can be a great differentiator.

- Skills and Attributes—What are your strongest skills and attributes? You should list at least three.

  This is where you get to describe not only the skills you have acquired, but also some personal attributes that you bring with you.

- Your unique fit—What about you, in terms of the working world, is unique?

  Using the combination of Experience, Knowledge, Skills, and Attributes you can quickly sum up what about you makes you a unique and valuable addition to a company or organization.

Sample Commercial Elements

Let's look at a sample list that I could put together for myself. Here is what I would include for each one of the bullets above:

- Passion—What activities are you passionate about in your job/career?
  - Helping others develop themselves
  - Designing training programs
  - Making presentations
- Education—What is your highest level of completed education?
  - Doctoral degree
- Experience—What are the number of years and your areas of experience and specific expertise?
  - More than 15 years career consulting experience
  - Expertise in résumé design, interviewing, and self-marketing techniques

- Knowledge—What specific knowledge within your experience and expertise do you bring to the table?
    - Design and development of training programs and course curricula
- Skills and Attributes—What are your strongest skills and attributes? You should list at least three.
    - Use of numerous self-assessment tools
    - Possibility thinking
    - Relationship building
- Your unique fit—What about you, in terms of the working world, is unique?
    - Gift for sensitivity

Making the Elements Flow

Creating the bullet list of components is an important exercise, but you can't hold a conversation in bullet points. Now that you've completed the components of the paragraph, your next task is to put those short blurbs into a usable format.

This can be a challenge. It is sometimes difficult to distill your work experience—and more specifically the essence of what makes you valuable—down to a few lines; but, again, you must. It's critical to be specific and succinct. It will take some thought to get everything down to a usable 30 Second Commercial, but the results will be extremely useful to you.

Remember when you put your elements together that the 30 Second Commercial is intended to be a bare bones description with little to no elaboration. If the person you're speaking with wants more detail, they will surely ask for it.

Sample Commercial

Refer back to the sample elements I listed for myself in the "Sample Commercial Elements" section. Using those sample elements, I can demonstrate how to use them to create my 30 Second Commercial. Mine would go pretty much like this:

"I'd be happy to tell you about myself. I have found that I'm very passionate about helping others develop themselves, designing training programs, and making presentations. In support of this effort I have a Ph.D. and more than 15 years of career consulting experience with expertise in résumé design, interviewing techniques, and self-marketing techniques. Further experience includes design and development of training programs and course curricula. Some specific skills include use of numerous self-assessment tools, possibility thinking, relationship building, and a gift for sensitivity."

Note that the paragraph captures such marketing bargaining chips as transferable skills, attributes, depth and breadth of experience. These things translate nicely into *value*.

A critical statement, saved specifically for the end, is what I call "something unique about you as a professional." It is very important to be able to articulate some particular thing that you do well that is uniquely different than other professionals like yourself. You must be able to separate yourself from your competition, and what better way than to highlight something about you that is unique? It can be difficult, and to capture it you may need to call for help from previous bosses, family, or close friends. Briefly explain the 30 Second Commercial to them and tell them you are trying to put one together to be more competitive. More often than not, they will offer up something useful.

Things to Avoid

As you'd expect, there are some things I recommend you avoid mentioning in your 30 Second Commercial.

> *It is very important to be able to articulate some particular thing that you do well that is uniquely different than other professionals like yourself.*

First, you should never mention company names. The logic for this strategy is to not offer potential prejudice to the listener. You have no idea if the listener likes or dislikes the company you mention, so don't give the person a chance to use any biases against you.

Second, avoid using specific job titles. While you might think that these are important to building a complete picture of your career, what they actually tend to do is box you into only certain jobs. You don't necessarily want to be tied down to a specific title, as this could jeopardize access into other exciting arenas.

Supplemental Information

In the event that the person does want more detail, you need to be prepared to have some slightly more in-depth information in reserve to expand on your 30 Second Commercial. You never know when the person may have a question or two.

For instance, they might ask where you went to school or under what circumstances you got your experience. Remember, you want to be succinct, but not incomplete, so in an equally concise way, you should have additional information at your fingertips to expand on your commercial if necessary.

Summary

You might have noticed that the 30 Second Commercial is very much like the "Summary" in the self-marketing instrument. This is not an accident. It provides consistency in your delivery and in your marketing campaign. In fact, you can sometimes use the 30 Second Commercial as a tool to improve the self-marketing instrument.

I'm continually amazed that such a simple narrative can be so crucial to the process but without a doubt, the 30 Second Commercial is a powerful tool. It's also another example of something that is almost always overlooked in the "typical" job search. In fact, many people have told me

I'm continually amazed that such a simple narrative can be so crucial to the process...

that this particular tool has been one of the most effective in their arsenal. So, make the most of it.

Spend some quality time developing your 30 Second Commercial. As time goes on and you gain experience, don't be afraid to modify it as long as it still captures the elements we discussed.

As we move through the process, you'll see that we come back to the 30 Second Commercial again and again. I think you'll find the time you spend working on it to be well spent.

Skills

Skills

14

Resource Development

One of the most important skills you can develop for an effective job search is resource development. Ever since the industrial revolution began it has been clear that the most effective way to access the best jobs is through development of contacts who can help you gain entry into companies or organizations. Although many things have changed over the years, the use of networking as the most effective tool to land a job has not. Even so, it's a topic that many people are uncomfortable with. In fact, many consider networking a four-letter word. As I'll demonstrate in this chapter, though, there's really nothing to fear. A person doesn't have to be connected to Wall Street or have a thousand friends to be able to utilize this part of the search process. What *is* necessary is that you learn to communicate with others and be willing and able to ask probing questions. Here is where slight variations from the method can mean huge differences in results. It's important to implement the concepts and methods in this chapter precisely as I lay them out.

The Old Way: Networking

Many people shy away from networking, and with good reason. In the traditional networking model, people contact their family, friends, or colleagues and ask them if they know of any jobs that are available or if they know anybody inside "Company X." This method was and still is helpful, but has its problems, and I believe the problems far outweigh the benefits. When I think about why this is so, I can point out two major causes:

- It makes people—both the searcher and those that are asked—uncomfortable.
- It simply doesn't work as well as most people think.

As a result, many people dislike old styles of networking as a tool in their job search.

What I find when people use this "old school" method of networking is that they are typically nervous about even asking others if they know of any jobs. Worse, often after only a few encounters the job searcher feels that network contacts are pulling away from him or her, and they're probably right.

The reason is this: this method tends to put network contacts on the spot. They may or may not be willing to refer you inside an organization. And even if they are willing to do so—or even specifically recommend you for a job—their reputation is on the line. If the situation doesn't work out for some reason, it reflects back on them.

In addition, there is still a stigma attached to individuals that are out of work. Although this has gotten better over the years, it is still out there. It is especially prevalent if the searcher comes right out and says they are looking for a job. The very statement places you in the position of being a disempowered victim.

The other problem with the traditional method of networking is that it just doesn't work very well. Statistically, the old style of networking yielded only about one useful lead out of five to ten approaches. The remaining 80-90% did nothing to materially advance the search.

The Concept in Action

Coincidentally, as I was writing this chapter, one of my colleagues who is a high-level professional salesman earning over $250K annually was asking me about my book and this particular chapter.

During the discussion, he mentioned that he's been fired on several occasions, but the very next day he picked up the phone and called as many as 50 people he knew. His anecdote ended with a statement that affirmed what I know is true: This old-style networking activity wasn't as effective as he would have liked.

Note that the average person I come in contact with usually wouldn't be willing or able to pick up the telephone the day after they'd gotten fired to begin charging up their network. And in this case, the network was significantly more substantial than most people who are looking for a job.

If he'd used my methods, who knows how quickly offers would have come in, how many offers he would have had, and how many additional people he could have added to his network of resources?

Part of the problem is the very questions that are asked:

- "Do you know of any jobs that are available?"
- "Do you know anybody at "Company X?"

These are both very close-ended questions. It's very possible that the person you are speaking with really doesn't know of any available jobs and knows no one at company X. But, given the way these questions are presented, if the answer to both is "no" then your conversation is finished. You're no closer to a job, no closer to additional leads, and your contact is on the defensive.

The New Way: Resource Development

I have a better idea. I suggest that you employ a *resource development* methodology that does not tax friendships, does not require people to put their reputations on the line, and does not put undue stress on the job searcher. What a novel idea! With some subtle—but fundamental—changes in the way you approach people, you can address the two major downfalls of the traditional networking model.

Remember back in Chapter 4, "Mindset" I mentioned that as you went through this process that you were *not* going to look for a job? This partially comes into play here in Resource Development. You will be looking around and talking to people about companies that might be the best fit for you, and when you find the company that is, then you will begin looking into positions in that company. Until then, you're just looking, nothing more, and that in and of itself

> *Instead of going to your contacts and asking for information about job openings or leads into companies, approach them from a different angle.*

helps people be more comfortable. When people are comfortable, they are much more willing to help you and to give you information. Here's how you do it.

You're going to use a method of Neuro-Linguistic Programming (NLP) to help you get the information you need. Instead of going to your contacts and asking for information about job openings or leads into companies, approach them from a different angle. After some brief introductory conversation, bring out your list of target companies and pass it to them asking— and here's the critical part—"What do you know about these companies"? If your contact is at the end of a phone, mail, or fax, then send them the list and ask the same question.

Note the difference. You did *not* ask if they knew about any available jobs. You did *not* ask them to put you in touch with people who might be able to "give" you a job. You simply asked if they had any information about some companies—and at this point you *should* be looking for information only. Psychologically, this approach makes all the difference. Also note that you did *not* say "Do you know anything about these companies?" Again, that is a closed-ended question where a "no" answer is a conversation stopper. A word or two can make all the difference between a good lead and no information whatsoever.

If they have any information about the companies in question, they usually offer it up. The interesting part is that if they have a contact name, they typically give that to you freely, as well. There is no discomfort on their part, because it was their decision to give you the name, since you were only looking for information about the company. Furthermore, in the process of developing your contacts you will come across individuals who offer you a contact individual who is then willing to give you some face time and mentor you into the company you've targeted. Again, the difference is you didn't ask, they volunteered it.

If they don't have any information about the companies shown, what is most likely to happen is that they offer up an idea about some other company that you *don't* have on the list. Add that company to your list. Statistically, this newer methodology nets a whopping one lead out of every *three* contacts made—much better than the roughly one in ten of the old method. In addition, it's much easier on the nerves—for everyone.

That's the power of NLP in this situation. In essence, you still got the information that the questions of the old method were intended to get. But, using the techniques and wording nuances of NLP, you went from an uncomfortable situation to one where people are usually happy to help you, and you aren't scared to ask.

The information-only approach doesn't stop there. You should go two steps further with the network contact person.

1. After they respond one way or the other to your first inquiry, you should then ask them "What other companies should I add to my list and what do you know about them?" This generally results in more information to develop your marketing campaign.
2. The final question to pose to your contact person. "Who do you know who might know something about these companies?" Phrased in this way it is almost impossible for them not to supply some information that could be useful.

The main point of the exercise is to keep the contact talking, keep them open to giving you information, and most of all, simply *keep the contact* so you can approach them repeatedly for further assistance since you will be constantly updating and modifying your list. This process opens the door for that potential outcome. Remember, it isn't as important that you get information about the companies specifically shown on your hot list. What you're trying to do is provide a safe venue for your contacts to assist you and continue to be available as you search. This method makes you much more welcome and non-threatening than using the traditional style of networking.

Getting Started

"That's great," you say, "but it still doesn't sound like something I want to do." Even after I explain the differences, many people still shy away from Resource Development. This may be because they feel it will be difficult for them and they still are not aware of how important it is. I have had many people give me all sorts of reasons why they can't use this part of the job search process. I've been told things like:

- "I don't know anybody"
- "I don't know people in that part of the country"
- "I'm not comfortable talking to strangers"

These may seem to be perfectly valid reasons why someone has fears about using effective resource development. But let me say that they amount to nothing more than excuses.

Let me go through them one by one:

- "I don't know anybody"—Unless you are a complete hermit, you know people. What you're really saying is that you don't think you have a wide network of people to confide in. That may be true, but consider that the smallest network of individuals that a client has ever brought to me was three. Just three. But, by following my method carefully and deliberately, they increased that number to fifty within a couple of weeks and still landed a job within the desired 90-day time frame.

The thing to remember is that your resources do not necessarily need to be business people or those who are even remotely involved in your target industry. Who are your friends? What family members do you have? Don't disadvantage yourself by discounting those around you. The person who might give you the lead you really need could be a 10-year-old child. First, it is absolutely critical to identify every single person you know. No restrictions.

Then, who are your colleagues, past and present? Other contacts to develop can be found in associations where you are currently a member. More importantly, you

A Resource Development Analogy

Suppose I provide you with a vehicle to go from point A to point B. It's a reliable, speedy car with a powerful V8 engine. Just as you are preparing to begin your journey, you reach under the hood and pull out six of the eight spark plug wires.

Can you still complete the journey? Possibly, but you have *severely* hindered your chances to do it as quickly and efficiently as possibly by limiting the abilities of the car.

The analogy may not make you like resource development more, but hopefully it demonstrates the importance of the activity.

Whether your journey is one of distance or one of job search, reaching your goal isn't going to be very easy using only a fraction of the available tools. I can't stress it enough: Resource Development is a critical tool in this process.

should begin participating in meetings with professional associations in the job arena you want to be in.

> *...let us not forget, in this digital age, there are Internet sites... that allow you to create a usable network not only of people you know, but your colleagues' associates, as well.*

Another place where you can easily develop contacts is at the church or synagogue of your choice. Perhaps one of the most common areas where you can develop contacts is at golf, tennis, exercise, or other athletic clubs. And let us not forget, in this digital age, there are Internet sites such as LinkedIn (www.linkedin.com) that allow you to create a usable network not only of people you know, but your colleagues' associates, as well—a concept we'll investigate more in the "Using the Information" section.

- "I don't know people in that part of the country"—While it may be somewhat more of a challenge, resources do exist for you to make contacts throughout the country, and in fact, the globe. If you've graduated from a college, then the career services department at your alma mater is available to you as a resource to find fellow alumni in any possible geographic area as well as industries and companies you are targeting. Many colleges and universities now also have alumni networking web sites. Again, you can also use professional associations that you belong to as a resource for finding contacts in other areas.

- "I'm not comfortable talking to strangers"—This may be a valid concern, especially for those who are naturally introverts. However, you don't need to start out talking to strangers. As I mentioned above, never discount those around you as the perfect starting point. Use them to practice and gain confidence using the process. Then, take your skills and branch out to those whom you don't know. I think you'll find that once you have built up your confidence level on the people you know, it will be much easier to apply the techniques to strangers.

This skill is so powerful that overall more than 75% of all jobs are obtained using this Resource Development method. In fact, there is a direct correlation between the amount of resource development needed to secure a position and the position level that is being sought. The higher the level, the more resource development becomes necessary.

The biggest jump in this relationship falls in the $80 - $100K range. Landing jobs through want ads and through Internet exploration has a rate of as low as 5% for people in the executive salary range. Likewise, use of recruiters or placement services is in the 5% range. You should, therefore, devote a proportional amount of your job search time to each type of lead generating activity, in other words devote no more than 10% of your time to these two methods.

In addition, the greatest amount of competition is in the want ad/Internet job

Other Contact Sources

For those of you who struggle with numbers of personal contacts available to you, there are a couple of other ideas that may help. There are numerous groups that meet both via the Internet and in person on a regular basis. These groups are for and by individuals who need to make contact with others who can assist them in gaining access inside organizations.

There are many, but here are a few ready-made career and job change networks for you to tap into:

- Execunet— www.execunet.com/
- Fast Company—www.fastcompany.com
- 5 O'clock Club—www.fiveoclockclub.com

pursuit. It only stands to reason that getting to the Unpublished Job Market through effective Resource Development is the most expedient use of energy, time, and resources. I've found that effective resource development reduces job search time by as much as a third.

Building a Resource Contact List

If you haven't done so already, you should immediately begin to develop a database of names and phone numbers of every single person you know. Again, it is important for you *not* to include only individuals who you think are important. *Everyone* is important in this process. Friends, family, colleagues, neighbors, bosses, barbers, hair dressers, people in places where you shop, people you may know at associations, and others. Your Christmas list and your personal phone directory are excellent places to obtain names.

You will not remember everybody that will eventually be included on your list at this very moment, but the important part is that you get the list started. Don't worry about how long it is at this point; just get it going. Make room on the form for:

- Name
- Phone Number
- Address
- Date/Time you contacted them.
- A brief summary of the encounter

- Whom they referred.

- Follow up date/time

- Space for "notes" which can include any other important information.

The most critical column here is the referral name, which then goes right onto the list as another network contact.

If you are computer savvy, you can use Microsoft® Access, ACT!, Goldmine, or other similar software packages for creating your database. If you are not computer literate, a handwritten list is fine, but much more limiting.

To make this exercise easier I have found it is also helpful to divide the names into an "A" list and a "B" list. While all individuals can be helpful, you may have determined that some individuals—especially those who are particularly well connected—may offer extensive resources to you in your efforts.

Computer Skills

If you do not consider yourself computer literate, I urge you to become as literate as possible, as quickly as possible. Hiring managers expect hires to be able to send e-mails and know their way around a computer.

In this age, it is almost impossible to find a job, especially at the executive level, that does not require computer usage in some manner. The more proficient and knowledgeable you are, the more valuable you are.

The same goes for being Internet-savvy. So much information is available on the Internet, both for the job search and for work itself, that it is foolish to ignore it.

One-day courses and continuing adult education classes are available for most popular software packages as well as Internet navigation—generally at very reasonable costs. If you are not familiar with these topics, I would consider training courses on these topics as money *very* well spent.

Implementing a Resource Development Process

Now let's take a closer look and structure the typical methodology of using the resource development tool. Expect to spend 75% or more of your job search time on Resource Development. The amount of time shifts dramatically from about 75% time commitment to over 90% committed effort when you get to the $80 - $100K salary range. Positions with salaries over $100K range require a time commitment that approaches 100% by the time you are looking at senior executive positions.

As you move forward, you need to be prepared for the Resource Development activity. One of the first areas of preparation is the procurement of new business cards. *Do not* use previous business cards for Resource Development; it isn't effective and presents the wrong image. You could spend one hundred dollars or more for professional business cards; however, for this exercise I usually suggest simple cards that can be purchased at many of the chain stationary and business supply stores such as Staples or OfficeMax for around $20 for a thousand.

Include only basic information on how to contact you on the card, for example, name, address, phone, fax, cell, and e-mail address. Unless you are specifically remaining in a particular position title—Financial Management, Software Engineering, Project Management might be areas within which you might stay—you should leave title out. In general, though, including titles on the network business card severely restricts your marketability and pigeonholes you into a single job type. People can get very hung up on titles and it immediately closes their minds to other options.

Other necessary tools needed in the Resource Development process include a "Target List" of companies, a fully memorized 30 Second Commercial, several copies of your résumé, your network list, and copies of your references printed out on matching résumé paper. The fully prepared job searcher has all of these tools with them in a folder at all times.

Gathering Information

Once you are armed with your tools, you are ready to start engaging your contacts. Follow these specific Resource Development steps. This is generally how they should occur, but everyone's situation is different, and adjustments may need to be made. Again, use any means available to reach these people, but face-to-face is most effective, if at all possible.

1. As I covered in the "Building a Resource Contact List" section, generate a list of every person you know. Additional names come to you as you "work the list."

2. Communicate with *each and every* individual on the list. Start with friends or family members whom you feel comfortable with. It may be necessary for you to write a script to work with until you get used to the process. You should be making at least two calls per day and increasing your contact list by a minimum of 10% per week to demonstrate true development of the contact list.

3. The communication should begin with casual conversation as if you were just calling to say hello. Somewhere in the conversation, the contact person will almost inevitably ask you, "How are you?" This is a nice segue to "disclose" that you are in the process of making a career/job change. This is the time to use your 30 Second Commercial.

4. At this point you have "warmed them up" for the target question. If you are face-to-face, pull out your "target" list of companies and say something like, "I've been considering positions like…, and I've been looking into several possible companies. What do you know about these companies?" Pass the list to them to examine.

5. Your contact will respond with some kind of answer, either affirmative or negative. Either way, the key is to *keep them talking*.

   Very often they may respond with, "No I don't recognize these organizations, but have you considered ABC company?" Probe that information and add it to your list for further investigation. It's important not to shoot down their responses with things like, "Thanks, I already know that," or "No that won't work, they're too small." Statements like these cause the contact to shut down and offer up nothing more. Worse, all future leads from this contact are gone. Instead, always respond with a thank you for the information, and keep them talking.

6. Ask question number two: "Do you know any other companies I should add to my list and what do you know about them?

   This usually has about a 50% positive result, which is excellent. They may need a moment or two to ponder the question and may even need to get back to you with information at a later time. This is fine. Again, avoid shutting them down as they come forward with information.

7. The third question is the most mission critical of all. *Do not fail to ask this question!* "Who do you know who might know something about these companies?"

   Between the two questions you should have netted somewhere in the neighborhood of at least one good lead out of three contact attempts. Most people do many times better than that, but I maintain the statistic for outside probability data.

About Multi-Level Marketing

Several cosmetic, household, and nutritional product companies use MLM to sell their products through a network rather than in retail stores. In general, the concept is for those who are selling to approach friends, relatives, and other people they know to attend a "get together." Here they chat about the value of these products and entice the others to "join," then replicate the process.

From a business standpoint it is about using socialization as a selling medium. From a model standpoint, it leverages the fact that a person first joining will approach people they know personally. This is known as the first level of sales. Those individuals in turn recruit people *they* know to join—the second level of sales potential. The second level people repeat the process—the third level or tier in relation to the original person. The pool of individuals at this point is often in the hundreds.

In terms of job search, this number is more than enough to get the job done. It takes some effort to get there, but it does develop quickly and effectively if you use my method.

This concept was designed from a Multi-Level Marketing (MLM) perspective. MLMs have known for decades that it is seldom the people we know that reap the largest dividends. It is the second and third levels of individuals that we do not know who are most likely to help us reach our goals, and in fact, it is generally recognized that it is the third level that produces the greatest potential. That is why the question from Step 7 is the most important one. It is the one most likely to get us to individuals we don't know.

Using the Information

The whole point of the above exercise is to obtain information about companies and contact individuals outside your immediate "circle of influence." We can assume from the statistics that we will be have leads to follow up on. Some of these leads are informational while others are individuals to contact. The most valuable of these leads are the ones that have the potential for "informational" interviews, which I cover in depth in Chapter 17, "Interview Types". This becomes a "hot lead."

So, once we've received our company contacts, now the second phase of the Resource Development process begins. This is the part of the process where, if done correctly, will pay dividends in the form of informational interviews, and eventually your "right" job.

1. Your contact has given you the name of a person inside an organization that you may or may not have originally targeted.

    In this case, the organization isn't as important as the referred person. Make contact with them. Introduce yourself by saying something to the effect of "My friend <*name*> suggested that I give you a call. I'm in the process of making a job transition and he/she thought you might be able to give me some information that would be helpful." Do not mention that your contact gave you a job lead or that the person to whom you are speaking could help you get a job.

    Continue with, "I have a few questions. I wonder if I could set up a short meeting, just 15 or 20 minutes or so, at your convenience?" The new contact may or may not agree to help, or may suggest a phone conversation, at which point you may need to go ahead right then, so you should be prepared for that possibility. If he/she agrees to meet with you, set up the time and suggest that you send them a résumé to peruse.

2. Do your homework on the company where this contact works. You might call the company and ask for a prospectus, look for news articles about the company, research competitor information, and not only visit their web site but also their competitor's web sites. Being well-informed when you meet the contact usually pays huge dividends.

3. These meetings with your newly-found contacts are your "informational interviews" and for the executive-level individual, you will find that the vast majority of the interviews you have are informational. This is because, for the most part, these jobs are typically not "open" at the time the searcher is looking. This is the Unpublished Job Market I spoke about in Chapter 8. And it is accessible mainly through the Resource Development process.

4. One last thing to remember is that for every informational interview you attend, you should leave with at least another contact lead and more information than when you came in, or both.

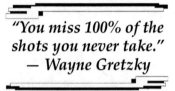

"You miss 100% of the shots you never take."
— Wayne Gretzky

What I have just described are the chronological steps involved in implementing the use of Resource Development. Using this approach could easily help you to feel much differently about networking than you ever have in the past and ease any discomfort you might have for future career and/or job change efforts. A quote I love regarding this section is one made by NHL Hockey great Wayne Gretzky: "You miss 100% of the shots you never take." When you see an opportunity, take your shot. All you have to lose is the opportunity.

If you believe any of the current information about the world of work being in constant transition, then you know that most of us are most likely going to engage in this process several more times before we retire. That being the case, the better you are at resource development the easier any future career/job changes will be. As I said earlier, the higher you go in functional level, the more resource development is needed. Even when you conclude the current search project it is very important for you to maintain your connections that you have worked so hard to develop in this campaign.

The Strategic Proposal
Marketing Method

One of the most important components of an effective executive-level job search is gaining access into specific company targets that interest you. You don't have to be connected to corporate VPs to accomplish this, but it does involve good detective work.

For upper management the Strategic Proposal Method I will discuss in this chapter has been among the most effective vehicles when engaging in a career change. It allows you to provide visible evidence that you have the skills, the experience, and the business savvy to perform at a level that corporate leaders respect. It might interest you to know that this project utilizes most of the high functioning skills of an executive: research, detail, documentation, organization, and the power of persuasion.

For many executive-level individuals who are seeking positions in organizations that interest them, the company has simply not provided budgets to support opening a high-level position. The onus is then on you to force the slot open by persuading the top decision makers of the company that you are an individual who can make their life easier, more profitable, eliminate a number of challenging problems, and above all, fully justify the expense of supporting another high-level individual in their organization.

It is interesting to note that many executive-level jobs and other big line item decisions are made on the golf course, in the executive lounge over a cup of coffee and a bagel, or at a restaurant over dinner. For that reason, I highly recommend that you combine aggressive resource development in those environments with excellent detective work in developing a powerful and difficult-to-ignore proposal. It is an extremely effective tool that works well for people at those levels.

Your Challenge

Your challenge is to perform some detective work on the companies in your hot list that you developed in Chapter 11. Through the use of the Internet, news articles, and other valuable data you can uncover company information that you could use to leverage your skills and knowledge in an unpublished position.

> *...you develop a proposal explaining what you've found... in a way that doesn't make them think you've exposed their "Achilles' Heel."*

From there, you develop a proposal explaining what you've found; however you must do it in a way that doesn't make them think you've exposed their "Achilles' Heel." Rather, only discuss how you believe you can help them improve their market position based upon your experience and expertise.

The point is for them to see how you would be of value to them, not that you've discovered a bad situation. The proposal is designed with the intent that you will follow up with a face-to-face conversation about the document. They will likely be able to read between the lines.

How To Build The Proposal

For people who find resource development methods to be more than a challenge, this approach can be used without the use of that advantage, but be warned that it will be much less effective. However, it is better than using recruiters, executive ads, or blind letter mailings.

For those individuals who are able to utilize their contacts, it will be important for you to have developed your contact list with special focus. In our usual Resource Development approach, we suggest taking just about any opportunity to explore when asking "what do you know about these companies?" However, for the Strategic Market tack, the first focus is to pull together your list of the six to twelve company "hot list" names, which should include any companies that you may be interested in. Then you must first use the hot list to investigate which companies your network of resources can actually help you with and to what extent. Once you have established that information, you can begin investigating the selected companies you want to include so that you can be assured that when you are ready you can tap back into your selected network and "rifle shot" your proposal inside the organization and onto the desk of a referred decision maker.

Research

When you research a target company for the purposes of developing a proposal you apply what you have learned about effective job search to your ability to uncover information about people, companies, and their vulnerability. You should already have developed a list of organizations that have your interest and narrowed it down to your hot list. The task here is to select the organizations one at a time and begin thoroughly researching them, carefully examining them for areas of weakness.

Do whatever it takes to get the information: look at their web site, order a prospectus, seek out news articles, compare competitors, and so on. You should look into every nook and cranny in an attempt to discover areas of weakness, particularly those where you could help them solve the problem(s) using your various areas of expertise, knowledge, and experience.

> *In examining the information you uncover you may find a variety of issues that you could address to help the organization...*

In examining the information you uncover you may find a variety of issues that you could address to help the organization become more profitable, avoid lawsuits, be more efficient, gain competitive edge, and more. This material becomes the foundation for your proposal.

Some other areas of research that I recommend to find the information you need include:

- **Media**—Trade magazines, journals, business sections of national business magazines, local newspapers or nationally known newspapers such as *The Wall Street Journal*.

- **Company Web Sites**—Research both the company you are interested in as well as competitors. These sites often contain a wealth of information that you could use to uncover areas where you might help them improve.

- **Dunn & Bradstreet**—Running a D&B report will provide much information that you could use in this effort.

- **Company Prospectus**—You can often call the company directly and order a prospectus and other information that companies are usually happy to provide. The information contained within can be used in furthering your research.

Details

It is important to gather as much detailed information about the target company as you can in order to make a convincing argument, but you should not include all of that information in the proposal.

You want to force a face-to-face meeting where you can apply all of your methods in the hopes of generating an offer.

Much of the detailed information you might obtain you want to keep for the "meeting" or informational interview. The proposal is predominantly intended to get their attention. The point here is to avoid laying out all your cards in the proposal. This provides some security by not allowing the company to approach someone else to implement the plan you laid out. You want to force a face-to-face meeting where you can apply all of your methods in the hopes of generating an offer.

Documentation & Organization

If you've done well, you should have been able to extract at least three areas to address. Three is the magic number. You want to explain what you have found via a "spin" that leans toward how you believe you can help them in more than one very generic way and explain some approaches you might take to improve the situation—without giving them the how. The document should not exceed two pages. One is better if you can be that succinct.

Of course, it is essential that you maintain well-organized files on each of your investigations since you don't know which one will actually become active and respond to your proposal. When they do call, you must be fully prepared to discuss in much more detail how you could be a benefit to the organization, again without divulging everything.

The Power of Persuasion

Once you have all the material organized it is a matter of sending the proposal to the decision maker of your choice, asking for an opportunity to make a presentation. Your powers of persuasion are needed to compel the company representatives to hear you out.

Wait about a week after sending the proposal and phone the person to whom you addressed the material. Request an informational session based upon your proposal. It will be common for secretaries or receptionists to resist putting you through to the executive. I have suggested that one way to get around this situation is to mention that you'd like to talk to the person about the "agenda items" in the proposal "before" you come in for a meeting. Most of the time the gate keeper will forward your call.

Now it is important to bring in the contacts you have been developing and let them know that you have been targeting some organizations. It is probably not in your best interests to let them know that you've developed some proposals, but approach them with the "information only" tactic mentioned in Chapter 14. Here you are more interested

Your powers of persuasion are needed to compel the company representatives to hear you out.

in direct information rather than the exercise of "adding new companies" since you've gone to so much work. As I mentioned, in developing your contacts you likely came across individuals who gave you a contact individual willing to give you some face time and mentor you into the company you've targeted. The ball is in your court to persuade decision makers that your ideas are sound and that you could make a clear and profound impact in their company and create an open position to you.

This process has been recognized around the world by top career counseling professionals as being one of the most effective methods of gaining positions in target companies. See a sample proposal in Figure 19.

(SAMPLE PROPOSAL)

YOUR NAME
Address, phone number
Email address

To: Date:

From:

Subject: Achieving Strong ROI with an Effective Project Management Office

Steps to ensure successful establishment & promotion of an effective Project Management Office.

1. Meet with key stakeholders and executives to gather their PMO requirements and goals.

2. Create deliverables based on requirements and PMO best practices

   Examples of PMO deliverables: policies, project methodologies and templates, support, guidance, training, tools, reporting, project management, quality assurance, resource management, risk management, budget management.

3. Create PMO high-level implementation schedule

4. Present and market to stakeholders and executives

5. Establish PMO, first focusing on short-term, high-ROI deliverables

6. Rollout long-term solutions

7. Support and improve

Sample of best practices to ensure PMO success

Mentor project managers to use accelerated project management techniques for initiation and recovery of projects

Establish four critical processes to support project success:
- Executive endorsement
- User involvement
- Project Charter
- Statement of Work / Scope Statement

Implement quality check lists and quality assurance audits

Figure 19: Sample Proposal

Interviewing

The Interview. It is true that getting an interview is the culmination of all of the preparation and legwork that we've discussed in the previous chapters. But many clients that come to me have a completely skewed impression about interviews. They think that once they get to the interview, their work is done. In reality, there is quite a bit of preparation and work that goes into a successful interview. In fact, interviews and the steps to get ready for them are so important that I've devoted three chapters to the topic. Even so, the information I'm able to provide here is heavily compressed: consider that entire books have been written on the subject. Because of this, I encourage you to pay close attention. Reread the material as many times as necessary until you are very familiar and comfortable with it. People who've absorbed and applied this information have empowered themselves significantly and avoided much needless anxiety.

In general, I've found that the interview and interviewing skills are widely misunderstood. Most people think that the interview is how an organization determines if the candidate is qualified for the job. So they go in ready to talk about strengths and weaknesses and some details to demonstrate their skill level. Many consider just getting through the interview as a success.

A recent article asserted that only about one person in ten can interview well enough to be hired. *One in ten!* The remaining nine struggle along until they get lucky, somehow manage to get it right, or find an opportunity through someone they know.

These interviewing chapters are intended not only to provide insight into the interview process, but to highlight strategies and tactics to help you interview better than you ever have before—so well, in fact, that if you follow the techniques provided here, you won't just be the one in ten, you will be the one in one hundred that so impresses the interviewers and rises far above the competition into an area where you have a remarkable chance of having multiple job offers to choose from. Now *that's* success. Most of the clients that I've coached through this process have had more than just one concurrent offer to negotiate. The record is in excess of a dozen. You may not need or want a dozen offers, but it's nice to know that the potential is there if the effort is made.

Keep in mind, too, that most searchers attend twenty or more interviews before the search concludes in the acceptance of an offer. Therefore, it is to your advantage to move through the interviewing process as quickly as you can *without any loss of due diligence to the quality of the thoroughness, research, and follow-through*. It is a balance between keeping your quality and focus, and sheer volume of interviews.

The Real Purpose of an Interview

The widely held misconception is that interviews are about determining if you are most qualified for the job within a pool of candidates. In truth, many experts believe that the process of job search is less about being selected as the best candidate and more about elimination. In essence, interviews are about trying to *dis*qualify you from the job, leaving the hiring manager with only a couple of choices to consider instead of a crowd. I've been told by many hiring managers that they had so much to do that they didn't have a lot of time to devote to the hiring process. The quicker they got through the group, the better.

In essence, interviews are about trying to disqualify you from the job.

What most people don't realize is that if the company has called you for an interview, your marketing instruments have done their job and the company believes that you are qualified for the job. Unless they are absolutely desperate, they aren't going to waste their time interviewing people who they don't think have a very good chance of fitting the bill.

Critical Interviewing Concepts

There are a number of interviewing concepts and techniques that are important to understand and implement in your interviews. We'll cover them here and revisit them throughout the interviewing chapters as required. If you follow these concepts and techniques, your interviewing *will* improve—in most cases dramatically.

Eliminating the Negative

The first concept is that you must avoid the use of negative words. This is harder than you might think. Remember that tough interview questions usually include embedded negative terminology that make it easy for the searcher to fall into a trap.

To win at the interviewing part of the Career Game Championships you must suspend many of the typical communication techniques and skills that you may have learned. From the first words we learn to our most sophisticated active listening techniques we practice as adults, we are taught to be as direct, clear, and forthright as possible. Communication concepts such as "reflecting" or "mirroring" and paraphrasing a conversation have greatly helped the workforce improve communications across many boundaries.

However, these very techniques can kill you in an interview where you are trying to eliminate all negative words.

The recurring theme of negative language in interview questions goes back to the concept of disqualifying candidates. For example, if an interviewer asks "Tell me about your biggest weakness," the natural thing is to reply with an answer that begins with "I think my biggest weakness is..." From your first words you are in trouble simply because you used reflection: Weaknesses are negative. While everyone has

Difficult to Resist

Eliminating negative language can be extremely difficult. I once had a top, professional-level coach as a client. His specialty was positive reinforcement, using it all the time in his role. He rarely, if ever, used negative language in his daily speaking. Yet, during practice interviews, he was surprised that I was able to lead him—several times—into providing answers couched in negative language. I was able to do this simply by the leads I provided in my questioning.

We are so programmed to use the language of the question to provide context for the answer that it takes practice and concentration to avoid falling prey to it.

them, and you can't avoid answering the question, you must answer in a way that plants a positive seed in the interviewer's mind and turns your weakness into a perceived positive.

The first clue to improving your interviewing technique is to be aware that this line of questioning is actually about your professional development. Suppose you consider organization to be a weakness. You might say, "I recognized earlier in my career that I needed to become stronger at organization. I attended a time management seminar, read some excellent books on the subject, and worked with a person who mentored me to a much higher level. Today, I continue to work on it and while I don't think it will ever be a strength, I've certainly come a long way." With this, you've turned what would have been an overwhelming negative and recast it in a positive light. It was a growth opportunity that you embraced and you're a better person because of it. Don't disqualify yourself with negative language. It is essential that you put a positive spin on every single interview question no matter what words the interviewer uses.

As you can see from the "Difficult to Resist" sidebar on page 159, it requires thought and concentration to remove negative language from your vocabulary under the best of circumstances. It is even more difficult to avoid negative language at interviews if you've recently gone through an emotionally stressful experience.

> *...when you are in a negative mindset, your chances for a successful outcome can be greatly diminished.*

This is especially true in the case of layoffs. Being fired, let go, downsized—whatever nifty euphemism the company used—tends to put people in a bad frame of mind. Additional influences can make a negative attitude even worse. Perhaps you were treated unfairly at work as a precursor to the layoff; maybe your spouse is pressuring you regarding the loss of income; or possibly family members and friends suggest that you should have handled things differently so you wouldn't have gotten the "axe." It is completely understandable that any of the above can put a person in a foul mood.

But you must be aware: when you are in a negative mindset, your chances for a successful outcome can be greatly diminished. You must take whatever steps are necessary to get your frame of mind back on track and be able to concentrate. Only then can you get the business at hand—your job search—under control.

Control

Control is important in the interview. Traditionally, the interviewer has been in control. Interviews and the questions that are asked have been designed to make that happen.

But from now on, you are going to be in control.

At the beginning of the book I mentioned neuro-linguistic programming (NLP) and we briefly mentioned it both in Chapter 9, "Résumés" and Chapter 14, "Resource Development". It is during the interview, however, where it really comes into play. Even here it is a simplistic application to the techniques, but it can be very effective. It is a method of using carefully-framed language to amend the thinking of the listener. Sales and marketing professionals have used these techniques for decades. Using the technique is not particularly complex, but you must be disciplined in its use to get the desired result.

When we talk about control of the interview we are saying that through good listening and preparation you will be able to avoid being placed in the victim role and simply surviving the interview. Instead, you will be able to use your knowledge to effectively lead the conversation to a place of self-empowerment and predictability.

Be careful to distinguish between taking perceived control away from the interviewer—it's not in your best interest—and saying things that will direct the interviewer to thinking that you come across as among the most professional candidates they have seen in some time.

The key considerations to having successful and predictable interview outcomes are putting

Control Can Turn the Tide

I recall a client of mine who, after going through this material, couldn't wait for their upcoming interview. They reported back afterward that it had been a textbook interview. The interviewer admitted that they didn't know much about interviewing but had a few questions to ask. As it turned out, they were exactly the questions I'd had my client prepare for.

Even though the interviewer opened with a definitive statement that the job wouldn't even be available for another two months and that he was simply trying to "line up" the best candidates for when the job became available, my client got a job offer on the spot.

What the interviewer didn't know was that my client was in control of the interview from the very beginning and that changed the course of the process.

together all of the critical concepts—avoiding negative language, this concept of directing the conversation, and the connect-the-dots concept I cover in the next section—and saying only what is necessary to make the point and answer the question. Too often, the more you say the deeper the rat hole will eventually become.

Ideally, you want to be able to control the direction of the conversation as soon as possible and maintain it throughout the interview. When you are in control, you can drive the direction of the dialogue and stay on track, continually coming back to the ways that you can marry your skills to the needs of the organization.

Connecting the Dots

If you remember nothing else during the interview, remember the key tactical concept that will give you the upper hand in any interview: *The more times you can connect the dots between the needs of the target organization and what you do well and are truly motivated to do, the greater your chances of getting the job offer.* The more ways you can answer questions in ways that demonstrate over and over how your strengths and motivations meet the needs of the organization the better your interview will be.

By following this simple edict, you will impress the experienced interviewer and stay out of their traps. If you are with an inexperienced interviewer, chances are that your answers will be so far removed from what they are used to or expecting that they will be completely blown away. How is that for generating a positive perception?

To me, true success in an interview is when you can continually connect those dots, unquestionably convincing the organization that you are the right person for the job.

Anatomy of an Interview

Most interviews, regardless of type, share a common, familiar pattern. We'll discuss the specifics of how each type of interview flows in Chapter 17, "Interview Types" but we can summarize the major components here. For good measure, I'll add one component that doesn't take place at the interview itself, but can have a huge effect on its outcome.

The Introduction

The introduction usually consists of the typical niceties, some small talk, and the sometimes awkward moment as the interviewer tries to move from small talk to the real meat on the interview. The segue from introduction to the Question and Answer phase usually takes the form of "Tell me a little bit about yourself."

As we discussed in Chapter 13, "The 30 Second Commercial", this phrase, or some variation thereof, is your cue to present your 30 Second Commercial.

Once you have presented your 30 Second Commercial, I suggest immediately asking a question. You choose the question depending upon what you know of the organization. Anything like, "That's a little about me. Now could you tell me a bit more about the position?" or "Could you tell me a bit more about the organization?" continues the control of the interview that you've established and moves you into the full Question and Answer phase.

Questions and Answers

This portion of the interview is where you have the opportunity to differentiate yourself from the other candidates so completely that a successful outcome is almost assured. One key element of this is "connecting the dots" as we discussed. Another is knowing how to recognize and answer difficult questions. There are two basic question types—Technical and Behavioral—and specific ways to answer each. I cover the Q&A process, including the question types, in Chapter 18, "Interviewing Questions". For now, keep in mind that the way you answer can be the difference between a slam dunk and a disastrous interview.

Technical questions are mostly about your ability to do the job based on your background and level of skill. From that standpoint you already know what you can do and it's generally easy to discuss. There are still some challenges, typically due to a lack of preparation. Well-prepared candidates take the time to capture quantifiable information, that is dollars, percentages, and numbers that demonstrate some level of competency.

Behavioral questions are often comprised of a "question behind the question." That is, the question appears to be asking for one thing, but in reality the way that you answer and the words that you use are more important to the interviewer than your actual answer. In addition, interviewers often ask a stream of questions that most candidates believe require different answers. In reality, there are only a small number of question types, and questions of the same type can generally be answered similarly, in a way that reinforces the connecting of the dots. The information in Chapter 18 helps you recognize the question behind the question and provides insight on how to answer appropriately.

During the Question and Answer phase, try to provide at least one concrete example from your

Know Your Interviewer

The majority of interviewers are not experts at interviewing. Most demonstrate their professional expertise in some other area, for example, engineering or finance. Their questions are most likely drawn from their own interviews—that is, they ask the questions they think they are supposed to ask—or the questions come from a list prepared by someone else such as Human Resources. Some, on occasion, even admit that they know little about the process. This can be troubling to a candidate whose future rests with the person on the other side of the table. Unfortunately it is reality.

However, you can—and should—exploit this weakness to its full potential. Think of the significant edge you have over the competition if you, the candidate, know more about the interview process than most interviewers. You can better control the interview, and its outcome. This means more job offers in the end.

résumé as part of your responses. This provides context between what you do well, what you can do for the company, and your experience in that area.

Realize that in a normal interview, there is only enough time to cover a handful of questions. Prepare by having several skills ready that you can relate. You've got a very small window of time to show the interviewer that you're the best fit for the job *and* a good fit with the people in the group. With that in mind, it follows that you can't afford any of your answers to be mundane or filled with "fluff." Each answer must be a winner, and each must serve a purpose. Chapter 18 explains how to do that as well.

A word of caution: It is important that you *not* try to memorize your answers like a script or try to internalize someone else's responses. Your answers must be in your words so they sound true to your personality.

Closing the Interview

After some period of questions, the interview will come to its natural end. This is usually apparent to both interviewer and interviewee; there simply comes a time when all the bases seem to have been covered and the conversation dries up. This is when most searchers breathe a sigh of relief. Then an overwhelming desire to leave comes over them: get out as soon as you can.

One of the most valuable tips I have comes into play at this exact moment. Avoid the temptation to shake hands and "get out of Dodge" as it were. Instead, take full advantage of that moment, because it is then that you are in an excellent position to do what you came to the interview for in the first place: build rapport and separate yourself from the typical candidate.

Most good sales and marketing people have a "closer" that they bring in to finalize the deal. Your closer is NLP. When you see the interviewer close the folder or shuffle in their seat indicating they are getting up to go, or say something like, "That should cover it," that's when you can go into overdrive and go for the win.

You might say something like, "If it's okay, can I ask one more parting question?" This is NLP in action because you are asking permission here, but it is exceedingly rare for them to refuse. Once they agree, fire away with something like, "given our conversation, what two key things do you think I bring to the table that would be a valuable asset to the group?" More NLP because this question locks in their mind that you are an asset. It reinforces the relationship between you as an individual and the specific attributes you embody that will help them reach their goals.

Only one searcher in a hundred or more ever attempts "a closer" as part of their strategy at the interview. Most people are far too insecure in the search process to remain in their seat and take a winning shot.

The Thank-You

After the interview, you must follow up. I believe that the best form of follow-up is the thank-you note. This simple step is often overlooked, but I have known candidates that have been given job offers *on this detail alone*. No matter what kind of interview you have—more on that in Chapter 17, "Interview Types"—always follow up with a thank-you note.

You can use either a thank-you letter or a card, but I always suggest a *handwritten* thank-you on professional looking stationery. We live in a fast-paced society where e-mail has become the de facto standard of communication. As such, an e-mailed thank-you is appropriate; however, a handwritten note goes a long way toward keeping you in the minds of the interviewers. It gets much more attention simply because is it *not* an e-mail. It stands out because of the time and care that was required to write and send it.

Thank-Yous for All

There is a challenge when there are multiple interviewers involved in the process. The "board room" or "team meeting" type interview challenges the job searcher to retain a lot of information for preparing the thank-you notes. But, you should make a point to send an individual thank-you to everyone in the room. It becomes essential, then, that you take very good notes and collect business cards to keep track of who said what.

The three main components of every handwritten thank-you card are:

- Thanking the interviewer(s) for giving you the opportunity to present yourself.
- Revisiting at least one (1) point in the discussion where you and the interviewer connected in some way, for example, "I felt like we both agreed about the need for attention to quality issues."
- Mentioning that you look forward to future dialogue where you can discuss how you might make an immediate contribution. I recommend using language similar to that from your cover letter.

One last point I want to make about thank-you cards: get them in the mail as quickly as possible after you've completed the interviews. I've known many candidates who took the time to fill out the cards in the parking lot of the organization and mailed them on the way home from the interview. This serves two purposes. It not only gets the thank-you note to the interviewer very quickly, it also allows you to include pertinent information about the interview while it is still very fresh in your mind.

Interview Types

When people talk about interviews, most people think of the "traditional" interview, that is, the type where you've applied for a job and the organization has called you in for a face-to-face meeting with one or more people. If they like you, they might call you back for additional interviews, possibly with different—and often more influential—people.

While these interviews still take place, they are being complemented with some other types of interviews. In this chapter I will cover those interview types: what they are, how to prepare for them, and what to expect when they occur.

Most of these interview types are cut from the same cloth, but I'm also going to include a special type of interview in the mix, one in which it is you, the job seeker, doing the interviewing.

Interview Types

There are a handful of interview types that I want to cover in this chapter. While there are similarities between them, there are also enough differences so that they warrant being discussed separately. I have broken the different types down into the following:

- **Telephone**—The hiring organization calls you to have a brief "qualification" conversation with you. This is a screening or abbreviated pre-interview where the company will decide whether you are qualified enough or they are interested enough to call you in for a face-to-face interview.

- **Traditional**—The hiring organization calls you to come in for a face-to-face interview with one or more individuals. Each of the individuals will meet with you to discuss your background and qualifications; they will then determine if you are the best candidate for the position.

- **"Board Room" or "Team Meeting"**—The hiring organization calls you to come in for a face-to-face interview with a group of people; however, instead of meeting them individually, you meet them all at the same time as a group. This type of interview may require a formal presentation from the candidate and it will include discussion about your background and qualifications. From that information the group/team will determine if you are the best candidate for the position.

- **Informational**—This interview type is unique because you are targeting a specific company/organization and it is you that is interviewing an individual who works at that company. These interviews are designed to be abbreviated—usually around twenty minutes—and the purpose is to determine and display common ground with the intent of being asked to come in for a traditional interview with a company official or hiring manager.

In the following sections I will describe each of the interview types in more detail, including how to prepare for the interview, what questions you should be asking, as well as what you can typically expect in terms of flow.

NOTE: Some of the information presented in the lists of material and interview flow is repeated from section to section. This is intentional. As you land these types of interviews you can refer back to the text and quickly review complete information for that interview type.

Telephone Interviews

With the constant evolution of technology and the prevalence of high-speed working environments, companies are relying more heavily on a twist to the interview process: the telephone interview. Although telephone interviews have been around for a long time, companies are realizing more and more that they can save time and cost by conducting initial screenings over the phone. It has become so pervasive that larger organizations even have full-time individuals dedicated to that specific job.

This telephone interview typically takes place after you have sent a résumé to an organization in response to a job advertisement or as a result of one of your network contacts. Someone within the organization then calls you to have a brief "qualification" conversation or to set up a convenient time to do that in the near future. Usually, the telephone interview is a screening or abbreviated pre-interview where the company will decide whether you are qualified enough or they are interested enough to call you in for a face-to-face interview.

There are some advantages and disadvantages to this interview type.

Usually, the telephone interview is a screening or abbreviated pre-interview where the company will decide whether you are qualified enough...

Advantages

- The interviewer typically avoids "trick" or behavioral type questions.
- The representative will not be tempted to make a premature judgment about you.

Disadvantages

- You are unable to see their body language and facial expressions.
- The removal of the face-to-face interaction puts additional pressure on the candidate. Not everyone has a great "phone voice" and the candidate cannot rely as heavily on their performance as if they were at the company site.

These disadvantages can be overcome and with good preparation it is possible to have a dynamic, convincing phone interview that will lead to a face-to-face interview.

These ideas are designed to enhance your efforts in conducting good telephone interviews. It is likely that if you follow these suggestions you will attain your goal, which, in this case, is to be invited to a face-to-face interview.

Preparing for the Interview

Most people today are quite comfortable speaking on the phone. However, when it comes to speaking to "strangers" or individuals who will make a judgment call about your continued eligibility for the position, many people can get a little rattled. They may feel that they don't come across in as professional a manner as they could.

It is important for candidates to prepare for their telephone interviews in advance of the event. Preparation may include a handy script of what you would like to speak about, especially regarding the depth and breadth of your experience and accomplishments. See Chapter 9, "Résumés" for some hints. You could also have the responses to your "tough" interview questions in front of you. Although reading them would likely not be as effective, just having them in front of you could easily prompt you as to what you want to say. It is a bit of work to type out this information, but if it helps you organize your thoughts and stay focused, it is more than worth the effort.

Why is it so important for candidates to be prepared ahead of time? Because many times the candidate is *not* informed of the interview until it occurs. This can easily put you at a disadvantage. You will not be able to conduct an effective presentation if you're in the middle of breakfast, in the midst of your morning routine, or walking around in your "bunny slippers." You can make a couple choices here.

- Screen the calls; simply do not answer incoming calls until you are prepared to be interviewed.

- Always be at the ready with all your materials available. While this choice might prove inconvenient to family members, it will guarantee that you're always ready to take the call.

After The Beep...

This is a good time to check and make sure that your answering machine or voice mail message is appropriate for corporate calls.

Poor quality equipment, music, chimes, children, pets or other background distractions should be corrected for the job search process. Make sure the outgoing message is clear, simply providing information about who you are and the number reached, without any cleverness.

Call your own machine and listen to the message that other callers hear. What you are currently using may be fun for the family, but could have negative repercussions in the professional world. There will be plenty of time for your creative message after you land the job of your dreams.

The materials that I am referencing are the same ones that you would have at a face-to-face interview. I suggest that you keep them right by the phone, if possible. These include:

- The original advertisement
- The original cover letter
- Copy of the exact résumé you sent or most current résumé focused on the job target if none was sent. See Chapter 9.
- Any available research on the company
- Company prospectus, if available
- Competitor research, if any
- Your list of questions that you want to ask

Any or all of these can be very helpful during phone interviews. Often, the conversation leads to specific details; if the information is right in front of you, it is much easier to recall the specifics. In these instances, the lasting impression to the interviewer is that you are well-informed, organized, and prepared. In addition, you will also have every tool you need at your fingertips.

Presentation Tips

Effective presentation skills similar to those I described in Chapter 14, "Resource Development" come into play here. Remember during the phone interview that it is important to stand up—and stay standing up. Standing significantly changes your presentation dynamics. You might even walk around a bit. While sitting, it is too easy to slide down into the chair or lean over the table propping your forehead with your free hand. These things seriously hinder an open, full breath, energy-oriented delivery.

Possibly the most important thing to remember is to smile. This is easy to forget in the midst of the interview; however, even though the interviewer cannot see it, smiling helps you sound enthusiastic, upbeat, and genuinely interested in the organization and the potential position. A

> *A moderately well-trained telephone interviewer can "hear" a smile on the phone.*

moderately well-trained telephone interviewer can "hear" a smile on the phone. The effort dramatically changes the entire facial muscle configuration and is actually quite easy to detect. The challenge is to remember to *keep* smiling during the entire conversation.

Typical Flow of the Interview

The telephone interview takes place after you send in a résumé and cover letter in response to a particular job ad or a network contact of yours has spoken on your behalf prior to the call.

Normally the telephone interview goes something like this:

1. A company representative calls you to have the interview right then or calls to set up a time in the near future to conduct the interview. The latter is more favorable to you.

2. The interviewer sets aside twenty to thirty minutes to talk and begins by asking you to tell them a little about your background. Make sure you use your 30 Second Commercial.

3. The interviewer will likely continue to ask you questions about your background as it specifically relates to the position. This is often known as the technical question part of the interview.

4. The interviewer may describe a little about the company and their benefits. This is optional and they may wait until a traditional interview to give you this information.

5. Usually the interviewer will give you the opportunity to ask them a question. Refer to the "Interview Questions"section for questions that you should ask at telephone interviews.

6. Often the interviewer will explain their traditional interviewing process and—assuming you have done well—tell you that they will get back to you at some later date to set up a formal face-to-face meeting.

Traditional Interviews

The "traditional" interview has been taking place seemingly forever. Most people in the working world have at some point been involved in a traditional interview.

This type of interview typically takes place after you have sent a résumé to an organization in response to a job advertisement or as a result of one of your network contacts. The organization then calls you to come in for an interview with one or more individuals at a time that is mutually convenient. Each of the individuals will generally meet with you for about an hour to discuss your background and qualifications. From that information they will determine if you are the best candidate for the position.

The type of questions posed to you during the traditional interview typically consist of behavioral and technical—that is job-function-based—questions. Some of these questions are designed to get you to say something that will eliminate you as a candidate. I'll discuss this in much greater depth in Chapter 18, "Interviewing Questions".

There are, of course, advantages and disadvantages to the traditional interview.

Advantages

- Ability to make a good first impression and have the opportunity to be asked to come back for the next round of interviews. Even better, you might get the job offer on the spot.

Disadvantages

- If you're not a good presenter, the interviewer may make an immediate conclusion to exclude you before you get the chance to prove your value to the company.

- Interviewers can be intimidating; a case of nerves can sabotage your efforts.

Despite the disadvantages, there is typically very little you can do to avoid the traditional interview, even within the career change process I'm describing. However, if you prepare well and use the methods I'm laying out, you are likely to have success over those who are "winging it" as many candidates do.

Preparing for the Interview

All your hard work has gotten you to this point. This is where the rubber hits the road, so to speak. It is critical for candidates to thoroughly prepare for the interview in advance of the event. Learn as much as you can about the company. Thoroughly know what you want to say in response to any question the interviewers might throw your way.

It is also a must to observe good grooming habits. Bathed, shaved, recent hair cut or hair do, nails trimmed, and conservative dress. Note that unless you are applying for a position in the fashion industry, avoid wearing and adorning yourself to make a fashion statement. Also avoid using strong colognes and perfumes. It is distracting and takes the interviewers off what is important: your qualifications.

Always have all your materials with you. These would include:

- The original advertisement
- The original cover letter
- Copy of the exact résumé you sent or most current résumé focused on the job target if none was sent. See Chapter 9.
- Any available research on the company
- Company prospectus, if available
- Competitor research, if any
- Your list of questions to ask the interviewer(s)

You may not need all of these, but they can be very helpful during interviews. Often, the conversation gets down to details and if the information is with you it is much easier to recall the specifics. In addition, the lasting impression is that you are well-informed, organized, and prepared.

> *...the lasting impression is that you are well-informed, organized, and prepared.*

Of course it isn't required, but if you are not familiar with the location of the company, take the opportunity to go to the job site in advance. Driving the route will help you to fix the location in your mind and possibly uncover traffic issues prior to the interview date. This simple precaution has averted many an anxiety attack on the day of the interview.

Presentation Tips

I want to reiterate a tip. These interviews are critical, so again, presentation counts.The goal here is to be invited back for another round of interviews or better, get the job offer on the spot.

As with all interviews it is important to sound enthusiastic, upbeat, and genuinely interested in the organization and the potential position. And don't forget to smile.

Body language is also important. Do not cross your arms, try not to fidget too much, and do not let a nervous habit, such as repetitively moving a leg up and down, creep in to your body language. Never eat, drink, chew gum, or smoke. Don't even ask permission to do so.

Typical Flow of the Interview

The traditional interview typically takes place after you have sent a résumé to an organization in response to a job advertisement or as a result of one of your network contacts. Normally the traditional interview process goes something like this:

1. A company representative calls you to come in for an interview at a time in the near future. The representative tells you the ground rules of the interview, for example, time slots, order of interviewers, and usually how many people you are meeting.

2. The interviewer sets aside a specific amount of time with each interviewer.

3. When you arrive at the appointed date and time, a representative will come and take you to your first interview appointment.

4. In most instances the interviewer will open the conversation with the question to tell them a little about your background. Make sure you use your 30 Second Commercial.

5. The interviewer will likely continue to ask you questions about your background as it specifically relates to the position, integrating a number of behavioral questions.

6. The interviewer may describe a little about the company and their benefits. This is optional and they may wait until a later round of interviews to give you this information.

7. Usually the interviewer will give you the opportunity to ask them a question. Refer to the "Interview Questions" section for questions that you should ask at the interview.

8. Most of the time the interviewer will explain their interviewing process and—assuming you have done well—tell you that they will get back to you at some later date to set up another interview.

Once the date and time is set, you may have a day to several days to prepare. I strongly suggest that you pull together all your materials the night before so they'll be ready the following morning. This would include your choice of conservative clothes.

Plan to arrive at least a half hour ahead of your appointment time. Planning to be there "on time" is a formula for disaster. If anything at all happens, you *will* be late, something you never want to be.

I suggest sitting in the parking lot and studying your questions and company information for a few minutes rather than make your presence known right away. This is also the time to visit the restroom and check yourself out to be sure all grooming points are taken care of.

Calm, collected, and prepared are the operative words when you arrive for an interview. Anything less is asking for trouble.

Take three deep breaths and let each out slowly. Then you're ready to walk in the door.

"Board Room" or "Team Meeting" Interviews

The "Board Room" or "Team Meeting" interview is similar to traditional interviews. However, they derive their name because instead of meeting with interviewers individually, you meet them as a group, often in a conference room or other large space. This is a large distinction from the other forms of interviews. This type of interview is often used for senior management jobs.

This type of interview typically takes place after you have sent a résumé to an organization in response to a job advertisement or as a result of one of your network contacts. The largest percentage of Team Meeting Interviews are as a result of a network contact who has spoken on your behalf. This is because 90% or more of higher-level management jobs are procured through network contacts.

The organization then calls you to come in for a face-to-face interview with a group of people at a time that is mutually convenient to everyone. As I mentioned, you meet them all at the same time as a group. These groups may number as few as three or four up to as many as a dozen. The group size usually depends upon the level of the position.

The largest percentage of Team Meeting Interviews are as a result of a network contact who has spoken on your behalf.

This type of interview process may take more than an hour and often requires a formal presentation from the candidate. It will also include discussion about your background and qualifications, as well as some behavioral questions. From that information the group/team will determine if you qualify for further consideration.

Preparing for the Interview

Preparation for this type of interview mirrors that of the traditional interview, but there are a couple of additions. These types of interviews almost always require the candidate to make some form of presentation. These could consist of charts, portfolios, business analysis, theoretical forecasts, and previous project plan samples.[1] Always have all your materials with you. These would include:

- The original advertisement, if any
- The original cover letter
- Several copies of the exact résumé you sent or most current résumé focused on the job target if none was sent. See Chapter 9.
- Portfolio components if appropriate and several leave-behind copies
- Any available research on the company
- Company prospectus, if available
- Competitor research, if any
- Your list of questions to ask the interviewers

You may not need all of these, but they can be very helpful during interviews. Often, the conversation gets down to details and if the information is with you it is much easier to recall the specifics. In addition, the lasting impression is that you are well-informed, organized, and prepared.

Typical Flow of the Interview

The typical flow for this type of interview is similar to the traditional format above. There are several important distinctions to be aware of:

1. A company representative calls you to come in for an interview at a time in the near future. The representative tells you the ground rules of the interview, for example, time, number of hours to prepare for, presentation subject, if any, and usually how many people you are meeting with and possibly their names and position titles.
2. When you arrive at the appointed date and time, a representative will come and take you to the interview room.

1.When determining what materials to bring, always take into consideration confidentiality concerns.

3. In most instances the lead interviewer will open the conversation with the question to tell them a little about your background. Make sure you use your 30 Second Commercial.

4. The lead interviewer will likely ask you questions about your background as it specifically relates to the position, integrating a number of behavioral questions.

5. The lead interviewer will pass the conversation to the next person at the table, and so on.

6. Someone *may* present information about the company benefit package, but this is not usually the case.

7. Usually the interviewer will give you the opportunity to ask them a question or two. Refer to the "Interview Questions" section for questions that you should ask at the interview.

8. Most of the time the interviewer will explain their interviewing process and—assuming you have done well—tell you that they will get back to you at some later date.

You may have several days to a month to prepare. Once again, I strongly suggest that you pull together all your materials the night before so they'll be ready the following morning. This includes your choice of conservative clothes.

Like the traditional interview, plan to arrive at least a half hour ahead of your appointment time. Planning to be there "on time" is a formula for disaster. If anything at all happens, you *will* be late, something you never want to be. I suggest sitting in the parking lot and studying your questions and company information for a few minutes rather than make your presence known right away. This is also the time to visit the restroom and check yourself out to be sure all grooming points are taken care of.

Take three deep breaths and let each out slowly. Then you're ready to walk in the door.

Informational Interviews

The informational interview is the most unique of those we've discussed. In this case, you are targeting a specific company or organization and you contact them to set up a face-to-face interview with an individual who works at that company. This has most likely come about as a result of a resource contact you've met. The biggest difference is that you are interviewing people in your target company. These interviews are designed to be abbreviated—usually around 20 minutes—and the purpose is to uncover common ground and impress the contact enough to be asked to come in for a traditional interview with a company official or hiring manager.

> *The greatest advantage of this type or interview is that you have little to no competition for the position and there is usually no "job in a box" to be forced into.*

The greatest advantage of this type of interview is that you have little to no competition for the position and there is usually no "job in a box" to be forced into. In fact, when you meet with the company representative, a position may not even exist. You may have the opportunity to design the position that best fits your skills. In all the other types you are competing with other candidates for the job. In this case, your philosophy is dramatically different.

Remember, when tapping the Unpublished Job Market, it is the onus of the searcher to "develop" the position during the course of the informational interview. The trick is to do it without saying it. However, this is not as difficult as it might seem.

If you have researched the company well, you should have been able to see how you can meet their needs. After you have completed your research and located the company that fits best, then you will be looking for a position within that company. It is startling how many good jobs simply appear *when you're not looking for them*. To me this is the very best and most productive kind of interview.

Informational interviews should turn into real interviews with other decision makers and offers should follow that. Most informational interviews do not directly result in offers. It is the two or more that do result in job offers that make the difference. That is the reason you are engaging in this process.

Preparing for the Interview

Of course you should always have all your materials with you. However, since there is no real job these include only:

- Copy of the exact résumé you sent or most current résumé focused on the job target if none was sent; see Chapter 9
- Any available research on the company
- Company prospectus, if available
- Competitor research, if any
- Your list of questions that you should ask; refer to the "Informational Interview Questions" section.

Presentation Tips

Since we know that interviews, informational or otherwise, are all about building rapport, the searcher must do everything he or she can to "warm" to the interviewer. If done well, there will be several more conversations or interviews to engage in. They may even take place that day. Your conversation with the contact may result in "I have a couple other people I'd like you to meet with. We may have some ideas that might interest you."

Typical Flow of the Interview

The typical flow for this type of interview is particularly unique. There are several important distinctions to be aware of:

1. You call the company contact to set up a meeting at a time convenient to both parties.

2. When you arrive at the appointed date and time, a representative or your contact will come and take you to their office or a neutral conference room.

3. In most instances the contact will open the conversation with a question about what they can do for you.

4. You begin by using a variation of the 30 Second Commercial to introduce yourself. Then move forward by saying that you've been researching their company and have a few questions you would like to ask.

5. The interview will usually end in a couple possibilities:

    -   They will suggest another person in the company who they think would be a good person with whom to continue your dialogue

    -   They have nothing going on, or you feel the company is not a good match and you can ask them for a referral to another organization that might be a good match

Like the traditional interview, plan to arrive at least a half hour ahead of your appointment time. Planning to be there "on time" is a formula for disaster. If anything at all happens, you *will* be late, something you never want to be. I suggest sitting in the parking lot and studying your questions and company information for a few minutes rather than make your presence known right away. This is also the time to visit the restroom and check yourself out to be sure all grooming points are taken care of.

Take three deep breaths and let each out slowly. Then you're ready to walk in the door.

Questions You Should Ask

At any interview it is very important to be fully prepared to engage in activities that help the interviewer determine your eligibility. At some point toward the end of the interview the person on the other side of the table will likely ask if you have any questions for them, even though they may have been very thorough. The best candidates ask poignant, relevant questions with the purpose of getting more information to determine if you want to work at that organization.

> *The best candidates ask poignant, relevant questions with the purpose of getting more information to determine if you want to work at that organization.*

You should come to the interview prepared with several questions, but you will only have time for one or two in most interview types—possibly up to five at informational interviews. Therefore, you need to be selective. Listen closely to the interviewer. Based on the direction of the discussion, take your best shot. The questions listed below are designed to arm you with as much information as possible about the organization you're looking at—for example, the health of the company and its industry, the nature and social environment of the company, and its politics.

Interview Questions

The list below has questions for the telephone, traditional, and board meeting type interviews.

- What are the three greatest challenges you see for this position?
- How is it that this position has become available (if appropriate)?
- If you were CEO of this company what would be the first two changes you would make? (Since you are CEO of this company what two things would you like to change?)
- What is a typical work day like?
- What kinds of challenges do you see in the foreseeable future?
- Where do you see the industry going in the next few years?
- Where do you see this company heading in this industry?
- What do you enjoy most about working in this industry/in this company?

Remember, it is not likely that you will be in a position to ask all the listed questions. Be selective and choose two that seem most appropriate.

Informational Interview Questions

For informational interview questions, the searcher is usually interested in turning the opportunity into further leads or an offer and are more geared to researching the company.

- Where do you see the industry going in the next few years?
- Where do you see this company heading in this industry?
- What kinds of challenges do you see in the foreseeable future?
- What do you enjoy about working in this industry/in this company?
- Based on my résumé, what kinds of jobs might I consider in this industry?
- What would you suggest as some next steps as I consider moving into this industry?

For the informational interview you may have time for up to five questions. Prioritize just in case the dialogue eats up the time. You will be expected to be the time keeper. If you run over they will likely not be happy, unless they invite you to stay longer—an excellent sign. Then you may continue.

18

Interviewing Questions

As I stated earlier, many of my clients completely underestimate the power and importance of the interview itself. Their thought process tends to be along the lines of, "How hard can an interview be? It's just some questions. Answer the questions honestly and it'll be okay, right?"

Wrong.

In the hands of a deft interviewer, a well-designed question can be a very powerful tool. The way you answer has a huge bearing both on how you are perceived—regardless of your skill set—and whether you are asked back. Therefore, it's critical that you answer the questions the way that the interviewer expects—preferably better than expected. Never be dishonest in your answers, but know that there are better and often stronger ways of answering—as well as a certain level of information filtering—that help to highlight your positive aspects, minimize the negative ones and as a result have a real effect on the success of your interview.

As I mentioned in Chapter 16, questions break down to two basic types: Technical and Behavioral. In this chapter we're not worried as much about the Technical questions—how did you put a particular skill to use at your last job, what types of processes did you use to solve problems, and so on. While those do have some potential pitfalls that we'll discuss, they are generally straightforward and can be usually be answered candidly. No, without a doubt, the difficult questions are the Behavioral ones. I believe the most neglected component of the interviewing process is solid preparation so that the candidate has effective responses to these "difficult" questions.

The psychologically-based Behavioral questions are intended to foil even the best candidate. They often seem innocent at first glance, but are actually designed to get you in trouble; that is, to make you reveal a problem, a weakness, or simply to say too much. With these questions, the interviewer is trying to uncover the negative, something that eliminates you as a candidate. Don't forget, the interviewer is trying to *disqualify* you. That problem, weakness, or revelation may be just the thing that does it. If you aren't ready for these questions, it is easy to fall into the trap. As you can see from Figure 20, because of the wide variety of behavioral questions types and subjects, most interviews rely heavily on the Behavioral question type.

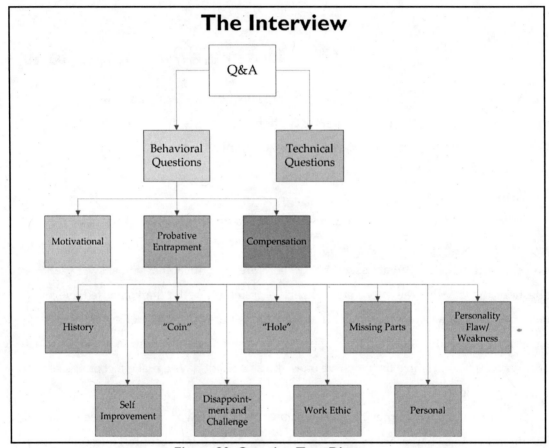

Figure 20: Question Type Diagram

You can see from the figure that there are many types of Behavioral questions, specifically in the Probative Entrapment section.

I want you to be prepared and to interview at a much higher level than you ever have before. To do that, you must be able to identify the difficult questions for what they are and to have effective answers to each and every one of them.

The operative word here is "effective."

Anyone can have an answer, but to have an *effective* answer—one that has the potential to change the course of the interview from "getting through it" to getting to the offer as quickly as possible—is a *very* different thing. For this reason, we'll spend much more time in this chapter discussing the Behavioral questions as opposed to the Technical.

As we go through the questions remember this: while a well-designed question is a powerful tool for the interviewer, a well-designed answer is a more powerful tool for *you*.

The Reality about Interviewers

As you go through your interviews, you will encounter some very experienced interviewers, that is, professionals who understand the importance of the questions, the meaning behind them, and the type of information they are looking to discern from your answers. These are worthy and crafty adversaries, and you should not underestimate the skills that they bring to the interview; that is why well-designed answers are so important. I approach this chapter from the perspective of providing answers specifically for them.

It is, however, important to know that more than 90% of all interviewers are *not* professionals at it. They are managers in some other field. This even includes some Human Resources (HR) managers whose specialties may be compensation and benefits or other HR-related activities.

While a lot of people in an organization may do interviewing, there are very few who do it as an area of expertise such as consultants like myself who have been brought in to conduct key

Assume Nothing

Strong interview responses cannot be assumed on the basis of a person's intellectual level. I was once interviewing a *highly* educated person. His response to one of my questions was, "I have difficulty with authorities who get in the way of letting me do my job."

As you see, an effective response isn't related to intelligence, education, or work experience; it's all about knowing what not to say, what you should say, and being prepared to say it when the time comes.

interviews and perform candidate analysis. It is still important to provide your answers in exactly the same way that you would with a very well-versed interviewer. If you do, by and large, you will have the upper hand in most interview situations.

Think about What You Do

The first step in preparing for interview questions is to simply think about what it is you do, and have done, in your career, specifically as it relates to the target job. This simple exercise will help you with both Technical and Behavioral questions. I asked you to do the same thing while analyzing yourself, but for this exercise you need to be more detailed and think about specifics. Similarly, the lion's share of that information is on the résumé, but again it is extremely abbreviated, so you must be prepared to expand on just about anything that you've listed there.

Very often, when people run into difficulty, especially with Technical questions, it is because they haven't taken the time before the interview process to think about their skills, how they've put them to use, and how that relates *to the opportunity at hand*.

By taking the time to think about how you've put your experiences and skills to use, you can be well-prepared for the inevitable questions about past activities.

Technical Questions

As I mentioned, Technical questions usually revolve around your experience and often take the form of the interviewer asking about projects, skills, problem solving, and so on. When answering Technical questions, it is important not only to connect the dots wherever possible, but also to present past activities and projects in a way that allows you to express your successes in a quantitative way. That is, always try to answer in a way that highlights solid numbers, dollars, or percentages, so long as they are reasonably accurate. This removes the often vague, subjective points and replaces them with solid, measurable information. Examples could include:

- "This project brought in an additional x dollars of revenue" or "This project saved the company x dollars per month/quarter/year."

- "The software solution we rolled out as a result of my research cut operating expenses by y percent."

- "The process improvements I put in place increased production by 100 units per shift."

Dollars, numbers, and percentages are usually closely inter-related, so you may be able to interchange the figures, so long as they're accurate and apply to the discussion.

"What if I Can't Quantify?"

For some professions, achievements can be difficult to quantify. A Software Engineer may not know how the feature that she worked on affected revenue. It is likely impossible for a Therapist to say "My patient improved 52%." This is where thinking about your achievements ahead of time can be indispensable. In these cases where information to base the quantification is either difficult or impossible to measure, it is that much more important that you spend the time to identify those areas that you *can* quantify and have them ready for when the question arises. If that still proves impossible, think about the biggest, most important project that you worked on. You can then focus on how it solved a problem for the client(s).

Behavioral Questions

Behavioral questions can generally be broken into a few categories. One type seeks to uncover a person's motivations, to demonstrate initiative, personal values, and energy. Another category contains what I call Probative Entrapment Questions. That's a fancy term for questions that probe into a person's past, current work experience, personality, or a combination of these, while looking for items to rule that person out. These can also include questions about qualifications, education, credentials, and specific experience. The last category are the salary questions. Some of these, in turn, can be broken down a little further into specific topics within the category.

In many cases, though, questions don't fall neatly into a single category. Some probative questions can also have motivational elements and vice-versa. Just to make it even more complicated, some technical questions have been specifically designed to have behavioral elements, as well. It's all in how the question is framed. So, you can begin to see why interviews can be so challenging to the inexperienced and in a way most people never realize.

Whether they understand it or not, the complexity of behavioral questions is why most people avoid the subjective and answer in an honest, straightforward way, attempting to keep things simple.

> *...the complexity of behavioral questions is why most people avoid the subjective and answer in an honest, straightforward way...*

As we discussed in Chapter 16, there is often a "question behind the question" element in the Behavioral arena. By using specific questions and terms, the interviewer is trying to uncover the answer to an unspoken question about your behavioral patterns rather than seeking the answer to the stated question. They will be making assumptions about your overall makeup based on the answer you provide. If you can recognize and answer the "hidden" question you will almost always be better off.

Concepts to Remember

The success of your interview depends on keeping some basic concepts in mind as you go through the question samples here, while you prepare for the interview and during the interview itself. Some of these are ones we covered in the "Critical Interviewing Concepts" section of Chapter 16. Others, while not what I would consider critical, certainly are important to a successful interview.

- Eliminate negative language from your answers.
- Do your best to maintain control of the interview.
- Always tell the truth, but don't always disclose every aspect. Put a positive spin on the interview question response, but don't elaborate on everything.
- Responses should not exceed thirty seconds or so. Questions that require a scenario or story will take more than thirty seconds, but should be less than a minute or two.
- If you find that the interviewer is "probing" or asking additional questions about your initial response, you've probably already made the journey down a rat hole. Well-structured responses lend themselves to a tidy, self-contained framework precluding further probing because the interviewer has the information they were trying to get.
- I can't stress this enough: If nothing else, with every answer *connect the dots between what you do well and are truly motivated to do and the needs of the target organization.* Remember, this will impress an experienced interviewer and bowl over the inexperienced.

Decoding Behavioral Questions

The stage is now set for preparing good interview question responses. I want to examine the nature of the questions, because knowing their makeup and intent will not only help you answer the questions, but also help you avoid needing a response for each variation. This should excite you—or at least relieve you. What it means is that you won't have to learn how to answer somewhere along the lines of forty plus different questions.

Using examples, we will examine some of the most difficult types of questions and offer some suggested answers for you to consider. Once again, it is important that you *don't* try to memorize the answers like a script to a play, or try to internalize someone else's responses. Your answers must be in your words so they sound true to your personality.

> *Using examples, we will examine some of the most difficult types of questions and offer some suggested answers for you to consider.*

In the sections that follow, I've grouped the questions by type and all of the questions within each type actually have very nearly the same answer. Use these as the basis for your own answers.

NOTE: In addition to what I discuss here, I also recommend another book dedicated completely to behavioral interviews: *Get Hired!: Winning Strategies to Ace the Interview* by Paul Green, Ph.D. A revised edition was published in 2006.

Motivation Questions

Motivation questions are often asked to help the interviewer uncover what it is that the candidate really enjoys doing. The trap of the motivational question is that they are often worded in such a way so as to draw out negative aspects of your personality. Since most behavioral questions tie back to motivations in one form or another, there are many variations on this theme. Questions in the Probative Entrapment category will also tie back to motivations as well, so you must be able to walk the fine line and answer well.

- What motivates you/What are your motivations?
- What are your short/long range goals?
- Why do you want to work for us?
- Why do you want this job?
- Why do you want to go into the _____ field?
- If you could have your choice of any job, what would you do?
- What do you expect to get from this job that you weren't getting from past jobs?
- How do you feel you can help our company/organization?
- If you were choosing someone for this job, what kind of person would you select?
- Why did you leave/do you want to leave your last job?
- How did you like working at your last/current company? Why?
- What did you like best/least about your last job?
- What do you do in your spare time?

Since you've completed the section on self-assessment, answering these questions shouldn't pose much of a problem. But I want to make sure that your responses go to a deeper level than the average candidate. The question behind the question here is "have you determined what you enjoy most, and how can those motivations help us?" These questions are also frequently asked because most candidates simply have not considered what it is that gets them out of bed in the morning or the kinds of activities they enjoy most. A poor answer will make that abundantly clear to the interviewer.

"What motivates you/What are your motivations?"
"What are your short/long range goals?"
"Why do you want to work for us?"
"Why do you want this job?"
"Why do you want to go into the _____ field?"
"If you could have your choice of any job, what would you do?"
"What do you expect to get from this job that you weren't getting from past jobs?"
"How do you feel you can help our company/organization?"

These are perfect examples of how many differently-worded questions are actually asking the same thing. All of these can be answered in practically the same way.

In these cases, it is critical that your answers offer a short list of top motivations, but I caution you that you shouldn't list just anything and everything that lights you up. Your response must include those personal motivations that also specifically correlate to what the target company needs. This goes back to connecting the dots as often as possible.

> *Your response must include those personal motivations that also specifically correlate to what the target company needs.*

For the questions that are company- or position-specific, make sure to mention that in your research on the company and/or the position, you felt that there was a connection between the direction that the company is headed and the things that motivate you, and give at least one example, if possible.

When asked either the "Why do you want to work for us?" or the "Why do you want this job?" question, I suggest responding in this way: "Based on the research I'd done on your company I became very interested, because I'm looking for a company that can fully utilize my analytical, strategic thinking, and customer service skills. Would you say that <Company X> is looking for someone with expertise in those areas Mr./Mrs./Ms. <Interviewer>?" You would, of course, name two or three top motivations of your own and fill in appropriate words for the company name and interviewer name.

Four core things took place in the above response.

1. I opened with the research statement letting the interviewer know that I'd done my homework on the organization.

2. I mentioned two or three key motivations of the kind that I consider critical to my work day but that also match their requirements.

3. I asked the interviewer a question. I controlled the interview by asking the question and was very specific about what kind of response I was looking for. It helps me to clarify that I'm on the right track and the organization and I are on the same page in understanding what is essential to the function.

4. By including these key points you used the essence of Neuro-Linguistic Programming (NLP) techniques. Not only have you locked into their mind the fact that what you bring lines up with what they're looking for, you've gotten them to verbally acknowledge that point.

You conveyed a lot of information into two or three lines and this is powerful. Compare that answer with the typical response of "I heard that this was a good place to work" and you can see the benefits of employing such a method. You should be aiming for this level of completeness in all of your answers.

"If you were choosing someone for this job, what kind of person would you select?"

Do not answer "someone just like me." Instead, this is another opportunity to tie the job requirements to the skills and motivations that you possess. While you are, in essence, saying "someone just like me," it is less obvious and if done correctly won't give the interviewer the impression of arrogance that the blatant comment would.

"Why did you leave/do you want to leave your last job?"
"How did you like working at your last/current company? Why?"
"What did you like best/least about your last job?"

These three are the questions in this group that could be a bit troublesome. It is very important to avoid the bullet and *not* answer the question directly. There are typically two possible scenarios: either you were let go, or you've decided that you no longer want to work at your current company or position. Neither is going to serve you well if you use them as a basis for your answer.

- For the first scenario, it's a cop-out to say that you were laid off. That puts you in the role of victim and no matter how you look at it that's not a positive spin. Instead, turn it into a positive by saying that it was a great company and when you got caught up in a downsizing it gave you an excellent opportunity to pursue organizations where you could focus on what you do well, at which point you'll once again connect the dots with more motivations and skills that will help the company. This is a strong approach to a typically negative situation.

- For the second scenario, you're going to use a variation on the first. Again, you're going to mention that is was a good company to work for, that you learned a lot, and that you've decided that it is time to seek out new challenges that address your specific motivations and allow you to focus on them.

In either case, remember the stated reason for leaving or moving forward should always be based on core motivations, otherwise there would never be a reason for transition. The key here is to have identified those core motivations and specifically articulate them to the interviewer.

> *...the stated reason for leaving or moving forward should always be based on core motivations...*

When responding to the "Why did you leave/do you want to leave your last job?" question, say something along the lines of "I've been working on my career plan and I am in the process of implementing that plan. I'm looking for a company that can fully utilize <name two or three top motivations>. Would you say that <Company X> is looking for someone with experience in those areas?" The difference here is that you make the events of your life look like part of a larger plan, even if they are not.

For the "What did you like best/least about your last job?" question, you should mention that it was an excellent position and you learned a lot. Now, you are looking for a position that can utilize your full skill base. Inherent in the statement is the underlying idea that the old job was not fully leveraging your skill base. However, by answering this way you aren't using the negative words. Once again, never bad-mouth your employer, and avoid negative language at all costs.

"What do you do in your spare time?"

Most searchers will answer with the activity that they most enjoy. This is okay—but merely adequate. An answer like that makes it difficult to score points because you can never be sure that the interviewer likes what you do. Don't leave this subjective area up to luck. You should keep the conversation to an activity that very specifically illustrates a passion of yours as it relates to the target job.

Examples might be "I like to work on crosswords because I really enjoy solving problems," in situations where solving problems is a key ingredient for the job. "I enjoy league sports because I'm very competitive," is a great choice for positions such as sales where competitiveness is important. With thought and preparation, you are likely to have a solid answer for this question highlighting your skill set.

> *With thought and preparation, you are likely to have a solid answer for this question highlighting your skill set.*

Probative Entrapment Questions

These questions are trying to probe into specific areas of your personality and personal makeup. It is not likely, by the way, that interviewers would ever ask two questions from the same category. They usually know what these questions are about. Still, I always recommend that it would be helpful to have a couple scenarios, just in case.

History Questions

The history questions are often asked at the beginning of the interview, and are intended to "break the ice" and give the interviewer an opportunity to know more about you at a higher level before moving into the more specific, pointed questions.

Questions in this category typically include variations on the following:

- Tell me a little about yourself.
- What have you been doing since you left your last position?

History questions give the job searcher some challenges when it comes to putting a positive spin on their response. Being forthright is almost guaranteed to land you someplace you don't want to be. Put a positive spin on your answer, and include only information that is relevant to your target profession.

"Tell me a little about yourself."

The answer to this question is one that every single job searcher should have down firm. Refer to your 30 Second Commercial from Chapter 13.

"What have you been doing since you left your last position?"

This one comes into play only when you have been obviously out of work for some time. The key here is to realize that interviewers want to hear you've been busy and staying current with your work. If you have been out of your position for more than a couple months it will be critical that you "line up" activities, reading material, perhaps a course, or something that you can discuss when you have an interview. Don't get caught with an empty gap there.

"Coin" Questions

"Coin" questions are those that have two sides. In these questions one side is fine but the other side can be damaging. Typically, answering the first part of the question isn't too hard, but it does have its traps. To answer the second half or negative side of the question requires some fancy footwork on your part.

Questions in this category typically include variations on the following:

- Tell me about your greatest accomplishment and your greatest disappointment.
- Tell me the best thing about your last job and the thing you disliked most.
- Tell me about your best/worst boss ever.

The question beneath the question(s) is "not only provide some work-related experiences and accomplishments, but give us an idea of how you respond to negative situations.

> **NOTE:** Due to their very nature, coin questions can show up just about anywhere and often contain elements of any of the other categories.

"Tell me about your greatest accomplishment and your greatest disappointment."

First translate the bad word for one that is more acceptable, for example, challenge instead of disappointment. Next, you must have selected a scenario that actually fits the situation—something that needed developing, what you did about it, and how it has made you a better person/supervisor/manager. Your answer must meet this criteria or you run the risk of getting into difficulty. A good response would be something like "Life is filled with challenges and I recall one situation that ultimately helped me develop as a manager…" Needless to say this scenario must be well thought out in advance.

The Flip Side of the Coin Question

The "flip side" of the coin question refers to those that you'd expect in the coin pair, but in this case the interviewer only gives you the "bad" half. Questions might be:

- Tell me about the most difficult problem you've had and how you overcame it.
- Tell me about your worst boss?

The strategy is the same: present as much of a positive response to these as you can. The difficult problem scenario above is the easier of the two, but must include a professional growth component. Keeping it reasonably brief is the toughest challenge to this question. Be cautious not to drag it out. With behavioral questions, one of the greatest challenges is balancing how much to tell. My recommendation is to keep it as short as possible without leaving out critical detail. All the more reason to have these responses well thought out in advance of the interview.

A word of warning—and this is what I was referring to when I said the first part could have its own traps—if you answered the "greatest accomplishment" portion of the question with something like:

- "my children"
- "my wife"
- "marriage"
- "time off"
- "vacation time"
- "I'm good at everything I do"
- "I work hard"

you are already in trouble. It's not that those things may not be true, but they have little to do with what the interviewer is looking for.

"Tell me the best thing about your last job and the thing you disliked most."

This question should feel familiar. It's really the same as the "What did you like best/least about your last job?" question I highlighted in the "Motivation Questions" section, only worded differently. It's here to illustrate that even though I've grouped these questions for the purpose of this exercise, there will be overlap between the different groups—especially when it comes to coin questions—and you need to be prepared to recognize the different types and address them with your responses.

In this case the stronger answer is to tie it back to how the job did address some of the things that motivate you, but that it didn't provide enough opportunity to engage in those activities, so you are searching for a position that will better leverage those things you really do well and enjoy. Remember, *never* bad mouth your previous company.

"Tell me about your best/worst boss ever."

The best/worst boss question has more to do with professional growth regarding mentorship than describing what a rat one of your bosses was. Answer from the perspective that you learned a lot from all your bosses even if it was what *not* to do. An appropriate response references how much you've always learned

> *Answer from the perspective that you learned a lot from all your bosses even if it was what not to do.*

from your bosses and possibly some specifics that have contributed to your success.

"Hole" Questions

"Hole" questions are usually asked when there are noticeable gaps in your résumé. Questions in this category typically include variations on the following:

- How long have you been out of work?
- Can you tell me about these gaps between jobs?

The question behind the question is "If you are such a great candidate, why were you out of work for a period of time?"

"How long have you been out of work?"
"Can you tell me about these gaps between jobs?"

If you recall I very specifically addressed this particular issue in Chapter 9, "Résumés" and told you how to avoid having to explain this issue. This question should not come up at all if you've done your homework here. Make sure you avoid having to explain this issue in writing or verbally.

There are, however, times when this is simply not practical. Situations such as a woman or man having spent time as a stay-at-home parent, a person having fallen victim to extended illness or other specific reasons besides the inability to land a job are perfectly valid reasons for a chronological time gap.

In these cases it's obvious that you can't simply gloss over the hole and you probably shouldn't need to. I recommend that if this is the case, be honest about the situation: let them know that you felt the time had come for you to enter/ re-enter the workforce and immediately follow this statement up with discussion of your areas of expertise.

As we discussed in Chapter 9, "Résumés", you should have registered for coursework that relates to your passion and have gotten involved with temp agencies to get some recent, relevant experience around your passion and to try and get a foothold in a company. If you have other related previous work experience then you should discuss that as well. This should adequately explain the gap, while conveying to the interviewer that you are serious about your return and still a good match for the company.

Missing Parts Questions

These questions can be a bit tricky for many people, simply because they are often unexpected. You've gone to the interview expecting that, since they called you, you must be qualified. These questions can throw you completely off balance since they seem to indicate you are not, in fact, a fit for the position.

- Isn't this a career switch for you?
- Aren't you overqualified/ under qualified for this job?
- What has kept you from progressing as fast as you would have liked?

The question beneath the question here is along the lines of "aren't you really unsuited for this position?" The best way to avoid the question is to not be in a position to have the question asked at all. Actually, this is easier than you might think. The key here is to target jobs that are the best fit for you and not go after jobs that are not. The self-assessment that we discussed in Chapter 5, "Analyzing the Self" and the 80/100 Rule we discussed in Chapter 7, "Establishing Career Options and Direction" will help you to determine how to target opportunities.

"Isn't this a career switch for you?"
"Aren't you overqualified/ under qualified for this job?"

If you do happen to get into a situation where these questions are asked, it is critical to avoid answering the question directly if at all possible. It's time to put on your "dancing shoes" to stay out of difficulty here. Again, don't sell what you don't have, but point to your résumé and specifically pick out the attributes you demonstrated on your résumé that parallel what is in their advertisement. Remember, they called you, so you must qualify.

Target specific experience, knowledge, and accomplishments that prior organizations have found invaluable and have resulted in good things for the company, and that you'll want to replicate at this firm, too.

You must demonstrate that you are, in fact, the right person for the position, and that you have progressed at your own, planned out, pace.

You must demonstrate that you are, in fact, the right person for the position, and that you have progressed at your own, planned out, pace.

"What has kept you from progressing as fast as you would have liked?"

This is a deadly question. The lack of progression that they are referring to could be any number of things, including a lack of a degree, frequent job changes, too long at one job/one industry, too young, too old, and so on.

Honestly, there are no winners here, but something like "I am currently implementing my career plans and the timing for this endeavor is right where I expected to be," goes a long way toward filling the gap without exposing any weaknesses.

Personality Flaw/Weakness Questions

The weakness questions can be the deadliest of all. In essence, these questions are looking at areas of your personality that continue to need development. There are several key things to know about this line of questioning before attempting to answer.

- Tell me about your strengths and your weaknesses./What are some of your weaknesses?
- With regard to the job we're discussing, what is your weakest suit?
- If you feel you have any weakness with regard to this job, what would it be?
- Everyone gets irritated at work about something. What irritates you?
- Everybody likes to criticize. What do your colleagues criticize about you?
- Tell me about a time when you made a serious mistake.
- Everybody has pet peeves. What are yours?
- What could management do to make you function more effectively?
- If you could relive your last fifteen years, what changes would you make?

The question beneath the question is "Are you aware of the areas where you need growth and what have you done to address them?" As such, the core response criteria revolves around identification of those areas of your personality that require more growth; what have you done about them, and how that awareness helped you to be a better person, employee or professional.

"Tell me about your strengths and your weaknesses./What are some of your weaknesses?"
"With regard to the job we're discussing, what is your weakest suit?"
"If you feel you have any weakness with regard to this job, what would it be?"
"Everyone gets irritated at work about something. What irritates you?"
"Everybody likes to criticize. What do your colleagues criticize about you?"
"Tell me about a time when you made a serious mistake."
"Everybody has pet peeves. What are yours?"

Never—*ever*—mention something that has always been *and continues to be* a large problem. Rather, a good example might be something like this: "I recognized earlier in my career that I needed to become stronger at organization. I attended a time management course, read a couple of books on the subject, and worked with a person who mentored me to a remarkably higher level. Today, I remain diligent in that regard and while I don't think it will ever be a strength, I've certainly come a long way."

The real power of the above response is in the closing statement where I bring the interviewer's attention to an area of the résumé where I clearly could demonstrate growth in the area that needed development. Would it ever likely be a strong suit?

Probably not, but it is key to show demonstrable results before you choose a particular topic to discuss. Note that this does *not* suggest the person was rotten at it then and still is now. It merely defines something that was a weakness that you continue to work on.

You'll need more than one example of weaknesses to properly cover yourself. I'd suggest at least three. If you have difficulty with thinking of several I suggest contacting colleagues and former bosses and asking them, "where do you think I've improved the most in the past few years?"

> *...it is key to show demonstrable results before you choose a particular topic to discuss.*

The question, "If you feel you have any weakness with regard to this job..." is the most disguised of this group because it appears that the interviewer is looking to hear you say something about your ability to come up to speed. In reality, they are looking to have you say something about the foibles you bring with you from every job you've had and likely will follow you into this job. Try a response similar to this:

"Well, it's interesting that you should ask that question. I have always felt that many of my strengths were still areas that continued to need developing. For instance, it has been important for me to develop my organizational skill set in order for myself, my staff, and the organization to meet our objectives. I find it an ongoing challenge to train, motivate, and mentor some of my support staff that need to meet the standard that we've set. As you can see from my résumé, I've managed several projects that clearly demonstrate success through effective team building."

A twist in the same type of question has to do with the "irritation and criticism" questions. These also have to do with professional development, but have more to do with how you behave when they are brought to your attention. You will be more successful with these questions if you think of them as "your weakness is also your strength." An example might be that you are aware that colleagues and others get on your case about how you get a little—or very—stressed when people around you aren't as organized are you are. An effective response might be something like: "Most organizations that I've worked for have greatly appreciated the level of detail I bring to the table and my passion for being thorough as contributing highly to the bottom line and I see it as a personal challenge to train and coach my team in how to be more effective in that regard."

> *...it might be of use to note that by and large your strength is likely to also be your weakness.*

As I alluded to above, it might be of use to note that by and large your strength is likely to also be your weakness. For instance, if you consider yourself particularly organized you are likely—though not in all cases—to be somewhat intolerant of those co-workers and support staff who are not as organized. The strength is your organizational skill. The intolerance is the area that needs developing. Once you have thought about that and properly identified these, it is extremely important to speak about them in ways that are positive and constructive.

"What could management do to make you function more effectively?"

This is a very deep trap question. In a nutshell, this question makes it easy for you to tell the interviewer what they need to do to make your life with them easy. But remember, interviews are about *them* and they are looking for you to bring strength to their bottom line, not the need to hand-hold you. A solid answer for this question is something similar to "I've investigated your organization and I believe the pieces are already in place for me to thrive in my position. I look forward to a partnership where we can operate as a team to reach the goals we both want to achieve." While it isn't a direct answer, wording like this usually draws their attention away from the tricky pitfalls of the original question.

"If you could relive your last fifteen years, what changes would you make?"

Reliving the last fifteen years is a trick question about flaws in the personality. Most positive responses here reflect a desire to make no major changes and always indicate that there has been an active career plan in place and that your current job search is the next step in that plan. You demonstrate a level of maturity that the interviewer is seeking if you can speak to a level of contentment with your current situation—without giving the impression that you are so content that you do not want to grow—and satisfaction with your chosen path.

Here, admitting that you didn't plan well and are dissatisfied with the path you've chosen is dangerous territory. You should show that you are aware that there is a lot of growth that comes from being a professional and that the path you've followed, regardless of any personal perceived sidetracks, made you what you are. Successful professionals are the ones who take up the challenge despite pitfalls and learn from them.

Self Improvement Questions

Self Improvement questions again pertain to your development, but from a slightly different perspective. Here you must think about what you currently do and will do to enhance your skill competencies. If the real answer is little or nothing you are in hot water.

Companies are most interested in individuals who keep up with the changing world of work. It is now a world of life-long learning and all employees are expected to keep pace with industry changes even if they have to do it on their own time. This is one area where you'll need to think about actually providing some concrete action to the words; otherwise you'll end up praying that they don't ask this type of question.

> *Companies are most interested in individuals who keep up with the changing world of work.*

- What have you been doing since you left your last job?
- Do you plan to get further education/degrees?
- What was the last book you read and what did you like about it?
- When was the last class or training you took and what was it about?
- What have you done to improve yourself during the last year?
- What are your short range/long range goals? How do you expect to meet them?
- Assuming we make you an offer, what do you see as your future?

These questions are typically not very disguised, but the trap with this line of questioning is that most people don't stop to think of how they have deliberately set time aside to improve themselves.

"What have you been doing since you left your last job?"
"Do you plan to get further education/degrees?"
"What was the last book you read and what did you like about it?"
"When was the last class or training you took and what was it about?"
"What have you done to improve yourself during the last year?"

However the question is framed, it is important for you to be able to specifically identify areas that represent professional growth. For the purposes of this exercise you should always think about and put together some information that is going to sound effective to the listener. Take note, however: If you haven't done anything about some of these items then it is time to do so. For instance, if you have no formal education, but most people in your field have a degree, I strongly urge you to register for at least a single class that is part of a specific curriculum appropriate to your field.

"What are your short range/long range goals? How do you expect to meet them?"
"Assuming we make you an offer, what do you see as your future?"

The interviewer wants to know that you have a sense of direction that includes forward movement, not just a job that you intend to stay in until the end of your days. Hints of your motivations come into play, too.

> *The interviewer wants to know that you have a sense of direction that includes forward movement...*

I suggest the following response: "Excellent question. I see myself working my way into executive positions and in senior management functions as I gain in experience and knowledge about the organization."

You don't need to go so far as to mention that you are a ladder climber unless you are motivated to do so. Future goals should always include generalized growth into positions two or three levels up from you. Broad based growth is very good too. Never say "I want your job" or "I want to be the company president," even if it's true. Even aggressive sales people should avoid this trap. "I see myself advancing over the next few years into higher levels of responsibility," is sufficient without being offensive.

Disappointment and Challenge Questions

The next set of questions have to do with dealing with problem solving, disappointments and challenges.

- Tell me about your greatest achievement / disappointment in life.
- Did you ever make suggestions to management? What happened?
- What are some of the more difficult problems you encountered in your past jobs? How did you solve them?
- How would you handle this problem? (After interviewer describes problem)

The question behind the question here is "how do you deal with situations where things do not work out the way you would like them to?"

"Tell me about your greatest achievement / disappointment in life."
"Did you ever make suggestions to management? What happened?"
"What are some of the more difficult problems you encountered in your past jobs? How did you solve them?"
"How would you handle this problem? (After interviewer describes problem)"

What the interviewer hopes to hear from you is some form of articulation about how much you love challenges, problems, and that you grow enormously from disappointments. "This is a great question because it opens the door for me to describe how much I thrive in seemingly chaotic or difficult situations. I'd like to bring your attention to my résumé where some of these projects <actually point to a bullet or two> were fraught with difficulties. I enjoyed working on these projects. In fact, when I was told that no one before me could figure them out I really became excited."

The disappointment question could more easily be addressed by talking about how you have grown professionally. "I recall a time that afforded me one of the greatest opportunities for practical learning. I'd made a bad decision and was very embarrassed about the result, but it turned out to be one of my greatest experiences because I learned <describe the learning> from it, which has paid huge dividends."

Work Ethic Questions

The Work Ethic questions are trying to uncover your commitment to the workplace. In today's corporate world there is an unspoken expectation that you will commit much of your resources to the company.

- How do you feel about evening work?
- Are you geographically mobile, either now, or in the future?
- In your last job, how much of the work did you do on your own, and how much as part of a team? Which did you enjoy more?
- Are you considering other positions at this time? How does this one compare?

The question beneath the question here is "How dedicated to the company will you be?" In the early stages, it pays to indicate a high level of time and effort to the organization.

"How do you feel about evening work?"
"Are you geographically mobile, either now, or in the future?"

Until you know a lot more about the job, I'd err in favor of responding that you are completely flexible. You can always back away once you get more information.

"In your last job, how much of the work did you do on your own, and how much as part of a team? Which did you enjoy more?"

With today's work world being so reliant on teams I'd focus on that. But always mention that you are very comfortable working on your own, regardless of the amount you've always been used to. It is important here that you be very much aware of what environment you

Avoid targeting functions that are opposite to your personal preference.

actually thrive in. Many functions are very solitary, while others are very team- and socially-oriented. Avoid targeting functions that are opposite to your personal preference. See your Myers-Briggs® results for guidance.

"Are you considering other positions at this time? How does this one compare?"

This question affords you to up the ante a bit. Simply saying "no" implies that your job search is weak. Saying "yes" could mean that you're playing the field for the best deal, which is likely the case, but again, isn't a powerful enough response. Here a little word play or NLP will work best. "I am considering other options at this time. However, I must say I am very interested in this position and this organization because <fill in a reason or two>. Do you have a feeling as to when you might be making a decision?"

Personal Questions

Personal questions can be very awkward. There are two types of personal questions: those that apply to your personal *style* and those that apply to your personal *life*.

The personal style questions are usually okay, but can be difficult to answer. Most personal *life* questions are essentially illegal to ask in the United States, since discrimination laws prevent disqualification solely based on sex, race, age, disability, beliefs, and so on.

- What else do you think I should know about you?
- What is your leadership style?
- What does success mean to you? How do you judge it?
- Tell me about your health.
- What does your spouse think about the kind of work you do? How about this job?
- Tell me about your family.
- What does your husband/wife do?

> *There are two types of personal questions: those that apply to your personal style and those that apply to your personal life.*

In all of these instances, whether advisable of not for the interviewer to ask, they are trying to uncover something about you as a person, which can then translate into some assumptions about how you will perform in the job. Don't fall prey to the trap of giving up much—if any—information that could hurt you here.

"What else do you think I should know about you?"

Offering up any information here is sometimes costly. It begs to have you cough up something secret, something not really related to the job itself. Don't do it. It is a question that likely won't be asked until near the end of the interview. You should, instead, quickly evaluate what has been discussed and plug in another couple motivations that would be very useful to them and the function you are targeting.

"What is your leadership style?"

The nature of this question has to do with avoiding the trap of telling them what you expect. The leadership style question is almost totally about how your personality relates to their company "personality." Treading carefully to reflect their style is key.

Good research should let you know what leadership trademarks interest them. If the fit is a good one for you, articulate a mirror image of what attributes reflect their approach. Say something like, "My research indicates that the management style of this company is supportive of <include applicable attributes such as positive reinforcement, mentoring, and overall employee development>. I think continued advocacy of those concepts can greatly enhance the bottom line and I have wholeheartedly supported and demonstrated use of that style in my past positions."

The leadership style question is one that in today's market almost demands that you are a team-oriented individual who is focused on mentoring and facilitative employee development. The only time this might be different is if your research indicates that they are specifically looking for a maverick personality to make immediate changes in the complexion of the organization. This is very rare, but if it's the case it is critical to describe your specific methods as they relate to the job description.

"What does success mean to you? How do you judge it?"

The "success" question is fairly straightforward. The question beneath is about knowing yourself well enough to know "it isn't about money and how much you have in the bank." Better answers usually revolve around attainment of measurable goals and acknowledged accomplishments so you know when you reach them will go a long way toward answering this question well. The process of setting goals, attaining them, then setting new benchmarks demonstrates personal growth.

> *The process of setting goals, attaining them, then setting new benchmarks demonstrates personal growth.*

"Tell me about your health."
"What does your spouse think about the kind of work you do? How about this job?"
"Tell me about your family."
"What does your husband/wife do?"

Because of the United States' discrimination laws, even asking certain personal life questions could be construed as fishing for such disqualifying information, which in theory could be used later to make illegal decisions. As such, most managers will not ask them to avoid possible trouble, even litigation. However, sometimes interviewers make errors and do ask these.

Don't be rude, but remember never volunteer the information that could disqualify you as a candidate. While I've even seen individuals put such information on their résumés, it is absolutely taboo. However, if you feel that you must address them, always put it in a positive frame that speaks to being available for work, family support, and full support of this new position.

Compensation Questions

The last questions are about the salary match and other compensation. They are also part of the Entrapment group, but are separate enough to warrant their own category.

Compensation questions are often the most difficult, especially if the interviewer brings it up too early in the process. Rather than simply state what they are willing to pay for the position, sometimes the interviewer chooses to put the candidate in the uncomfortable position of determining what to say about that. This turns into a throw the dice as to whether what you say will be too high and disqualify you or too low and forfeit dollars or demonstrate lack of confidence in what you are worth. Answering compensation questions early is almost always a lose-lose situation for the candidate based upon what they say.

This question comes in some variation of:

- What salary do you require?

The intent of the question is to get you to come up with a number without the company having to tip its hand as to how much they would be willing to pay. Ideally, the company will provide a number that you can then use as a springboard into negotiation, which I cover in Chapter 19, "Negotiation Information".

"What salary do you require?"

Frankly, the answer to this one is not easy. Since you never want to be the first to give up a number, you need to respond carefully. I have a three-stage answer to this very difficult, annoying, and usually inappropriate question.

1. "I was hoping that we would get a little further into the process before we got into discussions about money. I don't really know much about the job yet and you don't know much about what I can do for the company at this point."

If the interviewer presses further, move into stage two…

2. "I assume this position has been approved. Could you share the salary range with me?"

Many times I've heard interviewers give up the number. If they do, be careful to avoid reacting pro or con. You can always back out later if needed. If the interviewer presses yet further, they may be getting irritated and you may be forced into giving up a number. In that case, try stage three:

3. "Considering my experience, areas of expertise, and skill level, I am looking to be in a position that compensates in the <appropriate dollar amount> or better."

Three key points about this last statement: It should be a single, open-ended number that you select, and the number is usually about 15% higher than your last salary. By keeping it open-ended, it allows both you and the hiring organization flexibility and is less likely to be ruled too high or too low out of hand. Lastly, the overall structure of the statement allows you to press your best attributes prior to springing the number on them, which provides good support as to why you are asking for that figure.

Formulating and Testing Your Answers

Now you want to develop your responses to these questions. Take these suggestions and integrate them into your own words—they must ring true to your own personality.

Just sharing and reading your responses to yourself isn't enough. You need to verbalize your answers because your intonation, attitude, honesty, credibility, and believability are much more easily discerned when they are heard. Once that is done it would be a good idea to ask a partner, spouse, or trusted friend to listen and test how your responses come across.

Of course, it's beyond the scope of this book to include every question variation here. Based on what you've read here, you should be able to quickly analyze the question and determine roughly which category is close enough for you to work with. If all else fails, use the positive spin and connect the dots guidelines we've discussed throughout this section to help you to format a suitable response. If you feel you need further assistance, contact us via the Career Game Championships web site. Responses are usually within 24 hours.

Negotiation Information

Congratulations! You've got a job offer. With a formal offer in hand, you are in the home stretch toward getting that hard-sought job. But you aren't at the finish line yet.

One of the most important steps in the search process comes when the job offer is given to you. Once you have received an offer, it is then time to negotiate a compensation package to ensure that you earn what you are worth. This is not restricted to executives. Hourly wage earners can, and do, negotiate as well. It is important to remember: *The time to negotiate is only after an offer has been made.* The ultimate payoff to your self-marketing campaign comes when a final offer is negotiated.

Often, the searcher will accept the offer as initially presented by the hiring organization with no discussion about salary, vacation time, or any number of other benefits. This is a mistake. If you "leave money on the table" or don't negotiate a good compensation package for yourself, then you may have let a golden opportunity to capture your market worth slip away without a word.

After having gone through the process, you may think it is enough simply to have landed your dream job. You may be thinking things such as "it's not as much money as I envisioned, but I really wanted to get into this organization" or "I'm losing two weeks of vacation by moving to this company, but the job is everything I've been looking for." It is these types of "justifications" that may cause you to miss out on a great deal of compensation.

Many times these thoughts are driven by fear. It may be the fear that if you try to sweeten the offer in your favor that the company may balk and rescind the offer. It may also be a fear that you aren't good at the negotiation process and therefore may make a mistake or leave a bad impression.

On the other hand, it may not be fear at all. Many people simply dislike negotiating.

As you will see in this chapter, unless you back an employer into a corner, you generally do not have to worry about an offer being rescinded. In addition, I will show you a simple way to make negotiating very non-confrontational and allow you to cover the gamut of options, avoid mistakes, and make sure that the impression you leave as you start your new position is a favorable one.

The Process

Before we go too deeply into specifics, let's talk about the typical negotiation steps.

Like everything else we've covered in this book, there is a process to negotiating—a give and take that is common. The very first thing to do once you have received the job offer is to get the offer in writing if you can. Most organizations are willing to provide this document. It helps avoid the "but they said" or "I was sure I heard" problem.

> *...unless you back an employer into a corner, you generally do not have to worry about an offer being rescinded.*

Once you've had a chance to read over what is actually being offered, then you can begin to determine what can and should be negotiated and develop a strategy for this important activity. One key element to determining your strategy is to do some more research in regard to typical salary ranges, compensation, and benefits for the position and industry in question. As we'll see, this information is critical so that you don't price yourself out of the market.

With that information at your disposal, you can begin to negotiate. Different compensation aspects, as described in the "Negotiating Salary" and "Negotiating Much More" sections, can be discussed. Counteroffers may be made by both sides during the negotiation process. Negotiation ends either when you are satisfied with the package or it becomes clear that the company can add no more to the offer. At that time, you must decide whether to accept the offer, or pass on the opportunity.

Doing Your Homework

It is important to have a good grasp of the restrictions under which your target company is operating. Not all industries have the same salary ranges, even for a similar position, and other compensation in the way of benefits may or may not be available. Even companies within the same industry may have differences depending on their size, revenues, and other factors.

Organizations and companies generally have a salary range structure for each level or position. The range may be fairly broad—up to the tens of thousands for senior executives—but most positions have a few thousand dollars in their range. Searchers must remember that organizations do have a given structure that is typically not very flexible.

Most organizations or companies also have a compensation and benefit package. For companies and non-profits the benefits may vary widely, ranging from no benefits at all to complex and comprehensive benefit packages. The ability to negotiate these benefit packages can also vary widely, from no negotiation because it's a fixed package that the company or organization has "purchased" to being able to select and garner parts of packages depending upon individual need.

It is important to have a feel for these structures before you begin the negotiation process. Walking into a negotiation without background information could result in your requests being out of sync with the company's position. Remember that an important part of the whole process here is to be prepared and to have done research on your target market, even at this late stage of the game.

The Key to Negotiation: Four Simple Words

If you remember, one of the things that we covered previously when we were talking about determining your mindset was that it is 100% about the hiring company. This remains true during the job offer and negotiation process. When generating a job offer, the company is going to try to put a competitive offer together, but will also gear it towards their own best interests. To be clear, they are likely not trying to trick you or to intentionally give you less than you deserve, but they will try to make a deal that is best for them. As such, the offer they present will probably *not* include everything they could possibly offer.

The converse of this is that by the time an offer is made, they've already invested significant time, effort, and money into the process. They've decided that they like you and have a good match to their employment needs. They are not going to want to start back at the beginning without a good reason. This plays to your favor, as it is unlikely that they will perceive a gentle request for negotiation as a "good reason."

So, while many people are concerned that the company will at some point pull away from the negotiating table and change their mind about the offer, my experience has shown me that this is very unusual. Offers are typically rescinded only if the candidate begins to paint the hiring company representatives into a financial corner by insisting that if they don't submit to the searcher's requests then the deal is off. That kind of conversation *is* a show stopper and can kill an otherwise good deal. Remember, it's a negotiation, not a confrontation, so work *with* them. When they say, "This is the best we can do…" negotiations are over and you have a choice to make.

> *Negotiation comes down to four simple words.*

So, how do you broach the subject of what you want? It's easy. Negotiation comes down to four simple words. Memorize this phrase to open negotiation in a non-confrontational manner: "Can we talk about…?" This gentle question will ease you into topics of compensation. "Can we talk about…?" leaves the door open, isn't demanding, and you may reap unexpected benefits.

Using this phrase will keep the negotiations friendly and keep the conversation in the realm of "discussing" rather than "demanding."

Amazing rewards are available to you, in many cases, just for the asking. The key is not to shy away from the opportunity to negotiate due to the fears I mentioned at the beginning of the chapter. Remember the magic words: "Can we talk about…" If you use that phrase and follow the simple discussion tips mentioned above, I am confident that your experience will be a good one and you will be able to capture as much as you are able—without offending the hiring company or organization.

Much like the resource development process, I hope that by using this simple, non-confrontational phrase you will see how easy it is to discuss your options, you will see that there is nothing to fear, and that you will find you actually enjoy the negotiation process.

Negotiating

There are many things to think about when considering negotiation. Your comfort level in negotiation determines the outcome, but I hope my magic words will give you a sense of calm about the negotiation process and that you'll be more comfortable with it than ever before. When you negotiate, be flexible and keep the negotiation open with the "Can we talk about…" words.

The salary part of the compensation is where most negotiations occur. Most people leave money on the table when they accept a position, meaning they do not negotiate at all, or negotiate only a little money. Over time, non-existent or ineffective negotiation can result in tens of thousands or even hundreds of thousands of dollars being lost over the course of a career. (See "The Cost of Not Negotiating" for more about how the difference in a few thousand dollars of negotiated salary can affect you.) Again, research is key. You should also be aware that most companies will not pay you the top of their pay range. They know that if they offer that much you will have little to no future incentives. In addition, bringing someone in at the ceiling means that there is absolutely no way to capture a pay raise when/ if you deserve it.

Another common negotiating area regarding the salary area is to discuss earlier reviews. Many companies have a structure where new employees do not get reviewed— and therefore are not eligible for salary increases—until after roughly six months to a year. This time frame can often be negotiated to a shorter one, say ninety days, which can allow you to get a raise much sooner than their norm.

Other negotiation revolves around benefits and compensation other than salary. This is often overlooked completely by job searchers, but often when salary cannot be negotiated, headway can be made on the non-salary compensation items. Don't ignore these, as they can sometimes be better than increases in straight salary.

> *…often when salary cannot be negotiated, headway can be made on the non-salary compensation items.*

Finally, the searcher must be aware when discussions are complete. It will be common for organizations to counter-offer your requests, but this isn't an indication that negotiations are complete. Keep the conversation in the context of "Can we talk about…" As long as the response is "Yes," negotiations and counter-offers can continue, but when the answer is "No," negotiations are most likely over and you will be at the decision crossroads. If the package isn't there, escape graciously and move on to the next opportunity.

Negotiating Salary

It is here that "Can we talk about..." gets put into play.

For example, let's suppose you were making $80,000 and learned the range for your new job is $75,000 to $95,000. You believe you are worth $85,000. Ask the magic question, "Can we talk about salary?"

If offered $81,000, you could suggest $89,000. You may reinforce your interest and worth by saying: "I really want to work for you because the position is an excellent one, and I know I can produce results for you. Given my experience and my track record, I feel I am worth $89,000." Yes, it's more than your "expected" number, but still within their range. By going higher, it also gives the employer the opportunity to raise their initial offer and for you to come down in the hope that the salary will be the $85,000 you want. You may even get the unexpected benefit of the company agreeing to your $89,000 figure.

It is my general rule of thumb that you should feel confident in being able to negotiate about 15% higher than your previous salary for whatever position you are targeting. Again, it is important for you to do a little research to determine what the salary range is in the company and for similar positions in your desired geographic area.

Most searchers, however, can expect to negotiate up to about 80% of the total available range for that position. I have known people to push the envelope and negotiate more, but I don't recommend it, as I've seen that while those that push harder do sometimes get the extra money, it often causes major difficulties later.

Money Beyond Salary

A mid-level professional who I'll call John received a job offer, but wasn't going to negotiate. He really wanted to work for the organization he had targeted. In addition, the industry in question had a reputation for not negotiating.

I encouraged him to give it a try, since he felt that the offer was about $10,000 low. He really had little to lose except that money. He followed my instructions and they came back with a statement about he was already above the midpoint and would be making more than his colleagues. They declined.

The next strategy was for John to suggest that he was interested in the position if they could only agree on compensation. He asked if they would consider a signing bonus. The hiring person asked what it would take to have him across the desk come Monday morning. John responded, "a check for $10,000." The hiring manager countered with $8,000. John accepted.

The hiring manager promptly wrote out a check for that amount. He slid it across the table, saying "Congratulations. We'll see you Monday morning."

Negotiating Much More

People think most negotiating has only to do with salary discussions; while salary may be the predominant item on the list, there are many other things that are worthy of negotiation. I have put these in somewhat what I would consider a priority in terms of short and long term cash impact to your personal bottom line.

- Signing bonus—Quick, up-front money that is not viewed as part of the salary package, but can be banked in an accrual account where it can grow. This money often comes from another financial bucket and usually has a lot of flexibility. This is one of the most common money negotiations that help to dodge the salary issue.

- Performance bonuses—Negotiating this item can make the difference of thousands of dollars at the end of the quarter and year.

- Stock options—Some companies offer stock and other types of financial securities options to employees, depending on their level. Often, the amount and breadth of such options and in some cases even the time frame of eligibility, is negotiable. This area is especially powerful if a company is expecting funding injections, balloon growth, splits, and so on.

- Relocation Expenses—If the new position requires a move, there is often flexibility regarding the related expenses. Relocation can cost in the tens of thousands under certain circumstances. Some companies help a lot here, others don't. Packages range from no reimbursement whatsoever to the company paying for everything, including purchase of your old house while you settle in to a new one. Flights back and forth, hotel rooms, mortgage fees, mileage, car rentals, meals, new club fees, and so on are all things to think about when it comes to relocation.
  Some companies even have entire relocation service departments who handle all the details for such large activities. The onus is on you to negotiate the most beneficial package so it doesn't fall on your shoulders. Note that many companies that do pay relocation expenses will do so only if the move is over a certain distance and the move is required for the job.

- Educational Assistance—In today's professional work environment, it is essential for the professional to maintain a steady diet of learning. Many companies realize that keeping their employees competitive through education is an edge they can't afford to miss, so you can negotiate a variety of seminars, certification, and full degree programs that have the potential to benefit overall performance and competency. Often such programs are expensive and if you negotiate these as part of the package you can save yourself a significant amount.

- Transportation—Negotiating items like a company car, automobile expenses, public transportation passes, and various kinds of expense accounts can save you a lot of money over time. Many of these have become much more important since the turn of the century due to the significant increases in fuel expenses and traffic congestion in densely populated areas.

- Professional membership and activities—For many professionals clubs, fraternities, and other groups is where they find their network action. Again, having to take it out of your pocket is costly. Negotiating these items can get you a double positive.

- Title—Many times perceived position represents power and can equate to eventual big dollars in the longer run. In many instances, people have negotiated a specific title for their professional advancement. This can be especially important when deciding whether to go the management route or the individual contributor route.

- Job description—Careful crafting of your specific job description or some of its details can be important. You are only going to get one shot at this, but negotiating a favorable job description that has *more* of what you want to be doing in a job usually equates to personal

It's Not Always About Money

One high level professional I worked with—let's call him Frank—illustrated excellence in negotiating when it wasn't about the money at all.

In this case, it was about the job description. He had received an offer for a position he'd really wanted, but as his coach I noted that the list of duties was heavily lopsided in terms of administrative activities—to the tune of 4-to-1—which was not using his transferable skills any where near his potential.

I encouraged him to contact the hiring manager and discuss this. Reluctantly, he did what I suggested and found the hiring manager agreed it was in both their interests to focus on Frank's passions. The manager re-allocated some of the administrative side out and Frank was so successful due to the changes that within a year he had received a significant promotion and nearly doubled his salary.

performance, which soon equates to recognition and promotions in the short run, which, of course, gets back to more salary. I have known many people who've negotiated a "best fit" scenario for what they will actually do once they are in the position.

- Starting date—This one is sometimes more of convenience, but often it is necessary to negotiate this due to other obligations, tasks to finalize with your current employer, or vacations and other plans that could interfere with initial performance expectations. By setting time to "wrap things up" you can keep a good professional image at the company where you are leaving. Something else that can be negotiated are circumstances such as individuals have already planned trips or other events that have fallen within new start times. First good impressions are important, but one can negotiate these issues away so that candidate and company start off on the right foot.

- Vacations—It is common for companies to have a structure for vacation and holiday eligibility. Many times a person coming from one organization has earned a number of weeks of vacation, but in the new company they may be confronted with a complete new start and under the new company's policy may not be eligible for any time at all for a whole year. However, for many professionals it is important to avoid going backwards. Many times this is negotiable. I've known many instances where people have negotiated a total crossover transition where they have lost nothing in this regard.

- Insurance, medical, and retirement benefits—There may not be too many instances for this to be negotiated, but where you can, it's a good thing. Again, avoiding out of pocket expenses is to your advantage.

It is unlikely all of the above items are negotiable in a single situation. Make sure to mention *all* the options you wish to negotiate at the same time. Avoid discussing them one at a time so the company does not feel they are being unduly asked for too many concessions.

The Cost of Not Negotiating

A perspective that very few people consider when they think about negotiating or *not* negotiating is the long-term impact of leaving any money on the table. This is worse than most people think. The same laws of compounding that apply to retirement savings apply to salary, except this is money that you get to take away *now*. One or two dollars per hour or a few thousand dollars a year can translate to a difference in salary of tens of thousands of dollars by the time you retire. Can you afford to lose this much money simply because you are shy about "asking" for more money or are concerned about the offer being rescinded due to negotiation confrontation?

In the film *Jerry Maguire*, the character of Rod Tidwell demands, "Show me the money!" While this negotiation strategy probably won't work outside of professional sports or the movies—and I strongly recommend against trying—the sentiment behind it bears some discussion.

If you think not negotiating for an additional couple of thousand dollars won't mean much over the long term, think again. I'm going to show you the money... the money you'll miss out on if you don't negotiate.

Let's assume for a minute that you're 40 years old, and in the running for a job. They offer you $81,000 and you would like to get $85,000. Let's also assume that each subsequent year, you get a 4% salary increase and that you continue to work until you're 70 years old.

The chart in Figure 21 compares the salaries over that 30 year period using those assumptions. The white bars show your salary over time if you start at $81,000, the black bars indicate the salary growth if you started at $85,000.

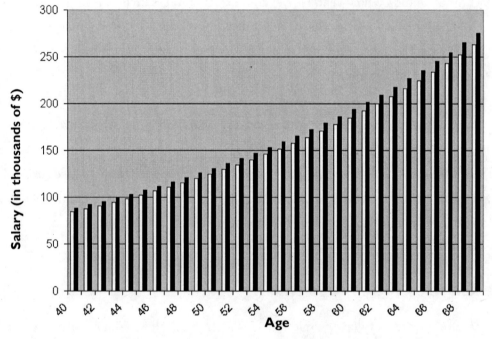

Figure 21: Salary Growth Comparison—Linear

As you can see, while salary steadily grows, the difference grows as well. By age seventy, the person who took the job for $81,000 would be making $262,715 per year. Not too shabby. However, the person who took the job for $85,000 would be making $275,688 per year.

What started out as a $4,000 difference in the first year grows to difference of almost $13,000 *per year* after 30 years. See Figure 22.

If that isn't enough, consider this: Over that 30 year period, $237,313.34 could be lost. Nearly a quarter of a million dollars over the course of a career. And all of that can be avoided by simply asking, "Can we talk about..."

If you think that not negotiating for an additional couple of thousand dollars won't mean much over the long term, think again.

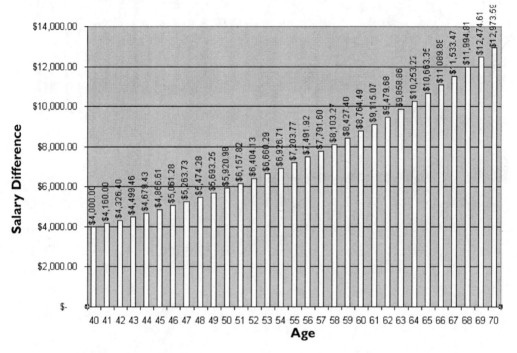

Figure 22: Salary Difference, by age, based on 4% Annual Increase

Just to drive the point home, let's take a slightly different look at the same situation. We'll start with the same initial assumptions, but we'll also assume that every five years, our job seeker moves to a new company, and each time negotiates the best deal he can get: a 15% raise over his current salary.

This time, as you can see in Figure 23, annual salary tops out over $480,000 a year in each case, but once again, the difference between taking $81,000 and $85,000 has a huge impact over the course of the career. Even with good negotiation skills later, leaving money on the table early can negatively impact your salary over the long haul.

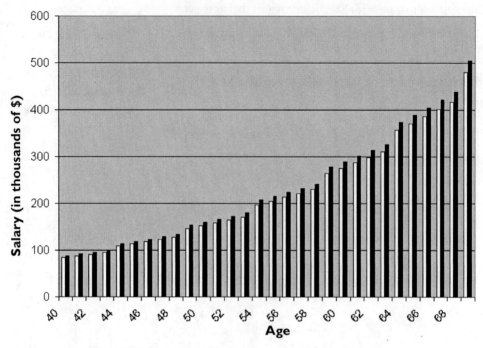

Figure 23: Salary Growth With 10% raise each five years

In this case, the difference during the first year is the same $4,000. However, in this scenario, by age 70, the difference per year has grown to over $23,000. The total left on the table over the course of the career in this case is nearly $335,000. See Figure 24.

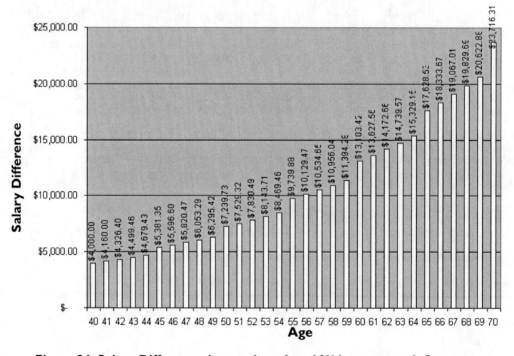

Figure 24: Salary Difference, by age, based on 10% increase each five years

Of course, these are just simple examples. As your experience, skills, and goals change, you may be in line for much better increases. As you move into higher levels of responsibility, the ranges will rise accordingly, but the point remains the same: by negotiating well, you can avoid leaving much by way of salary on the table.

Accepting the Offer

Once the negotiating has ended it is critical to request that the final deal be put into writing once more. Most organizations will not balk at the request. It is very important for you to have a chance to read and digest what has been discussed and the organization owes it to the new employee to know that promises said are promises kept by being in writing. A good rule of thumb is to take a day or two—no more—before accepting the deal.

Process Quality Assurance

Process Metrics and Quality

I believe my method integrates many techniques that make it unique. I believe, since you've read all this way, that you agree. This chapter covers one particular aspect of my method that I think truly makes it stand out above the rest.

As you might expect, I've spoken with many career counselors during the years I've been consulting and coaching. But in that time, I've never heard a single career counselor—besides me—who indicated that they coach some form of quality assurance surrounding their client's search campaigns.

I don't understand this. Your search, like any business project, needs to be measured. If you can't measure the process, how in the world are you going to be able to manage it? And if *you're* not managing it, who's running the ship? So, some way to measure quality and implement changes as needed during the campaign is a completely necessary part of a successful job search. The quality process is the primary focus of this chapter.

Don't underestimate the quality aspect. The quality assurance activities that I recommend are a big reason why my method generally results in obtaining a new job in roughly half the time of typical searches.

Take a moment to think about the typical search. Most people do not take the time—and even if they did they may not even be able—to determine if anything is wrong with their process. It follows, then, that they are unable to make any appropriate corrections. Instead, they complain that they can't figure out why no one is calling and keep sending out the same résumés and doing the same things, all the while hoping for a change in their "luck."

While luck might play a role in most other campaign searches, I'd much rather go with statistical probability and calculated observations that have the greatest potential to yield results.

When you can analyze what is and isn't working in your campaign, you will be able to make critical adjustments. Those adjustments can easily make all the difference around whether you have a successful outcome or not.

Throughout the text I've mentioned numerous benchmarks and measurable key indicators to be implemented and examined during your search campaign. We'll review some of those in this chapter as well as introducing some new concepts.

All the Process All the Time

The very first aspect of quality assurance in your search process is to be disciplined about being sure that you are using *all* of the processes described in the book throughout your campaign. Nothing impedes a successful outcome more than doing only some of the activities some of the time. You cannot skip activities, you cannot short circuit any part of the process, and you cannot let yourself slide into bouts of inactivity when things get tough.

Realize that there will be times in your search when little seems to be happening. While the quality assurance piece is excellent for checking to be sure that everything is working as it should, there are times during the search when nothing is wrong, it's just dead time. You must— absolutely must—keep your personal momentum going. Keep finding targets and keep sending marketing materials during those periods.

QC vs. QA

Very often in conversation, the terms Quality Control (QC) and Quality Assurance (QA) are used interchangeably. While they are similar, they are not the same.

QC describes any activity that examines products to determine if they meet their specifications. QA, on the other hand, includes any activity that tries to ensure that the necessary quality level is achieved. QC is meant to uncover defects, while QA is used to avoid them in the first place. Looked at another way, anything that is done after the work is substantially complete is QC, as opposed to QA activities which are done before the product is complete.

So, if we consider a successful job search the product in our scenario, you realize that the quality checks that we need to perform take place before the process is complete, and are, therefore, QA.

If you do a good job of "checking in" on your process and making sure that it's moving as described above then you'll be fine. Realize that it takes very little "slippage" for things to go back to the way they were before, with similar results. I cannot tell you how many times I've heard people say "this stuff doesn't work." Naturally, as soon as I asked them to show me the résumés they were supposed to keep track of and show me their list of network contacts that were supposed to be increasing, it didn't take any effort at all to see what didn't work.

In short, what you must realize is that quality assurance is not simply something that you can implement and it will suddenly take on a life of its own. You as the searcher must diligently examine and re-examine all your efforts all through this process. It is far too easy to let your guard down and then find yourself slipping back into old ineffective habits. For those who've persevered and maintained good records, the rewards have been astonishing.

Quality Assurance and Job Targets

Nearly every job searcher sends only one résumé in response to an advertisement. This is normal and appealingly typical. One of the many ways of distinguishing yourself from your competition and while doing so also implement a great quality assurance element, is to buck that trend and send multiple résumés.

It is the rare person who understands that multiple résumés are a more effective way to gain "exposure" in an organization. We determined right from the start in Chapter 1 that an ineffective method of job searching is to "paper the world with résumés." I submit to you that it is much more effective if you can "paper the *target organization* with résumés."

My suggestion is to make sure you get the most coverage in any given target company by using what I refer to as the "five résumé marketing blitz." This method ensures that you get at least five résumés into various contacts at the company, and if you're really doing your homework, you may be able to get even more. By its nature, it assures that you will get much more exposure than the average candidate who typically only sends a single copy of their résumé to a given company.

QA to the Rescue

I once had one client who was 8 weeks into his search. He was landing interviews, but he told me his gut said he should be getting more. Further, he clearly felt he needed more if he was to meet his target timeline. I agreed with both points.

Upon further investigation I determined that he'd only sent out about 20 targeted résumés, getting two interviews for his effort. I reminded him of the rule-of-thumb formula where a number of target résumés results in a certain number of interviews. A light bulb went off for him and he immediately stepped up his target résumé pace. In no time he was getting more interviews, met his deadline and got the offer he was looking for.

Using the QA metrics filter to see where his process was going off track—and then adjusting accordingly—got the desired result.

1. Respond to the ad with the usual electronic Internet résumé, which will end up in HR.

2. Send a hard copy of the résumé via snail mail to the company—which will also end up in HR—but as a more attractive-looking visual reinforcement.

Note that there may be occasions when you won't be able to do this. For example, you may run into situations where the company has specific instructions not to send a paper copy. There may also be situations, especially when responding to job listings from newspapers or online sites, where only a web site address is provided or the company has posted a "Company Confidential" ad and you are unable to determine their address to send the second copy. Fear not. The steps below will still ensure you are getting greater exposure than the competition.

3. Use network contacts to find out who the hiring person is and send them a private copy.

4. Use any means possible to obtain the name of the CEO, president, or whoever runs the target company or facility and specifically send them a résumé. Make sure you do *not* tell them you've sent other copies to other individuals in the company.

5. The target of the last résumé—and if you're good, the last two or more—comes from effective resource development. Once you have established that there is an open position in an organization, contact people you know and tell them that you have submitted your résumé to a target organization and that you need help in researching the company "before they call you in for an interview." The standard Resource Development questions, "What do you know about this organization?" and "who do you know who might know something about this organization?" can easily produce one or two resources.

Meanwhile, contact the individuals inside the target company from the perspective of "… a friend of yours <name> mentioned that there may be an opportunity there in the near future (even if the job is already open and been posted) and they suggested that you might be willing to forward this information to them." The "information" you are referring to is, of course, the résumé. At the same time ask them if they'd mind having a quick chat with you to tell you about the organization they work for. This is a great tool for building valuable rapport).

This process can be a very potent tool in gaining leverage in the target organization that few people ever have. You can easily go from being only one of many to being recognized as being one of very few showing enthusiasm and interest in the organization. This is a huge advantage over your competition and demonstrates an enormous amount of process quality assurance.

Another way of distinguishing yourself from your competition and implementing another quality assurance element is to always follow up after sending your materials. About a week after sending your information, call the target organization and ask the person involved in the process if they can tell you where they are in the selection process. You should also mention to them that you sent a résumé and reiterate to them that you are very interested in the position and their organization. Finish with saying you very much look forward to having a conversation with them about how you can make an immediate contribution.

Quality Assurance and Marketing Instruments

Statistics have shown that job searchers tend to take the easiest way out when it comes to cover letters and résumés, because the alternative is "so much work." This is unfortunate because the loss of quality with regard to effective cover letters and résumés is significant when people get even a little bit complacent and try to send résumés with little or no tailoring to the target position.

In Chapter 9 and Chapter 10 I discussed how the tailoring process is critical to an effective search method and a successful outcome. Take great care in arranging the cover letter and the résumé to very specifically reflect your talents as they relate to the needs of the organization. It is imperative to engage in the principle of my 80/100% rule. Only send targeted résumés to positions where you have roughly 80%

Another way of distinguishing yourself from your competition... is to always follow up after sending your materials.

or more of *all* the criteria for the position requirements and 100% of the critical needs as mandated by the ad. Such critical things might be a completed degree, thorough knowledge of a particular software, or other such items. You can gain a free pass to the 80% part if they say things like, "exposure to," "preferred," or words like "a plus."

Using these rules you can expect that for every 10-15 "targeted" résumés you will obtain at least one interview. Many people can do better than that, but statistically, this ratio holds true. This process provides you much more control than aimlessly sending résumés out but not knowing if or when you might get some kind of return on your investment (ROI).

If the above formula does *not* have the stated results, then you may not be targeting effectively or there may be a typo or some other detail that you overlooked. This has been the case in every single instance where someone I was working with was not getting the desired result. Once the damage was repaired things get back on track.

Don't overlook that time is a factor. In other words, if you sent out the 15th résumé this week, you can't necessarily expect a call tomorrow. Many companies often take up to four weeks to respond to résumés they have—this can result in the "dead time" I referred to earlier. Having said that, when I note that a person has gotten that far into the search pipeline without a result, I still suggest checking the details of the résumé and cover letter anyway rather than waiting the entire month and possibly sabotaging another five to ten submissions due to an error.

Should you discover an error in your materials, there is some possible recourse. I do suggest that you re-submit your cover letters and résumés with language indicating that you are sending a "revised" version for their consideration. This is better than just assuming that your "damaged" version has been found out and thrown away.

Quality Assurance and Your Interviews

Quality assurance at interviews is more challenging and demanding. Most quality breakdowns occur when people forget the answers they worked so hard to think about, or fail to prepare in the manner that we discussed. Another huge area where quality suffers is when the searcher didn't get the offer.

Untold numbers of individuals make various mistakes regarding the follow-up process, such as follow-up calls to discover how the selection process is going, or the most important follow-up: sending thank-you cards to each and every person you met for an interview.

Typically only a very small number of people will actually follow the suggestion to make a call to the company to try to gain more information.

QA and Time Frames

A recent success story involves a woman who was suspicious about the potential success of her search in a compressed time frame. "Will this get me a job within a few weeks?" she asked. My response was that it mostly depends on the diligence and attentiveness of the searcher, but that I expected it would.

She went along for a few weeks without much happening besides sending out résumés, developing resources, and having network discussions. However, she was diligent about following the process.

Six weeks after her launch she was rewarded with two offers on the same day, a full month earlier than her deadline target. She'd needed to be aggressive to meet her deadline and I'd informed her of that. And the results were there. Proof positive that the quality assurance element is critical to a desired search project outcome.

Most people take the "tail between the legs" approach and are so upset about not being selected they fail to ask:

- "How I could have been more effective?"
- "Would the company consider me for other opportunities in the future?"
- "Could you point me to another organization that might be able to use my skills?"

While you might come away with nothing as a result, in the process you come across in an incredibly professional manner and you may actually gain some valuable information and possibly another shot at a position.

Quality Assurance and Your Action Plan

Of all the places where quality assurance takes a hit, the action plan suffers the greatest damage. My experience has shown that searchers tend *not* to truly incorporate the many aspects of the search process of which they are capable. Again, it is easier to tackle the most visible jobs on the Internet and zip off résumés to known jobs. This is not only dangerous, but it makes for a much longer and—in many instances—much more difficult search. That area is where your greatest competition is. Why in the world would you subject yourself to that on a regular basis? Allocate your time accordingly and stick to the plan as it is most effective for you. Use all the ways to access good positions, all the time within any given week.

The amount of detail required in an effective search process is exactly where the quality assurance comes into play. Missed details usually result in missed opportunities. The worst part is you'll never know when or where you missed something and what the impact of that missed detail was. That is why it is critical to continually return to analyze your methods and make sure that you are always making efforts to hit all the details. You will, however, know when it's all done correctly. The process flows like a well-oiled machine and in a short period of time you'll be getting job offers.

Weekly Action Form

A great QA tool to help you be fully effective in your search is the implementation of the Weekly Action Form, shown in Figure 25. This helps job searchers maintain quality in the search, provides measurability of the project and instills motivation for helping job searchers obtain their goals in the search campaign process. As the name suggests, this form should be filled out weekly and maintained in a "results" folder for use in future campaigns.

WEEKLY ACTION FORM

NAME _____   WEEK ENDING _____

1. **Total number of hours committed to job search activities this past week.**_____
   (This total should include network time, research, resume tailoring, etc.)

2. **Total number of resumes sent out.**   **(Ad Letters)**   _____

   (Recruiter Letters)   _____

   (Blind Letters)   _____

   (Contact Letters)   _____

   (Other Letters)_____

   TOTAL Letters   _____

3. **Total number of NEW network contacts made this week.**   _____

4. **Total number of interviews this week including informational.**   _____

5. **Additions to company HOT TARGET list (from any source) this week.**

   _____

   _____

6. **New OPPORTUNITY additions to target company list this week.**

   _____

7. List at least *1 BIG WIN* (job search accomplishment) and (3) small *WINS* for this past week.
   1 BIG WIN _____

   3 SMALL WINS _____

   _____

8. **What did YOU DO to get the BIG WIN?** _____

9. **WHY was it a BIG WIN for you?** _____

10. **What single thing did you do better (regarding search) compared to last week?**

    _____

11. **What will you do to ensure a BIG WIN for next week?**

    _____

Figure 25: Weekly Action Form

Integration

Integration

The integration phase is where you put your Strategic Marketing Action Plan to work, ensuring that you pull in all of the components of the search. By integrating all the theory elements and not attempting to isolate or avoid certain parts, such as only engaging in activities that are more "fun," a person gains a significant advantage over their competition. Using all the tools at the same time and engaging in all the components as a single entity dramatically increases the potential for a successful and desirable outcome.

This is not as easy as it might initially seem. My experience has indicated that most people *think* they are engaging in all the activities they need to in order to achieve their job search goals. However, without exception, every client that had not been as successful as I knew they could be—that is, landing a position within 90 days, my typical target time frame for a successful job search—has been able to discover that, indeed, they were leaving out at least some portion of this very complex process. Knowing the information does not necessarily mean that everyone can implement the program as they are instructed. Old habits are hard to break.

I've said it many times throughout the book and I'll say it again: Integration, that is using all the tools, performing all the actions, and making all the checks, *must* happen all the time for this process to be effective. The interesting part about integration is that even though it is *so* important to the process, there isn't really much more to say about it than that. It is simply a matter of staying on top of everything and making sure that you are performing all of the activities that you need to.

Using the tools we've discussed—the Weekly Action Form, the Marketing Action Plan, and so on— ensures that you are indeed doing everything you can to integrate all of the activities.

Use the following checklist to make sure you're doing everything you need to:

❑ Continue developing resources, even if you've begun interviews. If the interviews do not bear fruit, it pays to have not fallen behind on locating new potential companies.

❑ Continually target your résumés and cover letters. Refine them as information becomes available.

❑ Each time you get a new company lead, investigate the company's website, review financial statements by obtaining a prospectus, and assemble a list of competitors. You will eliminate organizations that are not a good fit and connect with ones that are ideal.

❑ Continually perform your Quality Assurance tests on all aspects of your search as activities occur and get completed. Strive for continual improvement.

❑ Expect some periods when progress stalls, but don't let your *activity* stall. Continue performing all the items on this list. If things stall too long, re-evaluate your materials.

I recommend you look back to this checklist regularly. This will ensure you're covering all the bases and refresh your memory on the individual aspects and activities. Reread the appropriate sections of the book as needed to make sure that the information is fresh in your mind and that you are not missing any of the concepts we've discussed.

If you are studious about integrating the concepts, I **know** you will be successful.

Campaign Launch

Congratulations! You have completed the preparation and have the tools and knowledge to manage a self-marketing campaign to obtain a new job or career.

You have thoroughly assessed your work history, your current situation, and have considered and discussed potential opportunities. Throughout these phases, you have integrated information using innovative tools and strategies to differentiate you from the crowd. Now you implement the material and actions into a short-term marketing project.

Now is the time to put all of the information to work by launching your campaign. The methods assist you to organize and implement a plan to yield more results than you ever anticipated.

Self Marketing Launch Activity

You are now ready to launch your self-marketing campaign. The Marketing Action Plan is the structure to the project. You should have decided on an attainable target date for getting hired. Your campaign will focus on the following three primary activities.

- Contacting executive search firms/recruiters
- Leveraging advertisements/websites
- And most important, Resource Development

Recruiters and Job Listings

If you'll recall, statistically you won't do as well relying on recruiters and published job listings. However, it would be foolish to ignore them completely.

My recommendation for your first activity is to organize and submit letters to executive search firms and recruiters. Target these résumés to each firm's specialty as indicated by your research. Cover letters must reflect the same focus. For the most part, these are *one-shot deals.* Once mailed, you will only get a response if they have a suitable position to fill. However, you may initiate face-to-face interviews by calling them about a week after sending your materials or calling your contacts to see if any of them have used these recruiters or others. Gain leverage and practice by attending informational interviews with them.

The next step, usually the easiest, but also the least fruitful, is to focus on published ads online and in newspapers. Set up a number of search agents on Websites to receive target jobs by e-mail daily or weekly. Here, Cover Letter #1 shown in Chapter 10, "Cover Letters" becomes a powerful tool when accompanied with a tailored résumé.

Resource Development

Of the three areas where you can focus your energy, Resource Development is the most desirable and productive. Developing contacts will occupy most of your time, but it will generate

What Do You Have To Lose?

I would highly recommend that you test the process before moving into full-fledged launch. Practice your 30 Second Commercial and Resource Development process on very close friends or relatives who will not be as bothered by stumbling or other insecurity issues. Choose a company that you have no interest in working for and approach them just for the practice of getting the interview material down. These activities can help you to work through the jitters and false starts that result from an unfamiliar activity, get a feel for the process, and help you avoid making a mistake at a company where you really do want to make a good first impression.

leads within targeted organizations. Chapter 14, "Resource Development" discusses the process. You should devote 75 percent or more of your time, energy, and focus to this area. If you require a salary of $80,000 or more, spend 90 percent of your time developing contacts.

One reminder on resource lists. Remember how important the activity is. Make sure you have your list of the people you know who can assist you in your transition. Remember, include everyone. *Do not wait until you have a completed list to start your campaign.* If you do, you may find that your list is never truly completed and your campaign never gets off the ground. Simply start with whatever names you have and get them in print. Use research on companies to support the development of resource contacts. Don't use mass mailings and blind letters to companies, as they yield poor results.

You should gain useful information nearly every time you initiate a contact. Have your 30 Second Commercial prepared and know how to use the two Resource Development questions. Revisit Chapter 14 if you need to. When speaking with your contacts, don't forget to spend a little time asking people about their industry, plans for growth, direction, and potential as suggested in the "Questions You Should Ask" section of Chapter 17.

If you are worried about being nervous when starting to develop contacts over the phone, prepare a script. The script will keep you on track, allow you to practice getting your message across smoothly, and minimize your jitters.

Whenever you get a new company lead, investigate the company's website, review financial statements by obtaining a prospectus, and assemble a list of competitors. This information will prepare you to conduct a comprehensive informational interview. You will eliminate organizations that are not a good fit and connect with ones that are ideal.

> *If you are worried about being nervous when starting to develop contacts over the phone, prepare a script.*

The procedure may need to be repeated many times to reach your goals. It's worth it because getting the right job is very rewarding. Maintain continuity and focus, frequently monitor the quality of the project, execution of materials, and process, and persevere in every area of the job search. Avoid the temptation to slide back into old habits and take perceived shortcuts. Given the ups and downs of the market, expect to encounter *flat spots*, where progress stalls. When that happens, maintain self-discipline and keep focused on your goal. The activity will pick up again and your phone will start to ring.

Treat your job search with the intensity of a business project. Follow *all* the procedures and manage *all* the activities of the project and you will succeed.

Using a BIKE for a Successful Journey

One last metaphor as you move into your launch. Thanks to Lance Armstrong, many people today have taken up bicycling to keep in shape and maintain their health. You can use the metaphor of a bike to keep a career in shape and resilient as well as maintaining a healthy state of mind while you are in the search mode. A bike can help you realize a career vision that you previously may not have been able to reach. Your career BIKE is made up of Belief, Information, Knowledge, and committed Effort.

- **Belief**—You must believe that you are worthy of a better life and more financial security for yourself and your family. You must also believe that my approach will get you to where you really want to be.
- **Information**—You must gain information about what you want and why you want it for your particular situation. You must gather good intel on your target companies and job targets in order to reach your goal.

- **Knowledge**—You must have and use the knowledge I've provided about innovative techniques, effective strategic thinking and planning, as well as integration of quality into the campaign.
- **Effort**—You *absolutely* must commit to a focused effort and take planned and measurable action if you want to move forward. The best jobs do not typically fall out of the sky. You must create the vision, then manifest it through action.

> *You must create the vision, then manifest it through action.*

Wishing, hoping, and thinking about it will likely not manifest the vision you have of obtaining your goals. You must follow an action plan that is designed to keep you disciplined and focused on reaching your intended goals.

A bike is a vehicle that takes personal perseverance and effort to reach a good goal, but as you know, the end rewards can be spectacular. The same is true of your career BIKE.

It takes all four of these key attributes to get to your goal. Appropriate use of all four ensures that the trip will generally be smooth and relatively speedy. If any of the keys is missing or not fully utilized, the trip will likely be very uncomfortable. In fact, without all of the four keys being fully engaged the end goal has a high probability of not occurring at all.

Many hundreds of people with similar backgrounds to yours have made this journey before you. You can do it too, using *your* BIKE.

Implementation Checklist

Based on the activities we've discussed in previous chapters, you should have the following tools prepared and available for your launch:

- ❑ One or more résumés in a marketing-oriented format on your computer.
- ❑ One or more cover letter designs on your computer.
- ❑ A typed list of four to six references.
- ❑ A well-rehearsed 30-Second Commercial.
- ❑ An understanding of the two Resource Development Questions and how to use them.
- ❑ Practiced, positive responses to difficult interview questions.
- ❑ A typed list of questions for you to ask at interviews.
- ❑ Business cards to distribute to contacts.
- ❑ Professional-looking thank-you cards.
- ❑ A typed hot list of up to a dozen target companies on a single sheet of paper with space for taking notes.
- ❑ List of every possible contact who could help you.

Strategic Materials

In addition to the tools above, don't forget about your strategic materials. As we've mentioned, these are important items to have available on short notice.

- Reference list
- Letters of Reference
- Resource List
- Writing sample

All of these are discussed in depth in Chapter 11, "Company Lists and Other Strategic Materials". Review this material before you launch.

23

Succession Planning

The time will come when all your efforts pay off and you accept a great position. You will likely breath a sigh of relief, be very glad that the search is over, and hopefully be filled with excitement about your new job.

And that's it—at least in terms of thinking about your search.

With very few exceptions, virtually all career and job changers immediately stop the inertia of the campaign and dive headlong into full commitment to the new position. Don't misunderstand; I'm not suggesting that this commitment is wrong. However, for most individuals, the recently completed search is but the next step in a line of steps yet to come. The likelihood of you going through this process again within the next few years is very high. Rest assured, this is not because the process failed and you accepted a position that was a poor fit, but rather due to the realities of the working world.

As mentioned earlier, most professionals today will change *careers* three to five times before they retire and those numbers do *not* include the job changes within those careers. So let me pose this question to you: Are you sure you want to start from scratch the next time you have to do this?

> *Completion... is the first step toward new beginnings.*

The completion of this transition project is the first step toward a new beginning in another situation somewhere in your future. The one constant in all existence is change. This may not be good news to many of you, but you don't need a degree in quantum theory to know that it is true. They may be slow or fast, but change, irrespective of human desire, is inevitable. You do have choices, however. You can *guide* your destiny and be prepared for the future no matter what the river of life sets before you. Part of this preparation is to take some of the inertia of the job search and keep it moving even after you've gone into your new position. This will go a long way toward making the next search easier.

Evaluating the Process

In preparation for the next step—whenever that might be—I suggest that you take some time right now while the information is fresh in your mind and evaluate your experience. Whether your transition has been a lengthy one or a short one there is no doubt in my mind that the process has been rich in information and learning that could provide a significant foundation for future steps.

You have résumé records, resource lists, networking notes, interview notes, company target lists, company research information, and more. This information made it possible for you to accomplish what you have done in a very successful way. To tuck it away in a box to gather dust—or worse throw it away completely—is something I would hate to see happen and strongly recommend against. What I *would* suggest you do is take a little time and evaluate the data. Analyze what went well and what needed improving.

Interview Data

Examining the data around your interviewing results is extremely valuable. If you scored an interview for every 10-15 résumés you scored about average.

- If you did not score that well, then your résumé was not strong enough and it would be important to know why and what might need to change so that in your next transition, history does not repeat itself. Things such as lack of specific experience or lack of credentials in specific areas might have made your journey a lot more difficult. Before the next event, plan to plug these holes by getting what you need based upon the needs of the organizations you were targeting.
- If your score was better than average, then I congratulate you. But you're not off the hook. Just like the scenario above, you may have had an even easier journey if you could have presented and articulated yourself with stronger background experience and/or credentials.

Lining up the "Rights"

Even though my process discusses a good result as being an interview for every 10-15 targeted résumés sent, I must confess I've had many successful clients score an interview for every 2-5 résumés sent. Why? Because they had the *right* background experience in the *right* field and had the *right* credentials to easily meet the needs of target organizations and beat the competition. In other words, they were targeting very well.

Many of you were trying to get into fields that were right for you, but you did not have all the ammunition to compete as strongly as you could have. You may have to bite the bullet and get a degree. Even if this is the case, things could be worse: the next time you might be a lot older, have a higher position, and still have no degree. Sooner or later you will hit a wall and no amount of effective tools short of that degree will get you hired. There is no reason to repeat that history. Prepare yourself based upon this analysis portion of the project.

Resources

Take a look at your network of individuals and reflect on who was productive and who was not. Between now and the next event you should cultivate those people who've been helpful to you and continue a strong communication with them.

In addition, if you found that your network was always a challenge because it was small to start with, make the effort to improve that situation. I'm not suggesting that you become something that you're not, but your efforts in the future will be significantly easier if you have a larger, more potent network. Ignoring this situation until you do it again is asking for yet another difficult effort.

Record your Accomplishments

Another place where the analysis of the campaign results can come in very handy is to become sensitive to the fact that most people don't keep on-going records of their accomplishments. It would be very helpful to obtain hard documentation and computer copies of such things when they occur. Such items will make updating your résumé a lot easier and it will come together a lot faster than before, plus having the details available to you will help you refresh your memory of specific accomplishments that can help you during the interviewing process.

Development of More Effective Procedures

It is just as critical to analyze your campaign from the perspective of effectiveness and profitability.

Profitability?

Yes. Nearly every person I know who has undergone a career or job transition has operated out of their comfort zone, that is outside of the area where they have expertise. I really don't know anybody who ever wanted to be good at job search. So, just as in any endeavor where you're unaccustomed to performing, there has been a strong likelihood of errors occurring throughout the process. Whether you like to admit it or not, these errors have cost you time and dollars. In many instances, I've seen searchers cost themselves *thousands* of dollars.

Think about your interviews. What things did you say during the meetings that you could have avoided had you been a little more cautious? When you didn't make the cut and receive a job offer, did you call anyway and try to get valuable information such as asking "how could I have been a stronger candidate?" Make notes about those events so you do not repeat those mistakes and make damaging statements. Think about times when you didn't follow up and maybe let an opportunity slip by.

Documenting Accomplishments

As much as this analysis part seems to be about what you *did not* do well in order to avoid slip-ups in the future, it is just as important to document and remind ourselves of things we did well, too. Career and job change is one of the most challenging things a person will do in their lifetime. You have been thorough, well-planned, committed, and persevering, and I believe a person ought to take some credit for a project well done. I have found it extremely important to reward ourselves for the many things that we've learned, learned from, and successfully accomplished during the process. The way to do that is to document what occurred throughout the project.

As you went through the above exercise to determine what needed improving, you should have come across some items that worked very well and did not necessarily need enhancing. You should capture those things and document what you specifically did that caused those tasks and efforts to come out so well. This becomes great motivation for you. Most people wouldn't easily say they did a lot right concerning their job search except that they eventually got a job out of it. I believe this to be short-sighted.

Take the time to capture where, when, and how you believe you were effective in the process. Notes such as these will aid you greatly in your next search. And I think it's safe to assume there will likely be a next time. When that occurs, reviewing past searches will be an important part of the original self-assessment process that we began with. That is why I see this as a circle and the ending of this project is but the beginning of the next.

Planning the Next Steps

As a wrap-up of the full analysis of your career or job change campaign project readers would do well to capture—in writing—the next steps as they see them. As we discussed above, many people I work with come to the conclusion that at some point a more comprehensive education is needed before their next move. I strongly suggest that you do not wait too long before researching institutions to discover what is involved in that process. Don't wait until the wall is staring you in the face to begin looking.

Another thing: keep your marketing hat on. Make sure that fields and industries that you've been targeting seem to have a future in them where you can grow. Many people have been targeting various markets over the years, but markets change and some positions become obsolete in spite of our desires. I believe it is critical in the planning stages of your career plan to stay abreast of those changes and amend the plan accordingly to avoid painting yourself into a corner from which there is no escape. There is no substitute for being well-prepared for the unforeseeable.

Using All of You to Plan Your Future

In short, what I'm saying here is that you need to keep an eye on yourself and your career. I hope that I've impressed upon you the need to continually be proactive in planning your career, not to wait until circumstances force you to react. How many people do you know that have been blind-sided by a layoff or downturn in the economy?

You should always be asking yourself,

- "What do I do better than many other people?"
- "Are there employers or customers who are willing to pay for that expertise?"
- "If so, how much are they willing to pay?"

If you don't have answers to these questions at any given moment in time, you are vulnerable and that is not a place you can afford to be. Revisiting your career on a regular basis, staying actively engaged in the career management activity, and planning for the future will make it easy to stay on top.

Planning also means keeping all five senses tuned to opportunities. I've often mentioned keeping an open mind throughout the book and that is an on-going activity. In the larger scheme of things, this is an important step in planning for the journey to a much higher self plane if you so choose. It is all about the level of outcome that could be. When one evolves with the universe in the context of ones life, options are going to present themselves to you. If you are open to them, you will be there when they occur. As much as it is important to maintain focus on ones particular expertise, it is just as critical to keep a broad perspective of the greater horizon.

People who take this advice to heart will likely not be in financial or emotional difficulty no matter what happens to the rest of the world, because they are prepared and have insulated themselves from potential disaster. When professionals know what expertise they can market, how much it's worth, and how to research and persuade employers to pay for that talent, they have fully empowered themselves to move forward with their career.

Summary

Wow. We've gone through a lot in these pages. I know if you implement what you've read in a complete and integrated way, you are going to be successful. Many people would see this effort as the beginning of a very illuminating path. For others, it is a means to a better job.

I believe what I have described here is the most effective way through a very difficult process. The tools and processes have been made available to you. The philosophy of what I believe it takes to conduct a successful career or job change campaign has been discussed. You are now aware of how to successfully engage in an investigation process of determining more than how to get a job. You are able to determine what jobs to look for, in what industries they reside, how to research corporate cultures that resonate with you, what is needed to market yourself to those organizations, and be offered an excellent position.

To reach your goals, you may need to repeat the procedures described in this book a number of times, tweaking and modifying your presentation, questions, and answers along the way. But in the end, getting the "right" job is extremely rewarding. Done correctly, you will be very much in control of the process, which makes a huge difference when compared to the old way of getting a job. It will be very important for you to maintain continuity and focus, and make frequent quality checks on the materials and process execution, and above all, maintain a significant level of initiative and perseverance to each and every area as discussed.

And if you follow *all* the procedures and manage *all* the activities of the project in their appropriate priority, you will be successful and the rewards will be there. None of this is rocket science, but to get the desired result, a well-managed job search campaign plan needs to be handled with the same fervor as you would in implementing an effective retirement plan.

I have taken you through myriad concepts and ideas about how to identify and regain the career and job you deserve. It is now in your power to make your dreams come to fruition. There are literally millions of organizations in the world, with numerous positions whose tasks you would be delighted to do and even more delighted to be paid for. Your charge is to go find it. Now you know how to do it.

For my last recommendation, I'd like to suggest that you not only keep a positive frame of mind in this process, but strive to appreciate the journey along the way. This may sound unlikely, but I've found that many of my clients tell me that when they really take full advantage of the situation they sincerely find this to be a most exciting time for them. Many people have told me that, after implementing this process, it was the first time they had ever felt in control of their job search. They have also come to me and expressed that it was the first time they've ever enjoyed their search. I hope you do too. I offer my sincerest wish that you find this adventure one to embrace. Enjoy!

Appendices

Appendices

A The Career Path Indicator

This appendix contains an instrument that will assist you in your career and life planning. In it, put down information about your professional work history so that it becomes the foundation for a personal career evaluation to uncover your unique work competencies and motivations. When you have completed it, the information should provide you with many pieces of information regarding your search process.

By way of definition:

- Competencies are things that you are good at, whether or not you always enjoy the activity.
- Motivations are things that you really enjoy doing, whether or not you are really good at it.

The Professional Work History and Work Competencies /Motivations Assessment take some time to complete. I urge you to take the time. This information is critical to the development of an effective career plan and job search campaign management. The concept is to gain greater insight and obtain significant detail beyond what would typically be in a résumé.

This appendix is prepared in worksheet format so that you can record your answers.

Where have you lived?		
International travel? If so, where?		
Willing To Travel? (Check)	Yes:	No:
If Yes, Percent of travel time versus home time		
Willing To Relocate? (Check)	Yes:	No:
Relocation Preferences		

Languages	Speak	Read/Write
	☐	☐
	☐	☐
	☐	☐
	☐	☐
	☐	☐
Are you Employed?	Yes:	No:
If so, does your employer know you are looking?[a]	Yes:	No:
Is there a date at which you will end your current job?	Yes:	No:
If Yes, what is it?		
Date you want to target completion of your search and be in a new position?		
Target Geographic area.[b]		
Average hours per week you can dedicate to your search campaign.[c]		

a. This may determine if you wish to conduct a confidential search and whether you may be limited in use of network contacts.

b. Choose a reasonable target area. Extreme answers like "Anywhere" or "within two miles of my home" are unrealistic.

c. Consider that 15-20 hours is considered a full time search.

Career Path Indicator

Current evidence suggests that most of us working today will make as many as three to five career changes over the course of our working lives—not job changes, but full blown career shifts. Making informed decisions about career direction and the steps within that journey can smooth out the trip. Whether you are encountering a career change, a job change, or both, assessing what is important and motivates you can be valuable information to have. It can be used to determine your next step and more importantly help you to establish a real career plan. This could be crucial in helping you to avoid unplanned and often difficult career/job moves.

The Career Path Indicator asks you to think about the things that you truly liked about your previous jobs and clarify *new* passions you may have recently identified. Together these factors can help you focus on a variety of functions that could be possible job search targets and help you develop a comprehensive career path.

It is important to note that this instrument should not be used to identify a single job. Being that specific is too self-limiting. I suggest that if people have first identified these core attributes and look at a broader, more functional job/career view and identify a preferred work environment, then they will be much closer to finding the kinds of jobs they would like to be in and feel more like they are in control of their own destiny.

Section I: Competencies

Which of these competencies (things you are really good at) are most important to you to include in any job you might enjoy? Consider that these competencies are the kind of things that if they were a major component of the job you might want to perform it for the rest of your working career. Indicate your preference by checking the box to the left of the particular competencies that are most important to you. Try to limit yourself to ten or so.

☐	INVENTIVE	Enjoy the development of ideas through the creative process.
☐	COMPETITIVE	Enjoy winning. Being first to attain goals.
☐	NURTURER	Strong skill set to help others.
☐	MANAGING	Being in charge, supervising others, controlling.
☐	PLANNING	Enjoy setting up goals and implementing them.
☐	ORGANIZING	Very good at putting things in order.
☐	ACHIEVEMENT	Enjoy reaching goals and attaining benchmarks.
☐	INDEPENDENT	Excellent at working alone.
☐	LEADING	Demonstrating through action, how to do things.
☐	SOCIAL RESPONSIBILITY	Taking part in community action projects.
☐	TEAM BUILDING	Excellent at working with teams and groups.
☐	CHANGE	Enjoy doing different things, variety.
☐	INVESTIGATING	Searching for the right answer.

☐	STRATEGIZING	Making 3-5 year plans and making it happen.
☐	INFLUENCING	Enjoy convincing others of your ideas or concepts.
☐	DESIGNING	Creating new ideas, concepts, inventing, conceiving.
☐	HANDS ON	Enjoy working with your hands or getting physically involved in the project.
☐	ANALYTICAL	Figuring out what's wrong and possibly suggesting solutions.
☐	ARTISTIC	Sculpting, painting, drawing, designing.
☐	FACTS AND FIGURES	Like numbers, statistics, finance, figuring, inventory.
☐	ADVISING	Counseling, coaching, teaching others.
☐	BUILDING	Putting things together, making things, assembling.
☐	MEASURING	Calculating, testing, and inspecting things.
☐	NEGOTIATING	Making deals, selling, mediation.
☐	FIXING THINGS	Making things work again,
☐	GARDENING	Like growing things, plants, vegetables, flowers, creative landscaping.
☐	PROBLEM SOLVING	Assessing, figuring things out, troubleshooting.
☐	PERFORMING	Presenting things, acting in front of groups, speaking.
☐	BUILDING RELATIONSHIPS	Building trust, conflict resolution ability.
☐	MARKETING	Getting a product, concept, or service to market.
☐	OTHERS (List)	

Now, refer to the ranking sheet on the next page.

Section I Ranking Sheet

List all of the motivations you have identified, then rank them. This component of the Career Path Indicator is sometimes the most challenging because it asks you to prioritize what is most important to you. Pay particular attention to any competency you rate in the top five. Working for a company or being in a position that asks you to sacrifice any of these will likely cause you significant stress and misery. Use each rank number only once. Use scrap paper, if necessary, to work the numbers out.

Competency	Rank[a]

a.Use each ranking only once.

Transfer your top five competencies to the "Data Roll-up" section.

Section II: Motivations

What factors motivate you the most? Think of the activities that interest you so much that if your job consisted mainly of them you could be happy working at it for the rest of your working career. In the table on the next page, check the motivational factors that are most important to you.

☐	CHALLENGE	Enjoy performing beyond your average skill level.
☐	CONCEPTUALIZE	Enjoy coming up with new ideas.
☐	MOBILITY	Like to get up and get around, see new places.
☐	HELPING OTHERS	Help others attain a better quality of life.
☐	ENVIRONMENT	Need to work in the outdoors.
☐	CAREGIVER	Desire to serve others.
☐	STRATEGIZING	Motivated by planning and setting goals.
☐	ORGANIZING	Need to coordinate and correlate things.
☐	AUTONOMOUS	Need to be your own boss or person.
☐	ACTIVIST	Engaged in socially responsible projects.
☐	MEASURING	Calculating, testing, inspecting.
☐	TRANSITION	Seeks out opportunities to do different things.
☐	PHYSICAL ACTIVITY	Prefers active, physically demanding work.
☐	TROUBLE SHOOTING	Likes challenge of problems no one else can solve.
☐	ANALYTICAL	Enjoy analyzing information, data, or numbers. -or- Figure out what's wrong and fix it.
☐	SOCIALIZATION	Love working with/in groups or teams.
☐	PERFORMING	Always like expressing the self through music/acting/ speaking/presenting.
☐	PERSUASIVE	Enjoy influencing and convincing others.
☐	HANDS ON	Needs to be involved, tinker, build, operate.
☐	ARTISTIC/ CREATIVE	Must express self by writing, painting, designing.
☐	PROJECT MANAGMENT	Being responsible for projects but few or no people.
☐	MANAGMENT	Implementing policy. Being in charge of people. Hiring and firing.
☐	TRAINING/TEACHING	Helping others learn new information, techniques, methods.
☐	LEARNING	Always want to learn new things.
☐	CONFLICT RESOLUTION	Enjoy negotiating, mediating, resolving conflicts.
☐	OTHERS (List)	

Section II Ranking Sheet

List all of the motivations you have identified, then rank them as you did your competencies. Again, pay attention to any motivation you rate in the top five. When these activities are missing from your job you may feel de-motivated, bored, or listless. Use each rank number only once. Use scrap paper, if necessary, to work the numbers out.

Core Motivations	Rank[a]

a.Use each ranking only once.

Transfer your top five motivations to the "Data Roll-up" section.

Section III: Work Style and Environment

Most people can find "a job." Finding the *right* job—or even one that fits into a real career plan—requires more in-depth knowledge of the self. I find that most people find it very useful to identify their work style. This section examines your preferences regarding the kind of work style and work environment that is best for you.

Work Style

		Do you identify yourself as a person who is a (Score 1=most like; 2=Somewhat like; 3=Not at all like you)	
	Beginning Person	Prefer to start new activities and projects	
	Middle Person	Prefer maintaining activities and projects already in progress; like making projects run like "a well-oiled machine"	
	End Person	Prefer to complete things, clean up, etc.	
	My most preferred work style is: (#1) _____		

Transfer your #1 choice to the "Data Roll-up" section.

Peak Work Time

		Do you identify yourself as a person who is a (Score 1=most like; 2=Very much like; 3=Not very much like; 4=Not at all like you)	
	Morning Person	Does best work early in the morning, for example 5AM to 9AM.	
	Day Person	Straight "nine to fiver."	
	Flex Person	Flex-time person. Come and go when you want to. Don't care for schedules.	
	Night Person	Often does best work after midnight.	
	My most preferred work time is: (#1) _____		

Transfer your #1 choice to the "Data Roll-up" section.

Management Approach

	Your preferred management approach is:	
	(Rate as 1=most preferred approach through 6=least preferred approach.)	
No Approach		I have no desire to be in management at this time.
	Individual Contributor Type I	No employee responsibility; no profit and loss (P&L) responsibility, Usually given the project to implement. Jobs tend to be loner oriented, for example computer programmers, project managers, but may work on or with teams. Pay may be up to mid $60K mark. Answer to higher level managers.
	Individual Contributor Type II	One or few employee responsibilities; no profit and loss (P&L) responsibility; may have budget responsibility. Usually given the task to design and implement the project. Jobs also tend to be loner oriented, for example project managers, but may work on or with teams. Pay to low $80K. Answer to higher level managers.
	Line Management	Some employee responsibility; little to some profit and loss (P&L) responsibility; may be in charge of smaller groups of individuals—up to approximately 30. Responsible for employee development, employee evaluations. Pay to mid $70K range. Answers to higher authority on line items in budgets.
	Mid-Management	Some employee responsibility; some profit and loss (P&L) responsibility; usually in charge of larger groups of individuals—up to approximately 100. Responsible for employee development, employee evaluations. Pay to $100K range. Answers to higher authority on P&L line items.
	Staff Management	Full employee responsibility; profit and loss (P&L) responsibility; has managers answering to him/her. Pay usually $100K and above. Answers to V.P.
My most preferred management approach is: (#1) _____		

Transfer your #1 choice to the "Data Roll-up" section.

Company/Organization Type and Size

	Your preferred organization type and size is:	
	(Rate as 1=most preferred through 6=least preferred.)	
For Profit Companies/Organizations		
	Large Companies	Organizations with thousands of people. Sometimes pays better, has more comprehensive benefits. Often seems like a city unto itself. Highly structured, hierarchy—everybody knows their place, uses clock management.
	Medium-sized Companies	Organizations with smaller populations, may only have 1 or 2 facilities, doesn't have feel of "just a number" yet provides a measure of security.
	Small Companies	Has a more intimate culture, most everybody knows everybody else. Is generally established and often takes on characteristics of "family" owned. Often has little structure—matrix, quantum, team environment, flexible, open book, everyone invested.
	Start-up Companies	For the more dynamic at heart. Little stability, but high energy. Often has few, if any, benefits.

Non-Profit Companies/Organizations	
Government	
Private Sector	
My most preferred organization type and size is: (#1) _____	

Transfer your #1 choice to the "Data Roll-up" section.

Other Considerations

All companies have a culture – Some have strict lines of protocol while others have little or no protocols. Here are some things to think about as you move forward:

Other Considerations (Underline or circle all that apply most, unless otherwise specified.)			
Clothing/Dress	Casual	Business Casual	Professional
Culture	Open Door	Strong Autonomy	Hands On	Hands Off
	Mentorship	Independent Work	Team Style	Other
	If "Other" Specify:		
Gender Mix	Half/Half	More Women	More Men
Pace of the business	Very Fast	Fast	Moderate	Slow
Any Problem Flying?	Yes	No	Not fond of it
Your number one strength			
Your number one area that you believe needs development			
What else do you think would be important to know?			

Transfer all key factors from this section to the "Data Roll-up" section.

Data Roll-up

Top 5 Competencies In Priority Order		Top 5 Motivational Activities In Priority Order	
1.		1.	
2.		2.	
3.		3.	
4.		4.	
5.		5.	
Preferred Work Style			
Peak Work Time			
Management Approach			
Company Size and Type			
Clothing/Dress			
Culture			
Gender Mix			
Pace of the Business			
Any Problem Flying?			
Number 1 Strength			
Number 1 Area Needed Development			
What else would be important to know?			

Work History Documentation

Please fill out the following details about your work history. Start with your current or latest position. Once complete, you should be able to transfer the information to your Self-Marketing Instrument (Résumé) almost verbatim.

Remember, you typically do not need to go back more than 15 years for your work history.

Company Name	
Company Location (City and State)	

Date of Employment (Months not needed)	From:	To:

Job Title	

Pay range or other compensation (Salary)	

Specific Accomplishments
(Provide as much detail as you can.)

What did you like the most about the position?

What did you like least about the position?

Company Name	

Company Location (City and State)	

Date of Employment (Months not needed)	From:	To:

Job Title	

Pay range or other compensation (Salary)	

Specific Accomplishments
(Provide as much detail as you can.)

What did you like the most about the position?

What did you like least about the position?

Company Name	
Company Location (City and State)	

Date of Employment (Months not needed)	From:	To:

Job Title	

Pay range or other compensation (Salary)	

Specific Accomplishments
(Provide as much detail as you can.)

What did you like the most about the position?

What did you like least about the position?

Company Name	
Company Location (City and State)	

Date of Employment (Months not needed)	From:	To:

Job Title	

Pay range or other compensation (Salary)	

Specific Accomplishments
(Provide as much detail as you can.)

What did you like the most about the position?

What did you like least about the position?

Company Name	

Company Location (City and State)	

Date of Employment (Months not needed)	From:	To:

Job Title	

Pay range or other compensation (Salary)	

Specific Accomplishments
(Provide as much detail as you can.)

What did you like the most about the position?

What did you like least about the position?

Company Name	
Company Location (City and State)	

Date of Employment (Months not needed)	From:	To:

Job Title	

Pay range or other compensation (Salary)	

Specific Accomplishments
(Provide as much detail as you can.)

What did you like the most about the position?

What did you like least about the position?

Education/ Training/ Qualifications

Degree/Year	
School/University	
Major	

Extracurricular School Activities

Honors/Awards Received
Include dates.

Cite any current or past licenses or certificates, including years

Professional organizations or memberships
List past and current memberships. Include dates and offices held.

List your published books or articles

Industry List

Table 1: Industry and Company Options (Sheet 1 of 4)

Industry	Company Types
ADVERTISING/PR	Advertising Agencies
ASSOCIATIONS	Athletic and Sports Chambers of Commerce Cultural Eco Technology Educational Ethnic Fraternal Health and Medical Government Industrial and Manufacturing Public Affairs Religious Organizations Social Service Technical
ATHLETIC	Agents Coaching Olympics Special Olympics Sports medicine Professional Team Sports Management Teaching/ Training
BANKING	Commercial Banks Cooperative Banks Credit Card Banks Credit Unions Industrial Banks Private Banks Savings Banks Savings & Loan Banks Trust Companies Thrift & Loan

Table 1: Industry and Company Options (Sheet 2 of 4)

Industry	Company Types
BUSINESS	Franchise Fast Food Health and Fitness Land and Housing Development Trucking Real estate Restaurant Retailing Wholesaling
CONSULTING	Agricultural Business Computer and Technical Construction Finance Graphics Design Health and Fitness Human Resource Landscaping Management Manufacturing Marketing and Sales Medical and Safety Multi-Media
DAY CARE	
EDUCATION	Private Schools (K-12) Public Schools (K-12) Colleges and Universities (Associates Degree, Bachelor Degree, Masters, Doctoral)
ENVIRONMENTAL	City Planning Eco Management
FINANCIAL SERVICES	Mortgage Companies Independent Investment Companies Investment Brokers
INSURANCE	Accidental Health Life Long Term Care Surety Insurance Title Insurance
MANUFACTURING	Chemical Electronic Equipment Food Furniture Home Fixtures Industrial Equipment Industrial Machinery Instruments (medical, measurement, technical) Lumber Plastics and Injection Molding

Table 1: Industry and Company Options (Sheet 3 of 4)

Industry	Company Types
MANUFACTURING (cont.)	Plastics and Injection Molding Printing and /or Publishing Textile Transportation and Transportation Equipment Wearing Apparel Wood Pulp, and Paper
MEDICAL AND HEALTHCARE	Anesthesiology Cardiovascular Critical Care Dermatology Dialysis Emergency Family Practice General Practice Geriatric Group Medical Practice and Surgical Centers Hospitals Immunology Infectious Disease Industrial Internal Mental Health (Psychiatry, Psychology and Therapists) Neurological Nuclear Obstetrics and Gynecology Occupational Oncology Orthopedic Medicine and Surgery Pediatrics Plastic Surgery Podiatry Pulmonary Radiology Rehabilitation Sports Thoracic Urology Vascular Health Care Providers Assisted Living Health Maintenance Organizations (HMO) Nursing Homes, Hospice Care, Adult and Child Day Care Health Centers PPOs Hospitals Emergency Care Facilities Children Medical and Surgical Nursing Home Psychiatric Rehabilitation Medical Management

Table 1: Industry and Company Options (Sheet 4 of 4)

Industry	Company Types
MULTIMEDIA	Internet Radio Industry Television Industry
UTILITIES AND NATURAL RESOURCE	Alternative Energy Heat and Electric Industry Mining and Drilling
PRINTING and PUBLISHING	
NATIONAL AND STATE AGENCIES	
PARKS AND RECREATION	
PUBLIC RELATIONS INDUSTRY	
TECHNOLOGY	Automation Biotechnology Chemicals Computer Hardware Computer Software Energy Environmental Medical Telecommunication Satellite
TELEPHONE	Cellular Services Land Line Telephone Services

References and Bibliography

Benson, H. (1976). *The relaxation response*. NY: Avon Books.

Berman, E. (1987). *Successful back-to-work strategies for women seeking a fresh start*. NY: Crown.

Bolles, R. N. (1981). *The three boxes of life and how to get out of them*. Berkeley: Ten Speed Press.

Bolles, R. N. (1989). *How to create a picture of your ideal job or next career*. Berkeley: Ten Speed Press.

Bolles, R. N. (1990). *The new quick job-hunting map*. Berkeley: Ten Speed Press.

Bolles, R. N. (1994). *What color is your parachute?* Berkeley: Ten Speed Press.

Bradford, D. & Cohen A. (1990). *Influence without authority*. NY: J. Wiley.

Bridges, W. (1980). *Transitions*. Reading, MA: Addison-Wesley.

Bridges, W. (1994). *Jobshift*. Reading, MA: Addison-Wesley.

Bridges, W. (1995, September 19). "The end of the job." *Fortune*, pp. 62, 64, 68, 72, 74.

Brooke, J. H. (1991). *Postscript: Science and religion in the twentieth century*. NY: Cambridge University Press, pp. 321-347.

Brown, D. and Brooks, L. (1986). *Career choice and development*. San Francisco: Jossey Bass.

Capra, F. (1982). *The turning point—science, society and the rising culture*. NY: Bantam.

Charland, W. (1993). *Career shifting*. Holbrook, MA: Bob Adams.

Covey, S. (1989). *7 Habits of Highly Effective People*. NY: Simon & Schuster.

Crystal, J.C., & Bolles, R. (1974). *Where do I go from here with the rest of my life?* Berkeley: Ten Speed Press.

Danna, J. (1986). *Winning the job interview game*. Briarwood, CA: Palomino Press.

Enelow, W. S. (2001). *Best cover letters for $100,000+ jobs*. Manassas Park, VA: IMPACT

Publications.

Enelow, W. S. (2001). *Best résumés for $100,000+ jobs.* Manassas Park, VA: IMPACT Publications.

Enelow, W. S. (2006). *Cover Letter Magic.* Indianapolis, IN: JIST Publishing

Enelow, W. S. (2004). *Expert Resumes for Career Changers.* Indianapolis, IN: JIST Publishing

Enelow, W. S. (2004). *Insider's Guide to Finding A Job.* Indianapolis, IN: JIST Publishing

Enelow, W. S. (2007). *The $100,000+ Entrepreneur.* Manassas Park, VA: IMPACT Publications.

Farr, M. J. (1996). *The very quick job search.* Indianapolis, IN: JIST Works.

Felderstein, K. (1990). *Never buy a hat if your feet are cold.* El Segundo, CA: Serif Press.

Finley, G. (1996). *The secret of letting go.* St. Paul, MN: Llewellyn Publications.

Fox, M. (1994). *The reinvention of work.* San Francisco: HarperSanFrancisco.

Gardner, H. (1983). *Frames of mind.* NY: BasicBooks.

George E. (1980). *How to get fired today.* Lincolnwood, IL: VGM Career Horizons.

Green, P. C. (1996). *Get hired.* Austin, TX: Bard Books.

Hakim, C. (1993). *When you lose your job.* San Francisco: Berrett-Koehler.

Handy, C. (1989). *The age of unreason.* Boston, MA: Harvard Business School Press.

Hochheiser, R. M. (1995). "Throw away your résumé." Hauppauge, NY: *Barron's.*

Holland, J. L. (1985). *Making vocational choices: A theory of vocational personalities and work environments.* (2nd ed.). Englewood Cliffs, NJ: Prentice-Hall.

Johnston, W. B., & Packer, A. H. (1987). *Workforce 2000: Work and workers in the 21st century.* Indianapolis, IN: Hudson Institute.

Kaplan, R. M. (1991). *The whole career sourcebook.* NY: American Management Association, (AMACOM).

Kay, A. (1996). *Interview strategies that will get you the job you want.* Cincinnati, OH: Betterway Books.

Lavington, C. (1997). *You've only got three seconds.* NY: Doubleday

Lawrence, G. (1995). *People types & tiger stripes.* Gainesville, FL: Center for Applications of Psychological Type. (CAPT).

Lawson, K. (2000) *K-I-S-S guide to managing your career.* NY: Dorling Kindersley.

Lock, R. D. (1992). *Taking charge of your career direction.* Pacific Grove, CA: Brooks/Cole.

Martel, L. (1986). Mastering change: *The key to business success.* NY: Simon & Schuster.

Maslow, A. H. (1970). *Motivation and personality.* NY: HarperCollins.

Moore, M. (1996). *Downsize this.* NY: Crown.

Moreau, D. (1996). *Take charge of your career.* Washington, DC: Kiplinger Books.

Peters, T. (1987). *Thriving on chaos.* NY: Alfred A. Knopf.

Rifkin, J. (1995). *The end of work.* NY: Putnam.

Schein, E. H. (1993). *Career anchors.* San Diego: Pfeiffer.

Sinetar, M. (1987). *Do what you love, the money will follow.* NY: Paulist Press.

Straub, J. (1981). *The job hunt.* Englewood Cliffs, NJ: Prentice-Hall.

Super, D., & Sverko, B. (1995). *Life roles, values, and careers: International findings of the work importance study.* San Francisco: Jossey-Bass.

Tieger, P. D. & Tieger, B. B. (1995) *Do what you are.* Boston, MA: Little, Brown and Company.

Wheatley, M. J. (1994). *Leadership and the new science.* San Francisco: Barrett-Koehler.

Whitaker, U. (1992). *Career success workbook.* San Bruno, CA: The Learning Center.

Yate, M. (1991). *Knock 'em dead.* Holbrook, MA: Bob Adams.

About the Authors

Larry J. Linden, PH.D., CECC

Dr. Larry Linden has over twenty years of independent and corporate experience in international career management counseling, training program development, and implementation.

He has worked with leading out-placement organizations as a Division Manager, Senior Consultant, Job Developer, and is a Master Trainer of Career Consultants. He has consulted to individual career changers across the United States and in 16 foreign countries including those from Africa, Europe, and the Pacific Rim.

Dr. Linden has designed specialized tools and documentation for a fast-paced technology-oriented world, gaining the ability to deliver his services electronically and reaching and servicing individuals in remote areas of the world. In addition, he has designed curricula, conducted classes, programs, and workshops for all levels of employees and students, with emphasis on personal development through self-assessment, career management, and formal education.

Dr. Linden's projects have included development and facilitation of five unemployment support groups in the greater Massachusetts area; design and/or delivery of programs for Digital Equipment Corporation, The Counsel For Adult and Experiential Learning, Worcester State College, Cambridge College, Massachusetts Industrial Services Program, and The Franklin Public Assistance Program.

In addition to publishing articles on career portfolios and effective résumé design, Dr. Linden has conducted workshops and courses on portfolio development, career transition, résumé writing, tough interviewing, networking, job search strategies, self-marketing for success, critical thinking, effective oral presentation skills, graduate studies preparation, academic planning, and assessing diversity.

Dr. Linden received his Masters Degree in Education from Cambridge College in Massachusetts where he focused his attention on training and development and organizational psychology. He earned his Ph.D. in Sociology from The Union Institute in Cincinnati, Ohio in 1997. The focus of his dissertation was on the evaluation of a career portfolio as a transition and career management tool, affording him a unique perspective on career transition and transitional tools. He has resided on four doctoral committees and successfully coached the candidates through the dissertation process. Dr. Linden also conducts train-the-trainer seminars for Senior Career Consultant professionals.

Joseph Parker

Joseph Parker has over fifteen years of experience in technical and non-fiction writing in a variety of subjects ranging from hardware and software to music. He has worked in many facets of publications in the technical world. In addition, he has served as editor of the journal of the Chessie System Historical Society and is the author of numerous articles on model railroading and music. He also has years of experience in document design, graphic design, software development, web application development, and software project management.

As a successful client of Dr. Linden, Mr. Parker can firmly attest to the effectiveness of the methods described in the book. Mr. Parker received his Bachelor of Science in Technical Writing from Worcester Polytechnic Institute.

Glossary

This glossary of terms focuses on meanings mostly as they relate to job search, career change, and the numerous activities associated with a successful campaign. These terms may not necessarily reflect the literal or dictionary meanings you may be familiar with. Some of these terms have been coined by the author as a means of distinguishing his methods from traditionally known terms and approaches.

Accomplishments—Documentation of quantifiable (where possible) activities that you performed that resulted in savings or revenue generation for your organization. Usually used in conjunction with résumés and cover letters. Often referred to as *Achievements*.

Action Plan—See *Marketing Action Plan*.

Affiliations—Groups or social orders where one participates as a member, usually with the intent of movement—both physically and mentally—toward an established goal or outcome. Regarding résumés, the documentation of participation with these groups.

Aging—Regarding job search and career change, the state of mind one has when one determines that they may be or have been victimized by the workplace and assume that they may be beyond value to an organization. Usually, this is a false assumption.

Assessment—Thinking about and documenting ones progress over time throughout their career. Also, capturing that data and analyzing the information to be used as the foundation for future steps and jobs.

Associations—A group congregating for the purpose of social activity while working toward a mission as determined by its members. Regarding résumés, capturing the data as it might pertain to, and perceived as, "value" to a target organization or company.

Bio—A short document—usually a single written page—documenting the highlights of ones life. This document usually captures the most significant accomplishments, both personal and professional. It differs from a résumé in many respects, including the use of paragraph format, a lack of chronology, and a form that does not necessarily distinguish specifically between skills and work history.

Career Change—An activity where an individual identifies a different industry or job group than that from which they have previously worked and wishes to actively pursue a new direction. Examples might be moving from Assembler to Inventory Planner or Supervisor or moving from IS Programmer to Business Analyst or Project Manager.

Career Planning—See *Succession Planning*

Competency—The degree to which a person is able to demonstrate a high level of skill or ability.

Consultant—A person who gives professional or expert advice and/or services.

Contribution—Regarding jobs/careers, what you bring to the organization that makes or saves money and/or resources.

Credentials—Certificates, letters, diplomas, and college degrees.

Culture—As it pertains to the workplace, their philosophy, the way they think, their work and social habits, paradigms, behaviors, customs, attitudes, management structure, and often communication style.

Curriculum Vitae—An expanded version of a résumé that usually includes chronology of publications, personal accomplishments, and everything a person has done of note. These may be as short as a couple pages or may exceed 30 pages. Looks and is structured like a résumé, just longer. Typically used more in academia than in business settings. Sometimes referred to as a *CV*.

Deliverables—Work activities that will immediately or nearly immediately gain significant revenue or savings to an organization.

Disaster Recovery—A strategic, predetermined set of policies and procedures that have been laid out and documented to be used to restore order and return a company to normal operations with minimum negative impact after a catastrophic event. The event may be internal or external, and one that has the potential to cripple an organization.

Documentation—Written or printed piece outlining some specific activity or action to accomplish a specific goal or outcome.

Downturn—A negative economic swing of an organization or other social structure, which often results in loss of headcount or layoffs in a company.

Economic—Relating to, or based upon the production, distribution, and consumption of goods and services with or for financial gain.

Encompassing—That which encloses, completely surrounds and/or includes.

Entrepreneur—A person who owns a small or start-up business with a minimal number of staff or employees.

Environment—Circumstances, objects, or conditions in the workplace that surround a person. Sometimes referred to as *Work Culture*.

Ethics—A person's standards, moral principles, or work values. Typically, these reflect what is most important to an individual and those that they will not compromise.

Ethnic—Members of a group with common racial, national, tribal, or religious background.

Often a minority group.

Headhunter—See *Recruiter*.

Hierarchical Organization—An organization with a purely top down order regarding management. Everyone has a specific superior to whom they directly report. This can include socialization factors.

Hot List—A short list of target companies and organizations where you may wish to obtain employment. The Hot List identifies those targets that are high priorities.

Implementation—Taking action on a given plan.

Informational Interview—The candidate or job searcher informally interviews a target company about their culture, activities, and future plans. The interviews are normally very short, typically 15 to 20 minutes long, and intended to generate mutual interest and future discussions.

Job Change—An activity where an individual identifies and actively pursues a position in the same or similar industry or job group in which they have previously worked. See also *Career Change*.

Job in a Box—The kind of job you've always done and one that is available to anyone with similar skills.

Launch—The milestone when all of the preparations for your job search have been completed, and you begin to put the process into action.

Lead—An invitation for investigation, specifically as it relates to a job or target company.

List of References—See *Reference List*.

Low-hanging Fruit—The job that's easiest to get, as opposed to the ideal job that could be obtained with a little extra effort and time to learn how to get it.

Marketing—Presenting to another in a way that interests them enough to in engage in activities or a relationship.

Marketing Action Plan—The listing of activities in an organized and logical way, specifically with the aim of a pre-determined completion and outcome.

Marketing Instrument—A document that is specifically designed with the marketing of an individual in mind using the principles of marketing techniques to demonstrate key talents that specifically relate to a particular job target. Often perceived as a résumé, it is differentiated by the marketing focus.

Matrix Organization—Typically an organization where many of the components are "dotted lined", that is, an individual or group of individuals answer to superiors from other parts of the organization as well as directly reporting to a specifically named department head.

Measurability—The ability to evaluate whether any part of the process is working in a pre-determined way that will assure a planned, favorable outcome.

Methodology—A method or organized plan to accomplish a specific goal.

Matrix—A system or method of measurement.

Motivations—Those work activities that you truly enjoy doing. This may or may not include all of the skills applicable to a particular job or career.

Open Book Organization—See *Quantum Organization.*

PMO—See *Project Management Organization.*

PMP—Certification of achievement for completion of program and honors given to Project Management Professional graduates.

Portfolio—Presentation documents of specific accomplishments over time. These may be letters, certifications, diplomas, pictures, memos, graphs, videos, tapes, etc. May also refer to a binder or other medium filled with such documents as mentioned above.

Project Management Organization—An organization or division of an organization responsible for the development and management of all or integral projects.

Project Management Professional—An individual who has received certification of achievement for completion of a Project Management program.

Proposal—A document that demonstrates how you can make an immediate and significant contribution addresses the specific needs of an organization. Can also refer to the method in which such a document is used. See also *Proposal Marketing.*

Proposal Marketing—Creation and presentation of a proposal that demonstrates immediate contributions you can make to a target company. See also *Proposal.*

Quality Assurance (QA)—Any activity that attempts to ensure that the necessary level of quality is achieved. QA is used to avoid defects before they occur.

Quality Control (QC)—Any activity or instrument used to determine if a product meets predefined expectations. QC is meant to uncover defects.

Quantum Organization—An organization where every employee is considered as important as anyone else, including the CEO. Decisions are made with input from each individual including the lowest paid employee. The financial condition of the company is usually known to everyone in the company. Generally speaking, the pay in these companies is more evenly balanced than most other forms of organizations. Sometimes referred to as *Open Book* organizations.

Recruiter—A person who actively seeks individuals with specific skills and backgrounds to potentially fill a position within a company. Also known as a "headhunter" or "recruitment specialist." These individuals are most often paid by the company for having found and screened the "right" candidate for the position.

Reference List—A short but comprehensive list of individuals who will speak well of you with regard to your integrity, work habits, character, and general excellence as a potential employee. These usually consist of colleagues, supervisors, managers, and friends who know your work habits.

Remuneration—The determined pay, salary, or other compensation you can expect to receive for performing in a work-related activity.

Resource Development—Making use of friends, family, work colleagues, and superiors to gain access to positions within organizations. Often referred to as *Networking*, but substantially more effective than and distinctive from "traditional" networking. Also related to the development of a list of these people and asking them for information about specific companies you are targeting.

Requirements—In job search and career change, this is most often related to the skills, background, and credentials necessary to qualify for a particular job or position.

ROI—Return on investment. In job search it's "what do you get for your time and dollar investment" regarding a particular approach or activity.

Self-Marketing—The process of gaining corporate exposure in a way that places you in a situation where you will have the greatest potential for landing an ideal job.

Snail Mail—Using traditional methods, such as the US Postal Service, to deliver résumés, cover letters, and other correspondence.

Stakeholder—Usually a person or group of individuals entrusted with the funds and responsibility for the success or growth of a company or organization.

Strategic Plan—A careful plan or method designed to achieve success in a specific activity.

Succession Planning—Premeditated thought about a direction or goals—specifically regarding successive jobs or careers—and the development of actions and activities to achieve those goals. Often referred to as *Career Planning*.

Tactical Approach—An approach to job search that provides the opportunity to out-maneuver your competition and to have tools that are tactically more effective than those used by your competition. In more general terms, activities performed in an effort to obtain a strategic goal.

Target Jobs—Identifying and actively pursuing prospective jobs that interest you.

Target Organizations—Identifying and actively pursuing a company/organization where you believe you would like to work.

Time Management—The careful control and planning of time spent on various activities so as to be efficient, effective, and thereby ensure a successful outcome.

Transition—To make a change, that is, to move from one place, event, activity, job, or career, to another.

Typo—A typographical error. In résumés and cover letters, most errors are misspellings, inconsistent fonts or letter sizes, additional or incorrect spaces, tabs, and so on. A common typo is using the word "form" instead of "from." This can also include misused forms of words such as confusing the usage of "to," "too," and "two." A word processor's spell check feature is not likely to recognize and correct these errors.

Unpublished Job Market—Positions that are *not* published in newspapers, Internet job boards, and magazines, and are not generally known to the general public. This is not a listing of positions, but rather an actual market of opportunities that can be tapped by using the proper approach.

Work Values—Those activities and environmental factors that are *most important* to you, for example, work ethic, integrity, work hours, and so on.

Index

Mindset
    business project approach 41
    evaluating 37
    impact of unemployment on 39
    innovations and 57
    job search methodology 40
    rejection 38
    strategic perspective 40
Motivational Items
    importance of 48
Motivations
    dangers of ignoring 16
    defined 284
Myers-Briggs Type Indicator® 46

N
Negative language in interviews 159
Negotiating Other Benefits 215
Negotiating Salary 214
Negotiation
    accepting offer 221
    cost of avoiding 217
    four simple words 211
    other items 215
    process 210
    salary 214
    when to 209
Networking
    See Also Resource Development
    drawbacks of 139
Neuro-linguistic Programming 4, 141, 142, 160, 164, 191, 204
NLP
    See Neuro-linguistic Programming

O
Open Book Organization
    See Quantum Organization
Organization
    in your job search 22

P
Personality Traits 45
Power of interview questions 183
Probative Entrapment Questions 193
Process Management 120
Process Quality Assurance
    See Quality Assurance
Pyramid Résumé Design 96

Q
QA
    See Quality Assurance
QC
    See Quality Control

Quality Assurance 225
    all process all the time 226
    dangers of ignoring 17
    defined 284
    follow-up 229, 231
    interviews and 230
    job targets and 227
    marketing instruments and 229
    marketing plan and 231
    vs. quality control 226
    weekly action form 231
Quality Control
    defined 284
    vs. quality assurance 226
Quantum Organization 284

R
Recruiter
    defined 284
Recruiters 117
    inflexibility of 14
    job in a box 14
Reduction of rejection 38
Reference List 113
    defined 285
Rejection
    reduction of 38
Remuneration
    See Compensation
Resource Contact Lists 145
    engaging contacts 147
    informational interviews and 149
Resource Development 13, 120, 141
    benefits of 142
    countering inhibitions 143
    defined 285
    importance of 143
    informational interviews and 149
    process 146
    ratio of time to devote 146
    resource contact list 145
    two questions 142
    unpublished job market and 145
    using resource contact lists 149
Resource Development Process 146
Resource List 114
Résumé Challenges
    gaps 95
    missing credentials 93
    personal information 96
    too many credentials 94

While we firmly believe that this book contains what you need to get the job of your dreams, there may come a time where you feel like you need some personal guidance. To work with a professional consultant, please contact us at:

1-888-988-4360

or

http://www.CareerGameChampionships.com.

ISBN 142516130-8

9 781425 161309